speakout 2ND EDITION

Advanced Plus
Students' Book

with DVD-ROM

Frances Eales • Steve Oakes

BBC

CONTENTS

DVD-ROM: ⬛ **DVD CLIPS AND SCRIPTS**   ▶ **STREET INTERVIEWS**   ▶ **CLASS AUDIO AND SCRIPTS**

CONTENTS

CONTENTS

CONTENTS

PARTS OF SPEECH

1 A Read the article and complete the questionnaire.

Goals and growth

'If you know your goals, you're more likely to reach them.' [1]It's obvious that one could say that about a lot of things, including language learning. People [2]who devote time, energy and money to learning a foreign language [3]take up the challenge for many reasons; [4]what's surprising however is that a remarkable proportion of advanced learners of English are unable to describe their motivation in anything but the vaguest of terms. In a few cases, [5]not only [6]were respondents unable to identify their goals, but they also admitted to having [7]remarkably undisciplined study habits.

Are you an advanced learner of English? Let's see how well you do with our questions. For each question, circle a number from 1-3 according to [8]which answer fits you best.

A I'm learning English for

1 one single, overriding reason, [9]which is _____.

2 various reasons — work, travel, stimulation.

3 no particular reason [10]except the pleasure of the process.

B My opportunities for using English in my everyday life are

1 constant — I use the language [11]pretty much all the time.

2 occasional — there are perhaps 1–2 times a week when I need to use it.

3 rare — it's really only if I go abroad, for example.

C My language study habits can best be described as

1 structured, focused and [12]stress-free.

2 sporadic, random and sloppy.

3 non-existent, [13]much as I would like to say otherwise.

D If I were starting a language course today, by the end of the course I would like to

1 improve most of all in a few specific aspects of my language proficiency, namely _____.

2 make noticeable progress in my proficiency in all aspects of my knowledge and skill.

3 feel I've enjoyed the process but I don't have great ambitions [14]about improving specific areas.

Find out your 'score' by adding up the numbers you circled. Then read your results in the key at the bottom of the page.

B Work in pairs. Do you agree with what your results say about you?

C Match the grammatical terms below with the underlined sections in the questionnaire.

a) cleft sentence
b) collocation
c) comment adverbial
d) compound adjective
e) concession clause
f) conjunction
g) defining relative clause
h) frequency adverbial
i) introductory 'it'
j) inversion
k) negative adverbial
l) noun phrase
m) prepositional phrase
n) relative pronoun

MULTI-WORD VERBS

2 A Replace the word in bold with a multi-word verb made from the word in brackets. Make any necessary changes to word order.

1 What would you do to **decorate** the room you're sitting in to make it more exciting? (jazz)

2 Do you **defend** your friends even if they're wrong? (stand)

3 What tricks do you know to avoid **catching** flu in the flu season? (go)

4 Are you better at **making** plans or **executing** them? (come, carry)

5 When you're talking to someone and they **stop paying attention**, do you just **continue** speaking? (switch, carry)

6 What public behaviour can't you **tolerate**? (put)

7 Do children **respect** their elders the way they used to? If not, why not? (look)

8 Do you normally **consider** your ideas before telling others? (mull)

B Are the multi-word verbs separable? Replace any object of the multi-word verbs with a pronoun.

separable: jazz it up

C Work together. Ask and answer the questions.

PRONUNCIATION

3 A Work in pairs and say the sentences below. Mark the sentences wherever sounds a) change/merge, b) disappear, c) are added, d) are linked.

1 I went to India in between school and university.

2 I don't know this shop.

3 Would you like to eat mine?

4 My email address is on our website.

5 Could you remind me about the party?

B ▶ L.1 Listen to the sentences and check your ideas in Exercise 3A. Finish marking the sentences.

C Practise saying the sentences.

Key

People with more specific goals tend to achieve more in a given area. Therefore a lower score (4–6) predicts better progress in your language development. Furthermore, if you wrote specific answers for A1 and D1, you've significantly increased your chances of reaching those goals, as research shows that people who write their goals down are far more likely to achieve them than those who don't.

If you have a higher score (9–12), which portends less well in terms of progress, you could fault the questionnaire and simply enjoy being the way you are. But take a moment to identify one goal and write it down here: _____

1)) game-changer

TRAILBLAZER p8

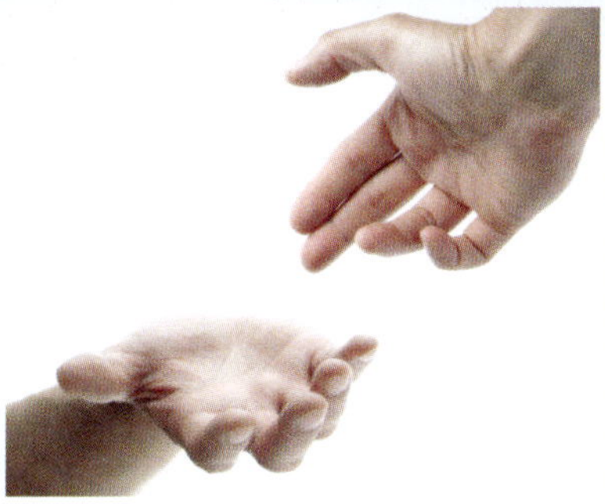

A LIFE AT A TIME p11

SHARING ECONOMY? p14

GENERATION RENT p16

SPEAKING 1.1 Suggest solutions to problems 1.2 Decide on which person gets help
1.3 Conduct a survey; Present survey results 1.4 Design a co-living space

LISTENING 1.2 Listen to a radio programme about a game-changing website
1.3 Listen to a presentation of survey results 1.4 Watch an extract from
a BBC programme about a co-living space

READING 1.1 Read about a trailblazer 1.3 Read about the sharing economy

WRITING 1.2 Write an article; Vary collocations 1.4 Write a proposal for a co-living space

1.1))) TRAILBLAZER

G verb patterns
P word stress
V transformation; prepositional phrases after nouns

SPEAKING

1 Work in pairs and discuss.

1 What would your everyday life be like if money were no object, assuming all your basic needs are taken care of?

2 In this situation, what can you imagine doing as a vocation?

READING

2 A Read the definition of 'trailblazer'. Then discuss the questions.

Someone who is an innovator in their field, who may develop a new method of doing something or a new approach which brings about change; often someone who opens the path for others.

1 Can you think of any trailblazers in these fields? What makes them a trailblazer?
   • science and technology • the arts
   • social networking • social reform

2 What five main qualities do you think a trailblazer needs? Make a list.

B Read the article about Boyan Slat, a modern-day trailblazer. How many of the qualities you identified are mentioned?

C Read the article again. Find information in the article that supports these statements.

1 Plastic waste is not distributed equally all over the oceans.

2 One solution to the problem is impractical.

3 Boyan's childhood experiences contributed to his later work.

4 He couldn't let go of his clean-up idea.

5 He has encountered setbacks on the way.

6 He's aware that his project is the first step in a longer process.

D Discuss with other students.

1 What is the aim of the writer of the article?

2 What do you think Boyan Slat is like as a person? If you met him personally, what questions would you ask him?

3 If you could be a trailblazer in any field, what field would it be? Why?

The ocean dreamer nears his goal

A Boyan Slat has a goal in life – to clean up the world's oceans. He was spurred on by an early experience, one that had a profound impact on him. 'I first became aware of the plastic pollution problem when diving in Greece, coming across more plastic bags than fish,' explains the Dutch-born pioneer. 'I wondered, why can't we clean this up?'

B Over the last half-century millions of tonnes of plastic have concentrated in five 'gyres', areas such as the Pacific Garbage Patch, a plastic soup stretching for millions of square kilometres. Conventional wisdom suggested the use of nets, but that would cost billions of dollars and take thousands of years to complete. Not only that, but emissions from ships would likely cancel out the benefits to the environment.

C Fired up by the problem, eventually Slat came up with a game-changing idea: 'I thought, why move through the oceans, if the oceans can move through you?' His innovative design involved constructing floating barriers which would collect debris for recycling whilst allowing sea life to swim underneath, all powered by naturally occurring ocean currents. The idea represented a paradigm shift, but had a long way to go before achieving recognition.

D Slat developed the idea as part of a school science project, for which he won Best Technical Design at the University of Delft, and that success set in motion a process that would lead to his current work. From childhood his creativity and originality were evident; he was always fascinated by engineering, building treehouses, zip wires and he even set a Guinness World Record for launching water rockets. Slat is clearly aware that his latest project, like some of his earlier ones, requires a leap of faith for those who devote their energy to supporting it. His message to participants in a recent research expedition gets this across: 'My sincere thanks go out to the crews of the participating vessels for making this crazy idea a reality.'

VOCABULARY

TRANSFORMATION

3 A ▶ 1.1 Replace the words in bold with similar words from the article and make any necessary changes. Listen and check.

1 Her election as prime minister **significantly changed** girls' expectations. (paragraph A)

2 This person is a **trailblazer** in the field of social networking websites. (paragraph A)

3 In this period, the **common understanding** was that the world was flat. (paragraph B)

4 This stone-age invention was **transformative** for travel. (paragraph C)

5 His election brought about a **fundamental change in thinking** regarding political campaigns. (paragraph C)

6 Its destruction in 1989 **initiated** a series of events that transformed the world. (paragraph D)

7 The discovery represented a **significant step forward** in eliminating polio. (paragraph F)

8 Scientists are **carrying out initial tests** to see if this could replace fossil fuels. (paragraph G)

E After school he went on to study aero-engineering at Delft University but quit after six months, as he was increasingly committed to developing the clean-up project and ready to dedicate all his time to it. The would-be entrepreneur set up a foundation, The Ocean Cleanup (TOC), but could find no sponsors. It was a disheartening experience, but the process, Slat says, helped him learn to communicate his ideas more effectively.

F But even when Slat contemplated failure, he never lost sight of his goal, and a major breakthrough finally came. A TED talk he gave went viral with millions of shares, and this enabled Slat to access financial support. He was just nineteen, but his youth, as one TOC volunteer pointed out, was anything but a disadvantage. 'Boyan's got this energy that simply takes you in. He never gives up, he works incredibly hard, and his persistence is infectious.'

G Slat now has over 100 scientists researching the oceans and is conducting pilot studies in various sites around the world. He acknowledges that the clean-up, if successful, is only the start. 'Although a clean-up will have a profound effect, it is just part of the solution,' says Slat. 'We also need to close the tap, to prevent any more plastic from reaching the oceans in the first place.' The words of a genuine trailblazer, undaunted by the enormity of the task at hand and the long road ahead.

B Cover Exercise 3A. Complete the collocations in the box. Put them into two lists: adjective–noun and noun–noun collocations.

| breakthrough | -changing | impact |
| shift | studies | wisdom |

adjective–noun: major breakthrough

C ▶ 1.2 **WORD STRESS** Listen and check. Listen again and underline the stressed words. What is the word stress rule in these collocations? Listen and repeat.

4 A Work in pairs and think of an example of a person, object or period of time for each sentence in Exercise 3A. If you cannot think of an answer, choose from page 128.

B Think of four people, objects or events that were transformative and write a sentence for each using expressions from Exercise 3A. Read your sentences to other students. They guess the answers.

GRAMMAR
VERB PATTERNS

5 A Complete the sentences with the correct form of the verbs in the box. Then check in the article.

| allow | construct | dedicate | develop |
| go | make | participate | study | swim |

1 His innovative design involved _____ floating barriers which would collect debris for recycling whilst _____ sea life _____ underneath.

2 The idea represented a paradigm shift, but had a long way _____ before achieving recognition.

3 'My sincere thanks go out to the crews of the _____ vessels for _____ this crazy idea a reality.'

4 After school he went on _____ aero-engineering at Delft University but quit after six months, as he was increasingly committed to _____ the clean-up project and ready _____ all his time to it.

B Look at the examples in Exercise 5A and complete the rules box.

RULES

1 Find an example of an -ing form after:
a) a verb. b) a verb + preposition.
c) a time linker. d) a noun and preposition.
2 Find an example of an -ing form used as an adjective.
3 Find an example of an infinitive after:
a) a multi-word verb. b) a verb + object.
c) an adjective. d) a noun phrase.

▷ page 104 **LANGUAGEBANK**

6 A Read the comments about Slat and his project. Underline the correct alternatives.

Dazzle: I admire him for [1]*try/trying* something so radical and I'm impressed that he's capable [2]*to do/of doing* so much so young. I've never had that sort of drive; I'll probably end up [3]*do/doing* something more ordinary with my life.

D2R2: It's hard to imagine him [4]*to live/living* a normal life. He seems destined for this sort of pursuit, as if his ambition was always to [5]*do/doing* something extraordinary.

May95: I can't help [6]*to wonder/wondering* what they're going to do with all the plastic they take out of the ocean. After going to such great lengths [7]*to gather/for gathering* it together, I'd hope there's no need [8]*to come up with/for coming up with* another invention to deal with the result.

Sunny1: There's simply too much rubbish [9]*to remove/for removing*. It's impractical and it isn't worth [10]*to fund/funding* projects like this. I think our aim should be [11]*to stop/at stopping* the pollution at source.

Sonar: He's doing this [12]*to make/for making* a difference, not for the money. Some trailblazers do things with a view to [13]*get/getting* rich, but he's not like that. Nothing wrong with wanting money, but I'm inclined to [14]*see/seeing* people like this guy in a different light.

B Work in pairs. Which of the sentences in Exercise 6A do you agree with?

SPEAKING

7 A Work in groups and choose a problem below that interests you or think of another problem. Brainstorm answers to the questions.

- Rubbish in city streets
- Water scarcity
- Youth unemployment
- The increasing gap between the rich and the poor
- Care of the elderly
- The isolation of young mothers
- A health system under stress
- Noise and air pollution

1 What are the causes of the problem?
2 What solutions can you come up with?
3 Which of your solutions is the most original?

B Choose one solution to present to the class. Prepare to talk about the causes of the problem, how you found your solution, and how the solution works. While you listen to other students' presentations, think of some questions to ask.

VOCABULARY PLUS

PREPOSITIONAL PHRASES AFTER NOUNS

8 A Read the profiles of three trailblazers. What motivated each person? In what way has each one had an impact?

B Complete the profiles with prepositions.

C Check what you remember. Cover the profiles and answer the questions. Use the noun in brackets and a suitable preposition.

1 Why did Marieme put herself through college? (necessity)
2 Why did she move into the field of technology? (talent)
3 Why did she start the movement IAMTHECODE? (aim)
4 Why does she deserve recognition? (success)
5 What effect did the sight of deforestation have on Jadav Payeng? (motivation)
6 When did he learn about how to plant trees? (course)
7 Why did he continue planting after the project ended? (hope)
8 Why has he received awards? (consequence)
9 How did young Michelle Payne feel about riding? (passion)
10 What could have deterred her in her aims? (risks)
11 Was she willing to speak about chauvinism in the sport? (hesitation)
12 Was Michelle's victory in the Melbourne Cup important? (implications)

D Check your answers in the profiles. Underline the nouns and circle the prepositions.

speakout TIP

When you keep a record of nouns, include the prepositions that commonly come after them, e.g. *the necessity of*, *a talent for*.

9 A Choose six nouns and prepositions from the profiles and write questions (on any topic) to ask the other students.

What's the main motivation for you to learn English?

B Ask and answer the questions.

▷ page 120 **VOCABULARY**BANK

Mariéme Jamme

Senegalese-born British businesswoman Mariéme Jamme has succeeded against significant odds. After being given away to an orphanage and surviving the horrors of being trafficked to France, Mariéme saw the necessity ¹_____ getting an education and later found she had a talent ²_____ generating sales in the tech industry. She is now a leading tech entrepreneur who recently launched the movement IAMTHECODE with the aim ³_____ supporting girls in STEAMD (Science, Technology, Engineering, Arts, Mathematics and Design). Her success ⁴_____ achieving so much no doubt comes from her grit and determination, but perhaps can be attributed to her maxim: 'You can make it if someone believes in you.'

Jadav Payeng

The sight of deforestation on Majuli Island was the motivation ⁵_____ the 'forest man of India' to devote his life to planting trees. In the course ⁶_____ taking part in a five-year government tree-planting scheme, Jadav found the inspiration for his remaining life's work: When the project ended he simply continued to plant trees, in the hope ⁷_____ creating a forest capable of supporting the wildlife that once lived there – and he has succeeded, with the forest now covering 300 hectares. As a consequence ⁸_____ his work, Jadev has been the recipient of many awards. 'My aim has always been to do good for the country,' he says.

Michelle Payne

The youngest of 10 children, Michelle always had a passion ⁹_____ horse riding. Determined to succeed in the sport, the young Australian was no stranger to the risks ¹⁰_____ riding, surviving a number of serious falls that threatened to end her career. When in 2015 she became the first woman ever to win the prestigious Melbourne Cup, she had no hesitation ¹¹_____ condemning the male-dominated nature of the sport, declaring: 'Women can do anything and we can beat the world.' The implications ¹²_____ a woman winning cannot be underestimated and in 2016 she received the Don Award for the sportsperson who has most inspired the nation.

A LIFE AT A TIME

G continuous and perfect aspect
P word stress: adjectives
V adjectives: needing and giving

1.2

VOCABULARY

ADJECTIVES: NEEDING AND GIVING

1 A Look at the pictures and discuss.

1 Would you help the people? How? What would it depend on?
2 Have you ever helped or been helped by a stranger?

B Match the beginnings 1–4 with the endings a–d.

1 Though their house was tiny, they were always **unstinting** in their generosity,
2 No matter how bad things got, she was always **compassionate** towards others.
3 Many donor companies wish to be thought **philanthropic** rather than commercial
4 After six months **on welfare**, with no hope of finding work,

a) he was **destitute** and unable to provide for his family.
b) but are their aims genuinely **altruistic** or are they in it for their own benefit?
c) 'I may be **hard up** myself but that won't stop me from helping people in need.'
d) often inviting homeless or other **vulnerable** people in for a meal.

C Work in pairs and answer the questions.

1 Which expressions in bold in Exercise 1B are about
  a) financial difficulties?
  b) giving to charity?
  c) giving without holding back?
  d) being capable of getting easily hurt?
  e) feeling care towards others?
2 What is the opposite of *hard up*, *altruistic* and *vulnerable*?

2 A WORD STRESS Which of the words or phrases in bold in Exercise 1B are stressed on the first syllable? Where is the stress on the other words or phrases?

B ▶ 1.3 Listen and check. Practise saying the sentences in Exercise 1B quietly to yourself and then aloud to a partner to check the word stress.

3 Tick the sentences you agree with. Then discuss your ideas in pairs. Give examples to support your ideas.

1 Unstinting generosity comes easier to those who have little.
2 A rich philanthropic person probably has other motives than simple generosity.
3 No one should be on welfare for long; it's always possible to find work.
4 A compassionate society can be measured by how it treats its most vulnerable citizens. That could be any of us, as in the future we could find ourselves hard up or in poor health.
5 When people help others I don't think it is for completely altruistic reasons.

▷ page 120 **VOCABULARY**BANK

LISTENING

4 A ▶ 1.4 Listen to a radio programme about an unusual charity organisation and answer the questions.

1 How does 52 Lives work?
2 What sort of help did **a)** Josie, **b)** the woman with the broken floor, **c)** Victor receive?

B Listen again and complete the sentences.

1 The simple key to the idea is …
2 Josie needed help because …
3 It's not the material things that make the big difference to the recipients, but …
4 The first woman Jamie helped had got away from …
5 The point of Victor having his teeth out was to minimise the risk of infection when …

C Work in pairs and discuss.

1 Would a programme like 52 Lives work in your country or home environment?
2 What sort of problems might arise? How could they be solved?

GRAMMAR

CONTINUOUS AND PERFECT ASPECT

5 A Look at the sentences from the radio programme and identify the tense of the underlined phrases.

1 … what I[1]'ve learnt over the weeks I guess at 52 Lives is that even though we give people tangible things and things that they need, that [2]hasn't been what[3]'s changing their life.

2 I got the idea when I [4]was shopping online for some second-hand furniture and I saw a 'wanted' ad …

3 … [she] and her children [5]had escaped quite a horrible domestic violent situation. They['6]d lived in a garden shed for a little while.

4 What are the latest things that people [7]have been asking for?

5 … what is the most unusual thing that anyone [8]has ever asked for … ?

6 There was a man called Victor in America, from Alabama, and he[9]'d had heart surgery …

7 What do you think this idea, this website, [10]will be doing five years from now?

B Work in pairs and discuss the sentences (1–7) in Exercise 5A.

1 Which sentences have the continuous aspect and which have the perfect aspect?

2 What continuous tenses do you know? Which can you find above? What do they have in common in terms of meaning?

3 What perfect tenses do you know? Which can you find above? What do they have in common in terms of meaning?

C Match the underlined verb phrases with the meanings.

a) an action before a particular time in the past

b) an action in a time period up until now

c) an ongoing action at a point in the future

d) an ongoing action at a point in the past

e) an ongoing action in the present

f) a repeated action

▷ page 104 **LANGUAGE**BANK

6 Complete the sentences with the correct form of the verb in brackets in either the continuous or perfect aspect. Sometimes more than one form is possible.

Interviewer: Are there people who come back, because their circumstances [1]_____ (change)?

Jaime: Occasionally, but to be honest, more often it's people who we [2]_____ (help) in the past who now [3]_____ (offer) to help other people. A few months ago we helped a little boy called Harry who [4]_____ (contract) a disease that meant he couldn't move very well. He [5]_____ (not be) out of bed for weeks, and his parents [6]_____ (try) to save enough money for a hoist to help him move around. We raised the money for the hoist in no time, and by next Friday we [7]_____ (raise) the money they need for a motorised wheelchair. His mum was so touched by what people [8]_____ (do) that now she [9]_____ (set up) her own kind of helping site where she [10]_____ (help) siblings of children who [11]_____ (become) unwell. They [12]_____ (post) their first person-in-need next week some time.

SPEAKING

7 A Work in pairs. Student A: turn to page 128. Student B: read the information below and make notes. Prepare to explain the situation to Student A.

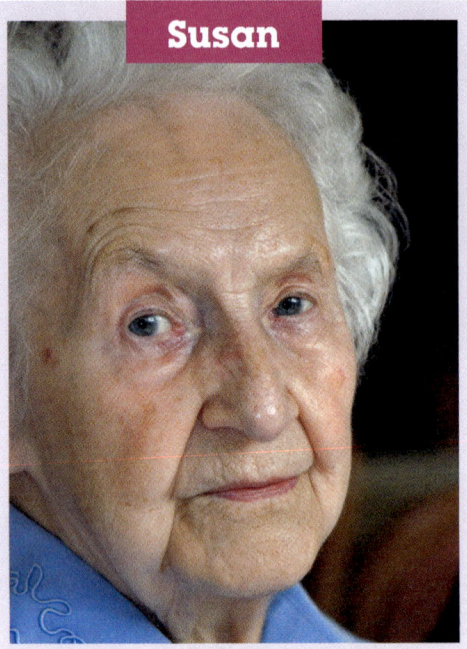

Susan

Susan is 87 years old and lives in Fargo, North Dakota (USA), where winter temperatures average below freezing. A month ago, in early December, she was phoned by a man who said that a roof in her apartment block was being repaired and she needed to pay $850 towards the repair. She was told that someone would come round to collect the money, which they did. Later she was phoned by someone purporting to be from the police who explained it had been a con and that the conman would be coming around again, asking for an additional $200. They instructed her to pay him and they would then arrest him. This was another scam. Susan no longer has enough money even to heat her apartment and winter is coming. She feels embarrassed and stupid and has no family to help.

B Work in pairs, A and B. You can only help one of the two people. Argue the case for your person, and in the end agree on who to help.

C Tell the rest of the class what you decided in the end and why.

WRITING

AN ARTICLE; LEARN TO VARY COLLOCATIONS

8 A Read the article and choose the best title.

a) What's on your Wish List?
b) Wishful Thinking
c) You Wish!

Have you ever wished you had a genie all of your own? You know, someone who would grant your every wish? Well, that's what the website Crowdwish sets out to do.

The basic idea is that people use 100 characters or fewer to express a wish, a hope or an aspiration. How it works is that during the day site members vote on the wishes and at 6p.m. the most popular wish is chosen and the founder of the site, Bill Griffin, spends the next day making that wish come true. As he says, people get '24 hours of industry and activity to create a new thing that didn't exist previously that goes some way towards fulfilling the aspiration articulated.'

So what kind of ideas do people come up with? Click on the FAQ button, scroll down and you'll find plenty of examples. Aspirations range from 'I wish I could take a decent photograph', (this teenager was invited for coffee with a top photographer) to 'I wish people would stop and help just one homeless person today with a blanket or drink' (Bill went out and distributed packs to people on the streets). Sometimes Griffin has to stretch his creativity to fulfil a wish — anything to avoid turning one down.

What I like about the site is that these days there's so much bad news it's good to see someone out there helping in a creative kind of way. If that idea appeals, then this is the site for you.

B Underline the best alternatives (more than one may be possible) and give a reason for your choice.

1 The article is meant to be read by *web designers/ students/travellers/anyone/entrepreneurs*.
2 The style of the article is *academic/formal/informal*.
3 The article is probably for a(n) *financial newspaper/ online magazine/suburban newspaper*.
4 The aim of the article is to *persuade/inform/ entertain/describe/provoke*.
5 It keeps the reader's attention by using *quotations/ examples/humour/anecdotes*.

C Work in pairs and discuss.

1 What is the purpose of each paragraph?
2 List the features of an informal article and find an example of each.
3 Turn to page 128 and check. Find examples of the features that were not on your list.

9 A Work in pairs. Close your book and brainstorm a list of verbs that go with the nouns 'wish' or 'wishes'. Then look at the article and check your ideas.

B Compare the collocations in the article with the extract from an online collocations dictionary above.

Verbs

make a wish (=silently ask for something that you want to happen) *Helen blew out the candles and made a wish.*

get/have your wish (=get what you want) *She wanted him to leave, and she got her wish.*

grant/fulfil sb's wish (=give them what they want) *His parents would now be able to grant his wish.*

express a wish (=say that you want to do something) *He expressed a wish to go to the United States.*

respect sb's wishes (=do what they want) *We have to respect his wishes.*

ignore sb's wishes *It is important not to ignore the wishes of the patient.*

reflect sb's wishes (=show what their wishes are) *The council is the voice of the people so it must reflect their wishes.*

http://global.longmandictionaries.com

The Longman Collocations Dictionary and Thesaurus

10 A Work in pairs and brainstorm verbs and adjectives that collocate with the nouns in the box. Then use a collocations dictionary to add ideas.

website   design   research   experience

B Complete each website description with an appropriate collocation.

1 The site allows you to get _____ experience of building your own blogsite.
2 The designers carried out _____ research over several years to find exactly the right combination of gaming and maths for a teenager.
3 The website is very easy to _____ with simple-to-follow links.
4 The creators of the site have _____ a fantastic, innovative design.
5 People share their _____ experience of travelling on a shoestring.
6 The _____ design is similar to other music-streaming websites but the functionality is much more sophisticated.
7 The results on the site are _____ on research from crowdsourcing of thousands of contributors.
8 The website was _____ only two years ago and now everyone I know uses it.

11 A Write a draft article describing a website that your classmates are unlikely to know much about. Aim to motivate readers to visit the site.

B Work in pairs and read each other's draft. Find the nouns (including synonyms) that occur most frequently. Work together and use a collocations dictionary to vary the verbs and adjectives that collocate with those nouns.

C Rewrite your draft, putting in a greater variety of collocations (220–260 words).

1.3)) SHARING ECONOMY?

F presenting survey results
P intonation: chunking
V collocations: sharing economy

VOCABULARY

COLLOCATIONS: SHARING ECONOMY

1 A Look at the photos. How are they part of the 'sharing economy'? What other examples do you know? Do you think that 'sharing' is an appropriate term?

B Complete the collocations in bold with the words in the box.

> access collaborative driven
> economy fringes model online
> on-demand terms

SHARING …
FOR A PRICE

Once a game-changing movement, the so-called **sharing** [1] _economy_ has long since gone from the **outer** [2] _____ to the mainstream, and, all along, economists and consumers alike have grappled with the terminology surrounding this **business** [3] _____. Also referred to as [4] _____ **consumption**, another term that emphasises the 'sharing' element, businesses that fall under these **umbrella** [5] _____ came into existence once [6] _____ **transactions** became the norm. However, there has been disagreement, above all, regarding the extent to which certain businesses really are about 'sharing', and a feeling that they are instead **profit**-[7]_____. As many businesses don't actually involve sharing, the term '[8] _____ **economy**' came into use, focusing more on the notion that the provider offers [9]_____ **access** to a product or service – for a price. In the end, has this revolution altered our idea of what sharing is about?

C Which collocations do you think are the best for the businesses you discussed in Exercise 1A? How would you answer the question at the end of the article?

D Work in pairs and take turns. Close your book. Student B: say the first word of a collocation from the article in Exercise 1B. Student A: say the whole collocation. Student B: use the collocation in a question. Student A: answer the question.

B: profit
A: profit-driven
B: Do you think the economy is run by the government or profit-driven corporations?
A: A mix of both, I would think. How about you?

FUNCTION

PRESENTING SURVEY RESULTS

2 A You are going to listen to the results of a survey on the sharing economy. Look at these questions from the survey and the pictures above. Which question would you find the most difficult to answer? Why?

Survey questions

■ How many examples of sharing-economy businesses can you think of?
■ What are the differences between them?
■ Which have you used?
■ Which would you like to find out more about?
■ Which would you like to try?
■ Which would you never use?
■ In what way are they 'sharing', and in what way are they for-profit businesses?
■ What do people's willingness to use the services or not depend on?

B ▶ 1.5 Listen to the presentation. Which of the survey questions do the speakers report on?

3 A Complete the phrases by writing one word in each gap. Then listen and check your ideas.

a) **On the** _____ , people expressed a curiosity about businesses that had less relevance for them.

b) **To** _____ **one example**, people who don't have pets _____ to be particularly interested in getting information about the pet-related services.

c) **Our** _____ **was simply that** these businesses had some novelty for them …

d) … and **their interest** _____ **reflected** amusement more than a genuine desire to use the service.

e) **Another** _____ **of this is** the number of people who asked for more information about the parking services, who, as it turned out, don't actually have a car.

f) _____ **speaking though**, … there was limited interest in trying out [services] that the survey participants hadn't used in the past.

g) **The** _____ **seems to be that** people are partial to what they already use or know about.

h) **One might** _____ **that** this reflects human nature.

B Put the phrases from a)–h) under the correct headings.

Generalising

_____
_____
_____

Exemplifying

_____
_____

Hedging/Speculation

_____
_____
_____
_____

4 A Work in pairs and look at these notes. Which survey question in Exercise 2A are the notes about?

Consensus/Examples:
- 'sharing' if community-based, e.g. Streetlife (neighbourhood-based social network) or if money exchange not involved, e.g. Freecycle (for giving/getting household stuff, etc. for free)
- but some are profit-driven, e.g. Uber – disrupt traditional businesses, undercut prices
- use of 'sharing' term not a problem; we know what it means

Comment
- people adapt to words (like 'sharing') taking on new meanings
- for-profit aspect seems inevitable – people need to monetise businesses
- maybe community-based/free services will eventually be monetised

B Decide which of you will report each point in the notes, and report them using the phrases in Exercise 3B.

▷ page 104 **LANGUAGEBANK**

LEARN TO

CHUNK LANGUAGE

5 A Look at the sentences in Exercise 3A. How could you chunk (group) the phrases? Mark the places where you think there are natural pauses between chunks.

On the whole, / people expressed a curiosity about businesses / that had less relevance for them.

B ▷ 1.6 Listen and read the sentences aloud with the speaker. Pay attention to chunking and pausing.

6 A Work with another student. Write down four sentences that you said when reporting the notes in Exercise 4B.

B Mark the chunks and then say the sentences, paying attention to chunking and pausing.

SPEAKING

7 A Work with a different student. Write a short survey (minimum five questions) about one of the topics below. Avoid *yes/no* questions.

1 Internet usage
2 Music-listening habits
3 Smartphone usage
4 Sleeping habits
5 Dealing with stress

B Work individually. Ask a number of other students the questions. Make brief notes on their answers.

C Work with your original partner and compare your answers. Write brief notes following the model in Exercise 4A, with consensus, examples and comments.

D Present your survey results to the class.

DVD PREVIEW

1 Work in pairs and discuss the questions.

1 Have you ever experienced a 'co-living' situation, for example a flat share or a dormitory? How was it?

2 What facilities and services would you want in a co-living space for you to feel comfortable living there? How much private space would you need, and what parts of a home could you share with others?

3 Consider a 'target group' of young, single urban professionals who can't afford their own flat. What facilities and services would they need?

2 Read the programme information. In what ways do you think the facilities and services reflect the needs of the target group of young Londoners? How similar is the description to your ideas in question 3 above?

◉) Generation Rent
BBC

A new building complex in north London is offering a different kind of accommodation aimed at millennials, mixing small private spaces with quirky shared spaces. 'The Collective' has 550 small bedrooms (which they call 'twodios', i.e. studios arranged in twos) and communal areas that include a spa, restaurant, games room, library and roof-top with plastic igloos – with most bills included in the rental price. Is this co-living a good deal, or just another way to exploit young Londoners in the property market? Video journalist Dougal Shaw went along for a tour of the building, which has just welcomed its first inhabitants.

DVD VIEW

3 A Watch the programme and take notes. In what ways does it present a positive image of 'The Collective'? How does it express doubt about the project?

B Read the questions the reporter asks, some of which are paraphrased here. What do you remember about the answers?

1 What do residents get out of it?
2 How do residents integrate (or not) with the local community?
3 Is the amount of private space enough for a young adult?
4 Do you have to be single to be here?
5 How are conflicts between occupants dealt with?
6 How much does it cost to live this way?
7 Doesn't the provision of services go against the idea of being independent?
8 Does 'The Collective' serve the needs of young Londoners, or does it exploit them?

C Watch the programme again and answer the questions in Exercise 3B.

D Work in pairs and complete the sentences with filler words or phrases. Then watch the programme from 3:50 and check your answers.

1 In a traditional house share, _____, if you've got personalities that don't quite work, you're _____ stuck in that small space together, whereas here there are so many people.
2 You are _____ stuck, but they've matched us on age, and interest and _____ career, so it works for us.
3 Once you _____ add in all of those costs, you're really not far off from what you would pay for a house share.
4 All those things that get done for you, is that not going against the whole idea of being independent? _____ 'Mummy's gone now and you've got to do these things yourself'.
5 It's about convenience. Rather than worrying about your internet and your utilities, and _____ life admin, you can focus on, _____, making friends.
6 _____ young working Londoners, that are the life blood of this economy, get completely ignored.

4 Work in pairs and discuss.

1 Is The Collective a 'game changer', or does it resemble existing co-living arrangements that you know of?
2 If you were (or are) in the target group, would you like to live in The Collective? Which aspects would appeal to you, and which would you find difficult?

speakout design a co-living space

5 A Work in pairs. How would a co-living space for the following groups differ? What facilities and services would one group need that the others wouldn't?

- The elderly
- Blind people
- Artists
- Single parents with children

B ▶ **1.7** Listen to two people planning a co-living space. Make notes on:

- who the space is for.
- why they chose that group.
- what facilities and services the space has.
- any problems they anticipate.
- proposed solutions to the problems.

C Listen again. Underline the alternatives you hear.

KEY PHRASES

… a kind of space that *addresses/meets* their specific needs …

Their bedrooms can actually *double/act* as their private rehearsal spaces.

That *would seem/seems* to me to be the key *consideration/challenge*.

… some *attention/thought* should be given to acoustics.

People living around this residence might have a *personality clash/an issue* with the noise.

That would *kill two birds with one stone/solve the public relations problem* for sure.

Knowing/Concerning my musician friends, the biggest problem would actually be …

These *kinks/snags* can be worked out in practice.

A few *setbacks/hiccups* are inevitable.

---

6 A Work in groups and choose a target group from the list in Exercise 5A, or define a group of your own choice. Plan a co-living space, using your ideas from Exercise 5A to focus your discussion. Make notes on your decisions.

B Briefly present your plan to the rest of the class. When listening to other students' presentations, ask questions about their plan and how they might address issues that arise.

writeback a proposal

7 A Read the following proposal for a co-living residence. What aspects of the residence do you think prospective residents will find attractive, and which might they not be comfortable with?

Foothold-in-the-Rock

Our proposed co-living residence, the Foothold-in-the-Rock House, aims to serve budding rock musicians who have not yet gained enough of a foothold in their field to earn a living with their craft and therefore cannot afford their own flat. Residents will also need to be selected based on who will best benefit from the co-living arrangement.

The facilities are specifically designed for this target group, providing the privacy needed for creative development, equipment and space for rehearsal and composition, and communal areas where the young artists can share ideas and simply unplug.

To keep costs, and therefore rent, at a manageable level, individual living spaces are small, bathrooms are shared between four studios, and all forty residents share a single cooking facility. Given the possibility of conflicts in using any of the communal facilities, in particular the kitchen as well as rehearsal spaces, a 24-hour rota system will be set up so that residents can reserve facilities in accordance with their own daily schedule. The unusually high level of sound proofing throughout the facility makes it possible for residents to work and play around the clock.

Developers of the Foothold House are seeking investors to complete the conversion of the building currently under renovation. Benefits to investors include access to facilities as well as direct income from shares of rent.

B Write a short proposal (220–280 words) for your co-living residence. Make sure the key selling points are prominent.

C Read each other's proposals. Which do you think best serves its target group? Which do you think is the most attractive for investors?

Ⓥ TRANSFORMATION

1 A Add letters to complete the expressions.

1 The one thing that's had the most p _ _ _ _ _ _ _ d
i _ _ _ _ _ t on my life in the past year is …

2 The one area where society really needs a m _ _ _ _ r
b _ _ _ _ _ _ _ _ _ _ _ _ h is …

3 … was a g _ _ _ e - c _ _ _ _ _ _ _ g idea which
brought about a p _ _ _ _ _ _ _ m s _ _ _ _ t. One
way our life is different as a result is …

4 Sometimes a historical event s _ _ s in m _ _ _ _ _ n
a change in how people think and live; for example …

5 If I could be a p _ _ _ _ _ _ r in any field, it would be …
and I would conduct p _ _ _ t s _ _ _ _ _ _ s to find
out …

6 When one is hungry, the c _ _ _ _ _ _ _ _ _ _ _ _ l
w _ _ _ _ m is to eat, but other options include …

B Complete four of the sentences. Discuss your ideas with
other students.

Ⓖ VERB PATTERNS

2 A Complete these questions by adding a verb phrase in the
correct form.

1 Are you able to concentrate while …

2 Are you trying to refine your English with a view to …

3 Can you imagine yourself …

4 To what lengths would you go …

5 Do you think it's worth …

6 Are you inclined …

7 Do you think that, when you get old, you'll end up …

8 In a life or death situation, are you capable of …

9 Is one of your aims in life …

10 Has it ever happened that you couldn't help …

B Ask other students your questions, and answer theirs.

Ⓥ ADJECTIVES: NEEDING AND GIVING

3 A Complete the words related to needing and giving.

The psychology of giving

Studies show that [1]phil_____ people aren't necessarily
wealthier or more [2]comp_____ than the average person,
but they have discovered a joy in [3]unst_____ generosity
towards the [4]vuln_____ in our society. A surprising number
of individuals who donate regularly talked less about
[5]altr_____ motives and more about the pure satisfaction
they found in giving.

Meanwhile, looking at those who give less frequently, most
find it easier to turn away from a whole group of [6]dest_____
people than one [7]har_____ individual. An appeal featuring
a photo of a poverty-stricken family on [8]wel_____ elicits
more donations than an article describing the situation of all
the poor in a given city or country.

B Discuss in pairs. Which ideas in the article do you agree
or disagree with?

Ⓖ CONTINUOUS AND PERFECT ASPECT

4 A Work in pairs and discuss. What tense and
aspect is used in each sentence? What is the
difference in meaning, if any, between the
sentences in each pair?

1 a) I've never been able to remember names,
so I …

b) I'm always forgetting people's names, so
I …

2 a) By the end of this year, I'll have been
living …

b) By the end of this year, I'll have lived …

3 a) A year from now my lifestyle will have
changed completely, specifically …

b) A year from now I'll be living in a
completely different way, specifically …

4 a) I'd been studying for most of my life, so
adjusting to the real world …

b) I've been studying for most of my life, so
adjusting to the real world …

5 a) I was planning on studying another
language, but …

b) I'd planned to study another language,
but …

B Complete one sentence in each pair so that
it is true for you. Then tell other students and
find out about their ideas.

*I've never been able to remember names, so
I avoid using people's names altogether so that
no one notices when I don't say their name.*

Ⓕ PRESENTING SURVEY RESULTS

5 A Correct the mistakes in the phrases in bold.

[1]**In the hole**, most of the people surveyed
[2]**tendency** to feel that there weren't enough
places for young adults to meet in public.
[3]**The census seems to be** that public spaces were
designed for children, families and the elderly.
[4]**To slight one example**, a group of university
students were kicked out of a playground for
being too old, then sent away from the park
benches, [5]**presumptuously** for being too young.
[6]**Another illustrator of this** is that nearly
everyone we surveyed said they meet their
friends in cafés, but hated spending so much on
coffee. [7]**One might specialise that** young people
would opt for cafés anyway, as they are so used
to frequenting such places. [8]**Genetically
speaking though** [9]**our compression was that**
young people desperately want to spend their
time in a healthy way, without the cost. To
that end, we have a few suggestions to make
regarding public spaces …

B Work in pairs and discuss. To what extent do
you agree with the opinions expressed? What
suggestions would you make to improve the
situation?

2)) learning

THE BEST MISTAKES p20   **ANOTHER WAY** p23   **THINK AGAIN** p26   **TEACHERS AND LEARNERS** p28

SPEAKING   **2.1** Discuss your attitude to mistakes; Participate in an experiment about memory
              2.2 Speak about your own education and educational values
              2.3 Lead a discussion; Improve interaction management
              2.4 Discuss the qualities a great teacher needs

LISTENING   **2.2** Listen to a radio programme about an alternative way of learning
               2.3 Listen to a discussion about creativity in education
               2.4 Watch people talking about different learning experiences

READING   **2.1** Read about the value of getting something wrong

WRITING   **2.2** Take notes; Write a summary   **2.4** Write about learning experiences

19

G *if* and related expressions
P connected speech: linking
V learning; idioms: feelings

VOCABULARY

LEARNING

1 A Look at the photos. What might have happened to make people respond like this?

B Work in pairs. What do the words/ phrases in bold mean?

1 Motivation is the **crucial element in** learning.

2 I need to get lots of **praise** for my efforts if I'm not to feel discouraged.

3 I think a teacher should never **deride** a student for making a mistake.

4 When I don't know something in English, I can usually **make an educated guess** about it.

5 I'm **something of a perfectionist**, so I don't speak in English unless I'm sure I will say things correctly.

6 Mistakes can be **highly beneficial to** learning.

7 I learn best when I'm **engaged** in a topic or conversation, and stop paying attention to my English.

8 I **steer clear** of making mistakes when I speak English, for example, by simplifying what I say.

C Match the words in bold with the definitions a)–h).

a) avoid

b) the most important thing

c) mock, make fun of

d) very good for

e) positive things said about someone

f) involved

g) try to answer, usually based on some information

h) someone who can't bear making mistakes (informal)

speakout TIP

When noting new vocabulary, decide how much of a phrase will be useful to help you remember and use it later. Look for and note typical grammatical collocations with associated prepositions e.g. *ridicule sb **for**, a crucial element **in***. Look at the examples in Exercise 1B. What patterns would you note for *praise, deride, beneficial, engaged, steer clear*?

D Work in pairs. To what extent do you agree with the sentences in Exercise 1B? Give examples to support your opinions.

Excellent! You got it wrong

What feeling do learners experience on making a mistake? Most report negative sensations – a sinking feeling in the pit of the stomach, a sense of embarrassment or even shame. Regardless of the subject matter, the desire to avoid making mistakes appears to be universal despite research which indicates we should welcome errors with open arms. **It seems as if** going through the process of guessing – and getting the answer wrong – can increase the likelihood of recalling information later.

In one landmark study of the teaching of maths, significant contrasts emerged between Japan and the USA. In the USA learners were given procedures and expected to follow them, and praise was only given **provided that** answers were correct. In contrast, Japanese learners were expected initially to struggle with the answers on their own and were **rarely, if ever,** praised for correct answers. **Whether or not** they made an error wasn't focused on, but rather the reason for the error and possible routes to the correct answer.

READING

2 A Read the article on the value of making mistakes. Which ideas in Exercise 1B are discussed in the article? What is the article's perspective on them?

B Read the article again. Are the sentences true (T), false (F) or not given (NG)? Where possible, underline the phrase that helped you decide.

1 Many people experience physical symptoms when they make a mistake.

2 In the USA, praise was given just for making an effort; the focus was not on being right.

3 Japanese teachers get their students to look at why they made an error.

4 American educators are supposed to write things down.

5 In one experiment, one group had more time to look at the target words than the other.

6 Involving oneself and one's mind in the learning process is considered important.

7 A psychologist said that the lack of stress in the experiment doesn't reflect most classrooms.

8 Teachers are more likely than students to value correctness highly.

C Work in pairs and discuss. What did you understand about these topics, and what is your opinion about them?

1 The difference between approaches in the USA and Japan.

2 The experiment on guessing.

3 The professor's ideas about using game-like activities.

Japan far outstrips the USA in maths scores. Is this because of the emphasis on the constructive use of error as a teaching technique? **If so**, perhaps U.S. educators should take note.

Another experiment explored the effect of 'unsuccessful retrieval' when learning individual words. One group of participants was asked to complete gaps in a sentence and **if in doubt** to guess the missing word, after which they were told the correct answer; correctly guessed answers, **if any**, were excluded from subsequent testing. Meanwhile a second group simply studied sentences already containing the words. The total amount of time allotted was the same for both groups, so the first group had significantly less exposure to the target items. Nevertheless, the first group – who had actually made a number of mistakes – scored significantly higher when tested on the items later.

Explanations for the positive effect of unsuccessful retrieval point to the key factors of cognitive and personal engagement, which have long been known to enhance the learning process. '**As long as** you have engagement, people will learn,' an educational psychologist commented. 'In fact I would say that **unless** you have engagement, people won't learn.' She also highlighted another crucial element: 'What is key to the process in this experiment is that nothing was at stake, really – there was no consequence to the error, and in fact the guessing itself was rather game-like in nature. Participants knew that they could not always be expected to get the right answer, and they were not derided for the so-called errors. **But for** the stress created by a fear of error, I believe all learners could learn more effectively, and probably have more enjoyment doing it.'

Without heeding the results from this type of experiment, practice may never benefit from the evidence at hand. Perhaps it's time for teachers and learners alike to rethink their quest for instant perfection; **otherwise** we may be missing out on an enormous opportunity for learning.

GRAMMAR

IF AND RELATED EXPRESSIONS

3 Look at the expressions from the article and underline the phrase that is closest to the meaning.

1 it seems as if = *apparently/probably*
2 provided (that) = *on the chance that/if and only if*
3 rarely, if ever = *never/almost never*
4 whether or not = *if something is true or false/if something is false*
5 if so = *if desired/if true*
6 if in doubt = *if you're not sure/if you don't care*
7 if any = *if there are some/if it's obvious*
8 as long as = *once in a while/if and only if*
9 unless = *if it doesn't happen that/if it happens that*
10 but for = *if it weren't for/except in the case where*
11 without = *if it weren't for/not having*
12 otherwise = *if this happens/if this doesn't happen*

▷ page 106 **LANGUAGE**BANK

4 A Read the quiz opposite and complete the sentences with the correct form of an appropriate expression from Exercise 3. Two items are not used.

B Do the quiz and compare your answers with another student. Check your score on page 128.

C Do you agree with the analysis? Which of you accepts mistakes more easily? Give examples from your own life.

HOW UPTIGHT ARE YOU?

Can you accept your own mistakes? Can you put up with others getting things wrong? Or does it drive you crazy when things don't go perfectly? Take this quiz and find out how uptight you are - or not! Circle the answer that fits you best.

How do you feel about your own mistakes?

1 Imagine you went to a dinner in your jeans and everyone else was wearing formal clothes. What would you do?

a) I would go straight home _____ people even noticed what I was wearing.

b) If _____ no one minded, I'd stay and make a joke if anyone commented.

2 Would you rather do a job on your own or with others?

a) On my own, so I could be sure of getting it right. I rarely, _____, make mistakes.

b) With other people. Few people, _____, get better results working alone.

How you feel about others' mistakes?

3 Imagine someone bumps into you on the street, quite hard. Which response fits you best?

a) Did they do it on purpose? _____ then I would feel really angry.

b) It doesn't bother me at all _____ that they apologise.

4 Your car is parked in a car park, and someone backs into it, leaving a tiny scratch. Would you make them pay?

a) I would, as _____ I would have to pay to have it repaired.

b) I wouldn't, _____ the scratch really was tiny and difficult to notice.

5 A cashier gave you change for a purchase, and you think she gave you too much. Do you keep it?

a) Yes, _____ I knew her. It's her mistake and that's her loss. I don't think many people, _____, would give the money back.

b) Well, _____ I would certainly count it in front of her, and give her back the extra. Everybody makes mistakes.

Count the number of a) answers you circled.

5 A ▷ 2.1 **CONNECTED SPEECH: linking** Listen to six questions and write down the answers.

B Mark the links between final consonant and initial vowel sounds.

Seldom, if ever.

C Prepare your own questions to prompt the same answers. Then work with other students and ask your questions. Pay attention to the linking when answering.

SPEAKING

6 A Work in pairs. You are going to try an experiment similar to the one in the article on page 21. Student A: turn to page 128. Student B: turn to page 133.

B Work in pairs and discuss.

1 How did Student B feel about guessing something likely to be wrong?

2 How do you usually try to memorise new words and expressions?

3 How important are the following when you study and memorise words and expressions?
   • Seeing the words
   • Hearing the words
   • Saying or writing the words
   • Using them in a sentence
   • Repetition of some kind
   • Knowing you will be tested

7 A Work alone. Turn to page 133 and write the words that you can remember next to the other words.

B Work in pairs again and discuss.

1 How many of the words did each of you remember?

2 How is the experiment similar to the one described in the article? Were your results similar?

3 Do you think there is any value in guessing?

C As a class, compile the results for all Student As and all Student Bs. Which group remembered more of the original items?

VOCABULARY *PLUS*
IDIOMS: FEELINGS

8 A In each of the following extracts from the article underline an idiom expressing feeling. What does each one mean?

Most report negative sensations – a sinking feeling in the pit of the stomach, a sense of embarrassment or even shame.

… the desire to avoid making mistakes appears to be universal despite research which indicates we should welcome errors with open arms.

B Work in pairs and write two new sentences using the idioms.

9 A Read texts 1–8 below. Where does each one come from? How can you tell?

B Underline the idiom expressing feeling in each of the texts.

C Match comments a)-h) with the idioms.

a) 'I wonder if she's really ill.'

b) 'That's terrifying. I wonder what happened next.'

c) 'I'd be very happy, too.'

d) 'Something must have happened to him in the past to make him so angry.'

e) 'He sounds rather frightening. He would make me feel uncomfortable.'

f) 'I'd be in pretty bad shape too if I were him!'

g) 'It seems as if they have no choice, but I bet they'll find a way out.'

h) 'That must have been incredibly uncomfortable!'

D Work in pairs. Write questions beginning *How did you feel when* … ? to prompt answers using the idioms. Work with a new partner and ask and answer the questions.

▷ page 121 **VOCABULARY**BANK

---

1 Sorry, I'm a bit under the weather, sore throat and cough etc., can't make it today.

2 She hated the way he looked at her. It made her flesh crawl. Like he thought every woman should be in love with him. And that was the problem – she was.

3 My wife and kids have left me, I've lost my job, and I'm coming apart at the seams. I'm desperate for any advice.

4 In the fifth week of strikes, workers are still blocking the factory gates and refusing to return to their jobs. 'Management has its back to the wall,' said one worker. 'They have to give in to our demands, or they go bust.'

5 Imagine, I arrived at the picnic in my jeans and T-shirt, and saw that everyone was dressed really smartly. I felt like a fish out of water.

6 He awoke to the sound of footsteps and breathing, and realised a stranger was in the room. His blood ran cold as the footsteps moved closer …

7 Oh you're so fine,
   And I'm on cloud nine,
   'Cause I know you're mine,
   And our stars align …

8 Dusty stared angrily at the man on horseback as the midday sun beat down on them. 'Got a chip on your shoulder, cowboy?' asked the man. 'Maybe this'll knock it off.' He went for his gun, but Dusty was faster.

ANOTHER WAY

G nominal relative clauses
P word stress
V collocations: education

VOCABULARY

COLLOCATIONS: EDUCATION

1 A Work in pairs. What sort of primary and secondary education did each of you have? What did you like or dislike about your experience?

B Complete the sentences with the words in the box.

curriculum   fostering   individuality   initiative   nurturing
path   respect   potential   standards   striving

The most important thing in education is:

1 a _____ environment, a context where you are cared for and helped to grow.

2 finding your own _____, discovering what interests you in life.

3 _____ for excellence, and never settling for second best.

4 _____ good relationships, that is helping people to get along in a positive way.

5 fulfilling your _____ and becoming as good as you're able to be.

6 a quality _____, educational content of a high standard.

7 rigorous _____, meaning challenging, even difficult, requirements.

8 taking the _____ and doing things first, not waiting to be told to do them.

9 mutual _____, or the belief between people that the other is as worthy as oneself.

10 a focus on _____, or not treating people as all the same, rather as unique.

C For each word circle the collocation or phrase it is part of.

2 A WORD STRESS List any words in the collocations in Exercise 1B which have a) three syllables b) four syllables c) more than four syllables.

B ▶ 2.2 Underline the stressed syllable in each of these words. Then listen and check.

C ▶ 2.3 Work in pairs. Listen and complete the sentences with one word. Then listen and check.

▷ page 121 **VOCABULARYBANK**

SPEAKING

3 Work with other students and discuss.

1 Which of the values in Exercise 1B were characteristic of your primary education?

2 Which do you think are the most important for a school to have?

3 Which do you think are irrelevant, i.e. not the school's job to provide? If not, whose role is it to provide them?

4 What other features of education are important?

LISTENING

4 A Work in pairs and discuss. Do you think children learn more effectively in a classroom with a teacher, or outside of a classroom in a play context? Why?

B Read about the radio programme and discuss.

1 What was the experiment?
2 What would you like to know about Sugata Mitra and SOLE? Write three questions.

BBC Radio 4

The Educators:
Sugata Mitra

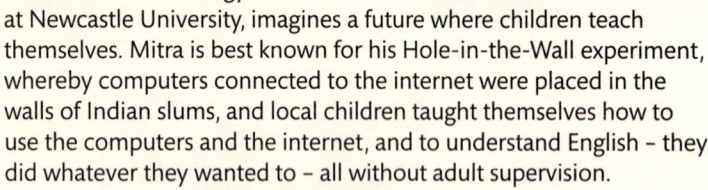

Sugata Mitra, Professor of Educational Technology at Newcastle University, imagines a future where children teach themselves. Mitra is best known for his Hole-in-the-Wall experiment, whereby computers connected to the internet were placed in the walls of Indian slums, and local children taught themselves how to use the computers and the internet, and to understand English – they did whatever they wanted to – all without adult supervision.

What he learnt from that experiment led Professor Mitra to develop a similar model inside the classroom. Now he and his team have set up several 'learning in the cloud' locations in schools, each called a 'Self-Organised Learning Environment' or 'SOLE'. A key element is the 'Granny Cloud', a group of volunteers available via Skype to support children in their SOLE learning. In this radio programme, Sarah Montague finds out how the concept works.

C ▶ 2.4 Listen to the radio programme. Note any answers to your questions.

5 A On a blank page, write the following headings and note any information you remember under each topic.

1 Elements of a SOLE
2 Where the Granny Cloud idea came from
3 Children's feelings about SOLE

B Listen again and complete your notes.

C Work in pairs and compare your notes. Then turn to page 132 and compare your notes with the model.

D Work with other students and discuss.

1 Would you like to have learnt in a context like a SOLE rather than a traditional learning environment? Why/Why not?
2 Think of potential difficulties if this idea were introduced in your country.

GRAMMAR

NOMINAL RELATIVE CLAUSES

6 A Look at the nominal relative clauses in bold in the sentences below and complete the rules box.

1 In this programme, Sarah Montague finds out **how the concept works**.
2 **What Mitra learnt from the original experiment** led him to develop a similar model inside the classroom.
3 **Who he was looking for** were adults with computers and spare time to help.
4 The students do **whatever they want** in order to find answers.
5 **Whoever wants to use the computers** can do so.
6 Children have to decide **when to ask a 'granny'**.

> **RULES**
>
> A nominal relative clause acts like a noun. Each nominal relative clause starts with a relative pronoun. Find a relative pronoun that means:
> a) anything that
> b) anyone who
> c) the things that/which
> d) the people who
> e) the way that
> f) the time that

▷ page 106 **LANGUAGEBANK**

B Correct the sentences using nominal relative clauses. Two sentences are already correct.

1 I practise speaking in English with who I can find.
2 Good subtitled films are exactly that which I need to improve my listening.
3 I've learnt a lot of English without any teacher telling me how to.
4 The language what we're studying today is the same in my language.
5 A good app for vocabulary learning is just the thing what I've been looking for.
6 Little and often. That's just why I like to learn.
7 I revise vocabulary wherever I'm on public transport.
8 What I do, I don't seem to be able to manage phone calls in English.
9 I'd like a list of who the best new novelists in English are.
10 I keep a record on my tablet of everything what we've studied.

C Work in pairs. To what extent do you agree with the sentences in Exercise 6B? Give examples to support your opinions.

WRITING

TAKING NOTES; LEARN TO SUMMARISE NOTES

7 A Work in pairs and discuss the questions.

1 When do you need to take notes?
2 What system do you have for taking notes when listening to English, e.g. a lecture?
3 Read these top tips for taking notes. To what extent do you agree with or follow them?

Note-taking: Top Tips

1 Give yourself plenty of space to write.
2 Prepare by writing down possible topics/ headings/questions, based on what you know the talk will be about.
3 Don't write down everything you hear.
4 Doodles, if any, should be useful, e.g. to illustrate an idea.
5 Paraphrase if possible – write meanings, not the speaker's words.
6 If in doubt what to write, don't. Listen.
7 Write down key words and phrases only, not sentences.
8 Use symbols, e.g. → can mean *therefore*, or *after that.*
9 Look back at your notes immediately after finishing, and check how well you remember. Fix anything that seems unclear.

B Look again at the notes on page 132 and answer the questions.

1 Which Tips did the person follow?
2 Comparing your notes from Exercise 5B to the model, in what three ways could you improve your note-taking skills?

8 A You're going to listen to another segment of the programme with Sugata Mitra where he talks about what we should and shouldn't teach children. Write headings for your notes (e.g. *Do teach, Don't teach*) on an empty page.

B ▶ 2.5 Listen to the segment and take notes. Then compare your notes with another student and the model on page 128. How could you improve your note-taking further?

9 A Read this summary of the notes from the first interview excerpt and compare it to the notes on page 132. What information is missing from each paragraph of the summary?

A SOLE is similar to Sugata Mitra's hole-in-the-wall experiment in that there are no adults present. However, it takes place in the classroom, and has the following elements: computers, a 'big' question to stimulate the pupils, no teacher, but a granny available via Skype IF the pupils ask for help.

The idea for the Granny Cloud came from an experiment Mitra did in India where he gave the impossible task of learning university-level genetics to twelve-year-old Tamil kids. They scored zero on the pre-test, but after doing research on their own their marks improved to thirty percent. Subsequently Mitra asked a local woman to work with the children, giving encouragement but nothing more. After two months they scored fifty percent on the test.

Pupils who were involved in trialling the SOLE were initially suspicious but curious about the process; however, they now feel positive about it. They see it as a valid counter-balance to teachers' conventional methods, which some students find boring. I think I would have a similar reaction.

speakout TIP

An effective summary can both help you remember content and also communicate essential facts to someone who didn't hear/read the original. It should:

• have a paragraph for each topic, each starting with a statement of content, similar to an essay.
• use discourse markers, but not overuse them, to help make the relationship between ideas clear.
• be concise, and paraphrase the original text rather than writing verbatim what was said.
• be accurate and include all <u>relevant</u> information from the notes; less important information can be left out.
• report objectively rather than giving an opinion.
• acknowledge any sources of information when available.

B Which points in the TIP does the writer follow well and which not?

C Write a summary of your notes from Exercise 8B (150 words).

F leading a discussion; managing interaction
P sentence stress; intonation: appropriacy
V creativity

VOCABULARY

CREATIVITY

1 A 'Everyone is creative, including you!' In which aspects of your life are you the most creative? Think about:

• home	• problem-solving
• hobbies	• computers
• the arts and music	• making things
• ideas	• work
• relationships	• other

B Work in pairs and discuss. Which phrases relate to promoting creativity? Explain any differences between each pair of phrases. Give examples to support your ideas.

1 stifle the imagination – fire the imagination
2 have a fertile imagination – have a vivid imagination
3 regurgitate facts – question facts
4 learn by rote – learn by heart
5 rely on intuition – rely on intellect
6 think outside the box – stick to the tried and tested
7 be spontaneous – do something on the spur of the moment
8 have a rigid outlook – be versatile

C Work in pairs and discuss the questions. Use the ideas in Exercise 1B to help you.

1 Does traditional education leave enough room to develop children's imagination and creativity or does it actually stifle it?
2 Should any changes be made to the curriculum in schools and if so, what?
3 Do you think testing is a good thing, a necessary evil or completely unnecessary?

FUNCTION

LEADING A DISCUSSION

2 A ▶ 2.6 Listen to a focus group discussion about encouraging creativity in schools. There are four people: Amy (A), Chad (C), Peter (P) and Sarah (S). Who would agree with these statements?

1 There is already enough attention to developing children's imagination and creativity.
2 There is too much attention paid to testing.
3 Testing in some form is a good thing.
4 It's up to the school to give attention to creative subjects.
5 Some people test better than others, and the system should accommodate that.

B Which speaker do you most agree with?

3 A Complete the phrases below. Then listen again and check your answers.

a) So our _____ today is to …
b) What I'd _____ I think is start with …
c) Could you explore _____?
d) Can I just check where _____?
e) That's certainly _____ considering.
f) Correct me if I'm wrong, but what you're _____ is that …
g) Who would like to _____ this one _____?

B Put phrases a)–g) under the correct headings.

Initiating a discussion or a topic

1 _____
2 _____
3 _____

Getting others to clarify ideas
Could you elaborate on that?
Could you run that past us again?

4 _____
5 _____
6 _____

Giving feedback/Evaluating
That's an interesting perspective.
I can imagine that working.

7 _____

C SENTENCE STRESS ▶ 2.7 Work in pairs. Which is the main stressed syllable in each phrase in Exercise 3B? Listen and check. Then listen and say the sentences at the same time as the speaker, paying attention to stress and linking.

▷ page 106 **LANGUAGE**BANK

LEARN TO

MANAGE INTERACTION

4 A Work in pairs and discuss.

1 How often do you take part in discussions? Where? At home, school, work, elsewhere?
2 Do you enjoy having discussions? Why/Why not?
3 What can go wrong?
4 How can the person leading the discussion make it a positive experience for everyone?
5 How well do you think Amy managed the discussion? Give examples of what she did or didn't do well.

B ▶ 2.8 Look at the sentences and think of other ways to express the words in italics. Then listen and write the words the speakers use.

1 Did you want to *say*/_____ anything, Sarah?
2 Let's *keep to the topic*/_____.
3 Can I just *finish*/_____ what I was saying?
4 I think we might be *getting off the topic*/_____ here.
5 Can I make a *suggestion*/_____ about that?
6 If I could just *add one point*/_____ here.
7 Can we just hear what Sarah *started*/_____ to say?
8 We're *running out of*/_____ time so let's move on to the next question.

C Which phrases help the speaker to:

a) interrupt/get a turn?
b) keep a turn?
c) deal with interruptions?
d) refocus people?
e) include everyone?

5 A ▶ 2.9 **INTONATION: appropriacy**
Listen to the phrases. Does the speaker sound impatient (I), tentative (T) or firm and polite (P)? Repeat the phrases copying the different types of intonation.

B Work in pairs. Write a key word from any of the expressions in Exercise 4B which are new to you. Cover Exercise 4B. Student A: say a key word. Student B: say the complete expression either impatiently, tentatively or firmly and politely. Student A: decide what the attitude is.

SPEAKING

6 A Work in groups of three or four (students A, B, C, (D)). Choose one of the topics below or a discussion topic which is relevant to your own context.

- Improve the transport flow in your town/city
- Practise speaking English
- Encourage greater diversity in your situation
- Improve the facilities in your institution
- Manage a shared work or living space
- Give opportunities for visitors to your town/city to meet local people

B Turn to page 129 and read your role card. Then discuss your chosen topic.

DVD PREVIEW

> a sport   a computer program
> cooking something   using a machine
> dancing   a musical instrument
> making/uploading a video   a game
> make-up skills

1 A Think of two things that you have learnt/studied in the past year or so, apart from a language. Use the ideas above or your own ideas and make notes on these questions.

1 How did you go about learning/studying each one?
2 When you learn something, how much do you think about how you learn?
3 Choose two other items from the list. How would you or do you best go about learning them?

B Discuss your ideas with other students. What differences do you find in how you learn different skills and subjects?

Michael
Presenter

Peter

Jeanne

Wael

Agnes

Hamza

Tricia and Jack

Priscilla

Sami

DVD VIEW

2 A Work in pairs. Tell each other about an inspiring teacher. What/When did they teach you? Why were they inspiring?

B Watch Part 1 of the interviews. For each speaker note a) the subject the teacher taught and b) why their teacher was inspirational. Whose ideas are the most similar to yours?

Michael: chemistry – did experiments in class – patient + good-humoured

C Watch again and complete the phrases.

1 She _____ a real interest in the subject for me.
2 She inspired me to always _____ instead of just looking at today.
3 He managed to make it incredibly _____ to us.
4 He's got the _____ attitude and he makes you really feel that you can do it.
5 He doesn't just do research, but he _____ practice.
6 This one actually inspired me to go further and _____.

D Work with another student and talk about the same teacher as in Exercise 2A. Try to use at least four of the phrases from Exercise 2C.

3 A Work in pairs. List the qualities a great teacher needs.

B Watch Part 2 of the interviews. Tick the things on your list that the people mention. Add any other qualities you hear. Which quality is mentioned the most? Why, do you think?

4 A Work in pairs and discuss. Is it always necessary to have a teacher when you learn something? Give examples of where you have or have not had a teacher and how well you learnt something.

B Watch Part 3 of the interviews. Which speakers feel most strongly about having a teacher? Which speaker is closest to your point of view?

C Watch again. Which speaker mentions each of the following concepts, and what do they say about it?
• Human interaction
• A steep learning curve
• A point of reference

speakout

5 A Work alone and look at the list of qualities from Exercise 3B. Put them in order of importance to you.

B Work with other students and agree on the five most important qualities. Give reasons for your choices.

6 A Read these quotations about learning. Which two or three do you agree with most? Make notes on your ideas, including examples from your life that support your point of view.

> 'Tell me and I forget, teach me and I may remember, involve me and I learn.'
> (Benjamin Franklin)

> 'The more I read, the more I acquire, the more certain I am that I know nothing.'
> (Voltaire)

> 'Education is the kindling of a flame, not the filling of a vessel.'
> (Socrates)

> 'Educating the mind without educating the heart is no education at all.'
> (Aristotle)

> 'Live as if you were to die tomorrow. Learn as if you were to live forever.'
> (Gandhi)

B Work with other students and share your ideas.

writeback a learning experience

7 A Read the forum entry describing how the writer learnt salsa. What have you learnt that is similar to learning to dance? How similar or different is the author's experience of learning to yours?

 SalsaJim

How I learn

I've always been interested in Latin American music so, a few months ago, I decided to join some local salsa classes. I was quite nervous on day one because I went into the hall early and I was hanging around for a while before anyone came. Then this Cuban guy comes in and he's the teacher and we follow his moves. No allowance is made for some of us being beginners. Each week the teacher shows us the steps and then we try to fit the steps to the music and that's incredibly hard, hearing where the beat comes in. I don't get a lot of personal attention but that actually suits me because I get flustered if people focus too much on what I'm doing wrong. I tend to learn by copying other people. Watching their feet. The only trouble is when you dance salsa you want to watch the person's face, engage with them, look in their eyes. Anyway, after three or four months it was going quite well. I'd learnt some routines and when the teacher calls out 'sedenta' I know what to do. My main method of learning is to go over and over the steps in my kitchen, practising by myself.

I did die horribly once, which put me off a bit. It was at the end of a lesson and I asked this woman to dance and I did two moves and my mind went blank, I just could not think of what to do next, and so I just stood there, died, and another guy came in and took her off me! And I realised that as a man in salsa you have to lead and so you have to have an armoury of different moves in your mind to lead your partner.

Reply

B Write a forum entry about something you learnt and how you learnt it. Draw on the experiences you talked about in Exercise 1 (250–300 words).

V LEARNING

1 A Add vowels to complete the expressions.

When a patient tells me they're ¹s__m__th__ng __f __ perfectionist, it quickly becomes apparent how often they ²d__r__d__ themselves for the simplest mistakes, at the same time ³st__r__ng clear of people who criticise them. The perfectionist is hungry for ⁴pr__ __s__, and at the same time sceptical of positive feedback. As regards treatment, the ⁵cr__c__ __l element in becoming more tolerant with themselves is for them to achieve what's called a state of flow, where they're so ⁶__ng__g__d in an activity, in the actual doing of it, that the result is no longer the goal. Discovering what gives them that state of flow is the key – in fact for anyone it is highly ⁷b__n__f__c__ __l. I suffered from perfectionist's depression myself, so I'm not just making an ⁸__d__c__t__d g__ __ss about treatment.

B Work in pairs and discuss. Why do you think the psychologist's treatment is effective?

G IF AND RELATED EXPRESSIONS

2 A Complete the sentences with the phrases in the box. You do not need all the phrases and sometimes more than one answer is possible.

| as long as   but for   if any   if in doubt   if so |
| it seemed as if   otherwise   provided that |
| rarely, if ever   unless   whether or not   without |

1 **A:** How often do you watch films in English?
   B: _____ .

2 **A:** If you saw someone drop some money, would you give it back?
   B: That would depend on _____ they saw me pick it up.

3 **A:** Would you ever consider living abroad?
   B: Yes, _____ I had a good job and a place to live.

4 **A:** When would you leave a football match early?
   B: If _____ my team were going to lose badly.

5 **A:** There's a rumour that your best friend is saying nasty things about you. What would you do?
   B: I'd ask him/her first if it's true. _____ I'm not acting like a friend myself.

6 **A:** You've just finished dinner in a restaurant with a group of friends. No one has money on them. Do you pay the bill?
   B: Not _____ they intend to pay me back.

B Work in pairs. Which 'B' sentences might *you* say?

C Choose three of the phrases that were not used above. Write a question for each that <u>could</u> use the phrase in the answer.

D Student A: ask Student B one of your questions, and tell him/her which phrase to use in the answer. Student B: answer the question using that phrase.

V COLLOCATIONS: EDUCATION

3 A Complete the collocations.

1 finding your own pa_____
2 a focus on in_____
3 fostering good re_____
4 fulfilling your po_____
5 mutual re_____
6 a nurturing en_____
7 a quality cu_____
8 rigorous st_____
9 striving for ex_____
10 taking the in_____

B Work in pairs and discuss. Think of a different context that is relevant for each phrase.

G NOMINAL RELATIVE CLAUSES

4 A Complete each sentence with a relative pronoun.

What are your strategies for developing your speaking skills?

1 I chat with _____ I can, in English of course.
2 I speak slowly, as I like to think about _____ I'm going to articulate my thoughts.
3 If a conversation hits a point where I'm not sure _____ the other person is saying, I pretend I do.
4 I talk to people on Skype in English every chance I get, _____ I find a willing partner.
5 I let the words come out of my mouth _____ they happen to come out, right or wrong.
6 I just talk about _____ happened to me that day. It's easier to talk about concrete things.
7 If I don't know _____ to say, I just ask a question and get the other person to talk.
8 If I get stuck choosing between two grammatical forms, I simply pick _____ is simpler.

B Discuss. To what extent are the statements true for you? Change any others to make them true.

F LEADING A DISCUSSION

5 A Add a missing word to each sentence.

1 So our today is to discuss how to deal with online bullying.
2 What I like to do is start with your ideas.
3 Who would like to kick this one?
4 Could you elaborate that?
5 Could you run past us again?
6 Can I just check you're coming from?
7 Correct me if I'm wrong, but you're saying is that this really isn't an option.
8 That's interesting perspective.
9 I imagine that working.
10 That's certainly considering.

B Discuss the issue of online bullying. Each time you include one of the sentences above, tick it off.

3 prospects

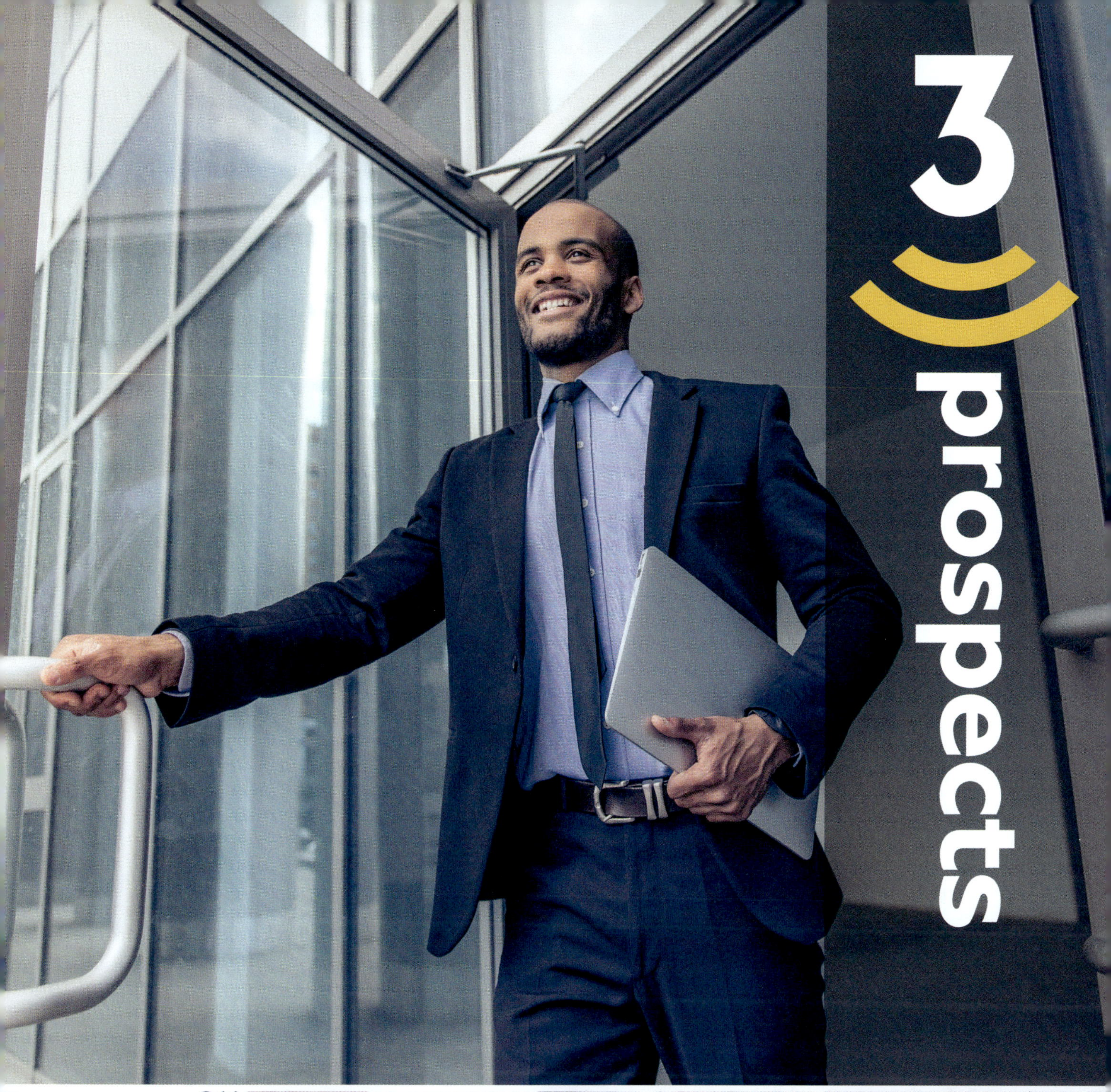

READY OR NOT p32

FIRED! p35

WHAT I'M SAYING IS ... p38

FUTURE JOB p40

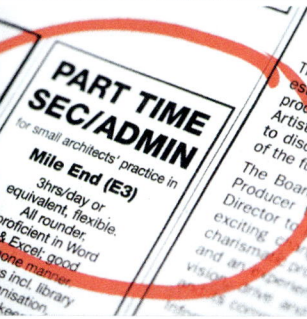

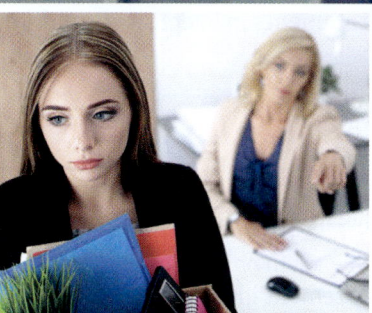

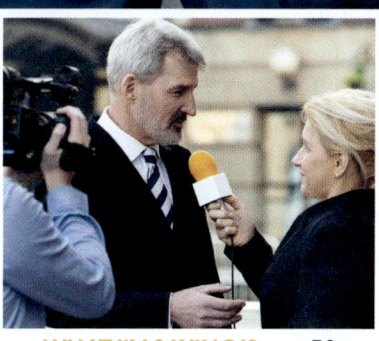

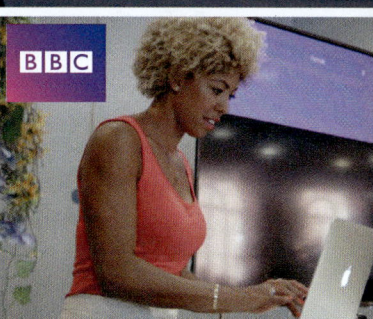

SPEAKING **3.1** Take part in a job interview **3.2** Hold a mediated discussion
3.3 Discuss questions about politics; Participate in a radio interview **3.4** Recommend a career

LISTENING **3.1** Listen to a question-and-answer session about finding a job **3.3** Listen to a political interview **3.4** Watch an extract from a BBC programme about artificial intelligence and work

READING **3.2** Read about people who were fired for social media mistakes
3.3 Read advice for public figures

WRITING **3.1** Write a cover email; Improve use of formal language **3.4** Write a fact file about work and artificial intelligence

3.1)) READY OR NOT

G expressing modality
P sentence stress
V job hunting

VOCABULARY

JOB HUNTING

1 A Work in pairs and discuss.

1 Have you ever looked for or applied for a job? If so, what was the process like? If not, what job(s) would you like to do and what qualities do you think you would need?

2 How competitive is the job market in your city or country? How can you get a job in a competitive job market?

B Complete sentences 1–8 with the words in the box.

> buzzwords   convey   footprint
> hard   jeopardise   literacy   novice
> play up   record   selling   soft
> stand out   strengths

1 There are tricks to make your CV _____, to get it to the top of the pile.

2 The three essential skills employers are seeking can be summed up in the job ad _____: 'communication', 'organisation' and 'flexibility'.

3 Employees are expected to have high social media _____.

4 Communication skills include the image you _____ of yourself on the internet, and a problematic digital _____ is likely to _____ your chances for a job.

5 Having _____ skills like working well in a team is more important than showing _____ skills such as technical know-how.

6 A _____ in the job market has no relevant experience or proven track _____ to point to in applications.

7 It's good to _____ your _____ and achievements when applying for a job.

8 Having a degree is no longer a strong _____ point; it simply helps the employer narrow down the choice.

C Match the definitions with words and phrases from Exercise 1B. Sometimes you need to add words to complete the collocation.

a) show knowledge-based abilities or those linked, for example, to relationships and creativity
    demonstrate hard or soft skills

b) someone doing something for the first time

c) everything about you that's on the internet

d) exaggerate your personal qualities and what you've done

e) put your opportunities at risk

f) the ability to use social networking sites skilfully, for example

g) a particular quality that makes something more desirable

h) the picture of yourself that you put across to others

i) words from a particular field that suddenly become popular

j) past achievements that can be shown

k) make your resumé likely to be noticed by whoever reads it

D Discuss. To what extent do you agree with the statements in Exercise 1B, and why?

LISTENING

2 A ▶ 3.1 Listen and make notes on the question-and-answer stage after a talk on job hunting.

B Work in pairs. What did the speaker say about each statement in Exercise 1B? Listen again and decide if the speaker agrees (√), disagrees (x) or gives no specific answer (?).

C Work in pairs and discuss.

1 List six job advert buzzwords or phrases mentioned. What do you now understand by them?

2 Think of two questions that you would ask the speaker if you were in the audience. How do you think she might answer them?

D Write a summary of the session (maximum 150 words).

GRAMMAR

EXPRESSING MODALITY

3 A ▶ 3.2 Listen to the conversations. What is the responder's job in each case?

B Listen again and write the response in each conversation. Then circle the modal verb in each case.

C Match the modal verbs in Exercise 3B with the meanings below.

- probability/possibility/impossibility (P)
- certainty (C)
- necessity/lack of necessity (N)
- obligation/lack of obligation (O)
- ability/lack of ability (A)
- permission/prohibition (PP)

4 A ▶ 3.3 SENTENCE STRESS In each phrase in Exercise 3B, mark the word with the main stress. Listen and check. What pattern do you notice?

B Listen again and repeat the phrases.

5 A Look at the underlined modal phrases from the talk. Match the phrases with the meanings in Exercise 3C.

1 These days there <u>are bound to</u> be a very large number of applicants for any given position.
2 It'<u>s absolutely essential that</u> you have the skills to enable you to manage large amounts of information efficiently.
3 You <u>need to have the capacity to</u> select and prioritise in a way so that nothing gets lost.
4 <u>Being able to</u> articulate your ideas clearly is key.
5 It <u>could be that</u> you aren't concise or articulate enough.
6 It'<u>s obviously your responsibility to</u> choose the appropriate platform to convey the right impression of who you are.
7 If there's a problem with your digital footprint, <u>inevitably it will</u> come out at some point.
8 Every job advert I look at says you'<u>re supposed to</u> have experience and a 'proven track record'.
9 It'<u>s vital</u> that anyone entering the job market … understands what these are.
10 It <u>seems totally unimaginable</u> that you've never had to apply your creativity …
11 Indeed, you <u>may well</u> have done all these things.
12 … there'<u>s a potentially strong likelihood</u> that you'll get to the interview stage.

B Which phrases in the box can replace the underlined phrases above? Sometimes more than one phrase is possible. Make any necessary changes to form.

be capable of   be crucial   be expected to
be guaranteed to   be highly unlikely   have to
I would guess   most probably   will undoubtedly

▷ page 108 **LANGUAGE**BANK

speakout TIP

Widening the range of language you use is a key 'quality step' you take in becoming a truly proficient user of English. Learning and using phrases to express a particular notion is one way to do that. For example, how many ways can you think of to express advice using modal verbs and phrases? e.g. *You should do it. It would be good if you did it.*

6 A Write something that

1 is bound to happen to you within three years, and is a good thing.
2 is absolutely essential for you to have in your home, but not everyone has.
3 you have the capacity to handle even though it's difficult.
4 being able to do is normal for a particular occupation (you choose).
5 people could think about you but which isn't the whole truth.
6 is obviously not your responsibility to do but you like to do it anyway.
7 will inevitably be invented, and will make life easier for some people.
8 you're supposed to do this week, but probably won't.
9 is vital for a visitor to your country to know.
10 once seemed totally unimaginable to you but now seems normal.
11 you may well decide not to do in the next week, even though someone expects it.
12 has a potentially strong likelihood of happening and will affect many people.

B Work in groups and take turns. Student A: read out your answer to one of the sentences in Exercise 6A. Other students: guess which sentence Student A is referring to, and ask him/her questions about his/her answer.

A: Tidy the chairs after class.
B: Number six?
A: Yes, it's not my responsibility but I like to do it.
C: Why's that?

WRITING

A COVER EMAIL; LEARN TO IMPROVE USE OF FORMAL LANGUAGE

7 A Work in pairs and discuss.

1 Have you ever written a cover email/letter for a job in your own language or in English?

2 In what ways is a cover email/letter different from a) a CV b) an informal email/letter?

3 Read the main body of the email below and check your ideas.

To: ....

I am writing to apply for the graphic designer position advertised on the SBI company website. I was particularly excited to discover this opening as SBI International has an excellent reputation in the profession, and I have been especially impressed by your recent online anti-hacking campaign.

To point out a few relevant aspects of my background, which are further detailed in my portfolio:

- In my three years as a freelance designer I have been involved in projects very similar to the anti-hacking campaign.

- I have extensive experience working with the full range of relevant design programs.

- My freelance experience has taught me to adapt to the demands of different project types essential for a graphic designer in a corporate context.

As I believe my referees will affirm, along with a flexible style I am also accustomed to working under pressure and to short deadlines. I am a good team worker, with strong communication skills and nearly all of my freelance projects have involved working with a group of designers.

Finally, I am dedicated to the profession and see myself working long-term with a company. I consider SBI to be an ideal context for me to show my best work and to develop further as a professional in the field. I feel my expertise, initiative and enthusiasm would be a real asset to your company.

As requested, I am attaching my CV, which includes contact information for three references, as well as copies of my degrees. A link to my online portfolio is at the end of this email.

I would be grateful for the opportunity to discuss my application with you and to explore my suitability for the position you have advertised. Please contact me at your convenience. Thank you for your consideration.

B What information is included in each paragraph? Make a list. How would you describe the tone of the email in three words?

8 Cover the email in Exercise 7A. Look at these extracts from cover emails and letters and rewrite the underlined phrases in a formal style. Then compare your ideas to the phrases in the email in Exercise 7A.

I'm writing to apply for the post advertised on the JobsRight website. I was [1]very pleased to read about the job as I know ExcelHotel [2]is well thought of.

In my previous work [3]I've done very similar jobs to those mentioned in your advert. [4]I have a lot of experience working with all the typical computer programmes. [5]I've also learnt to change based on what's needed.

I have good organisational skills and [6]am used to having a lot to do in a short time. [7]I plan to stay in the field and with one company for a long time. I feel my previous experience and skill set would make me [8]a great member of your team.

[9]I'd be happy to have the chance to talk about this and [10]see if I'd be good for the job. [11]Please drop me a line whenever you can and thank you for [12]taking the time to read this.

9 A Look at the job adverts on page 130. Choose one and draft your cover letter. Use the formal expressions from Exercise 8 where appropriate.

B Work in pairs. Swap your drafts and check them against the list you made in Exercise 7B. Does your letter address all the requirements of the advertisement? Would you consider the applicant for an interview? Give each other feedback.

C Rewrite your cover letter, taking the feedback into consideration (220–260 words).

SPEAKING

10 A Work in pairs. You are going to role-play an interview. Student A: turn to page 130. Student B: turn to page 131.

B Student A: when you finish, discuss with other Student As what the interviewees did well, and what they could have done better. Consider the following.

---

general impression   confidence   motivation
other personal qualities   relevant experience
concise, relevant answers

Student B: when you finish, discuss with other Students Bs whether you feel the job is right for you. What went well in the interview and what could you have improved?

FIRED!

G passives
P connected speech
V honesty; metaphors

3.2

READING

1 A Read the introduction to an article about people who lost their jobs because of something they posted on social media. What reasons can you think of for firing someone for a social media posting?

B Work in pairs. Student A: read the article on this page and write five words for each story to help you remember it. Student B: turn to page 130.

C Tell your partner about the stories. Who should and shouldn't have lost their jobs? Who do you feel most sympathy for?

D Read your partner's stories quickly to see if he/she included all the key aspects of the stories.

VOCABULARY

HONESTY

2 A Work in pairs. Look at the underlined words or phrases in the article on this page and on page 130 and match them with these definitions.

1 To finally be honest about something which you have been hiding.
2 To tell the truth even when it may be unpleasant or embarrassing.
3 To exaggerate something.
4 To be honest and factually correct in all the details about something.
5 To catch someone in the process of doing something wrong.
6 To be humiliated or become less respected.
7 To avoid talking about something unpleasant or say as little as possible about it.
8 To do something which shows what your real attitudes or qualities are, even if these are bad.

You're fired – for a Facebook posting!

It seems that some of us can't resist <u>showing our true colours</u> in our social media postings, even when we know deep down that they might be seen by someone who shouldn't. Did these people deserve to be fired, or should their employer work on their sense of humour?

Come fly with us (if you dare)!

Six crew members were fired from their position with a major airline after they <u>made candid comments</u> about, well, pretty much everything – the condition of the planes, the inflight meals, their salaries and the cockroaches crawling around the galley. 'It was a private conversation and we shouldn't have been fired for it,' complained one of the crew members, 'but my account got hacked and whoever it was posted it all over the place.' The airline director was unsympathetic. 'These crew members have not <u>presented an accurate picture</u> of our service,' he said. 'We can no longer consider employing them. There's nothing to be done.'

LIKE

Guilty … not guilty … guilty … not guilty …

A man serving on the jury of a double murder case was having trouble making up his mind, so naturally he appealed to the internet, setting up a poll on Facebook so that the public could help him decide. The result was his dismissal from the jury and a mistrial was declared, at an enormous cost to the city. When interviewed, Canadian-born Noah Martin <u>glossed over</u> his action. 'It was just a simple mistake and I don't want to discuss it any further.'

LIKE

Need a better costume

When her supervisor got a text that Isabel was taking the day off for a family emergency, he believed that his normally conscientious employee was telling the truth. Then when a photo of the São Paolo-based 30-year-old turned up on Facebook the next day, showing her in a carnival costume, he sent her on a permanent vacation. To her credit, Isabel <u>came clean</u> about the real situation. 'I admit that it wasn't a major emergency, but my mother really was ill and I dressed up in a costume partly to cheer her up.'

LIKE

B Correct one error in each option. One item is correct.

1 You are being interviewed for a job that requires fluent German. Your German is elementary. Do you:
   a) overdo the case and say you are fluent?
   b) present an accurate photo of yourself and hope for the best?
   c) count rapidly in German so that you don't lose your face?

2 A colleague you strongly dislike overhears you saying negative things about him/her. Would you:
   a) be candied and repeat what you said but say it was a joke?
   b) paint over the problem and change the topic?
   c) show your true collars and say what you really think?

3 You look at another colleague's texts while he/she is away, but then see there's CCTV in the room. Would you:
   a) come clear before anyone checks the video?
   b) do nothing and risk getting caught red-footed?
   c) damage the CCTV to cover up your actions completely?

C Work in pairs. How would you react in the situations described above?

GRAMMAR

PASSIVES

3 A Check what you know. Complete the sentences from the texts on page 35 and 130 with the appropriate passive form using the words in brackets.

1 We know deep down that they _____ by someone who shouldn't. (might see)

2 Did these people deserve _____, or should their employer work on their sense of humour? (fire)

3 It was a private conversation and we _____ for it. (should/not fire)

4 My account _____ and whoever it was posted it all over the place.' (hack)

5 'We can no longer consider employing them. There's nothing _____.' (do)

6 The result was his dismissal from the jury and a mistrial _____. (declare)

7 'I _____ work _____ on my back and the therapist recommended the rodeo.' (have/do)

8 People should realise there's a lot _____ for honesty. (say)

9 '_____ a second chance is just plain wrong.' (not/give)

10 'Can't someone post something without fear of _____ by Big Brother?' (spot)

B Look at the texts and check your answers.

C Check what you know. Look at the passive forms in the sentences and answer the questions.

a) What form or tense of the verb is used for each passive verb?

1 modal passive

b) Which sentence(s) include a named agent of the action and who or what is it?

c) In the other sentences why is the agent not mentioned?

d) Which sentence(s) sound(s) informal? Which sound(s) impersonal? Why?

D ▶ **3.4** **CONNECTED SPEECH** Listen to passive phrases from Exercise 3A. Mark the main stresses and any sounds which are lost, weakened or changed when said fast.

they might be seen by
     /bɪ/   /m/

▷ page 108 **LANGUAGE**BANK

4 Read the article and underline the most appropriate form, active or passive. Give reasons to support your choices.

Keep the change

[1]*Being disrespected/Disrespecting people* is something that makes waiter Alan Sanford angry. When [2]*a customer left him/he was left* a one-cent tip, he [3]*had the person's photo taken/took a photo of the person* and named and shamed them on the web. When Sanford's colleagues and boss found out, [4]*he was fired/they fired him*. '[5]*I could have been given/He could have given me* a warning,' complains Sanford, 'instead of [6]*being sacked/be sacked* straightaway.' Much to the chagrin of the service staff at the restaurant, the one-cent tip is now the norm!

The clown-burger

Flipping burgers at a fast-food restaurant [7]*can't be said/isn't said* to be the most interesting job in the world but Jackie Levine found a novel way to jazz things up – by juggling frozen burgers. However, Jackie didn't want [8]*to have her video taken/to be videoed* and posted on a popular social networking site. When a colleague posted a video of Jackie's routine, showing her occasionally dropping a burger and then tossing it onto the grill, neither the customers nor Jackie's employer were amused. Jackie has to practise her juggling at home now. 'I'm very angry with my colleague,' says Jackie. '[9]*The video shouldn't have been posted/ She shouldn't have posted the video*. I just want to get my job back. Now I realise there's something [10]*to be said/to say* for keeping your head down and just doing your job. I was just trying to liven things up,' she said. 'They're blowing it out of proportion.'

SPEAKING

5 A Work in groups. Choose one of the situations in the article on pages 35 and 130 or in the article above.

B Student A: you are the employee. List the reasons you should get your job back. Student B: you are the manager. List reasons why the employee should be fired. Student C: you are the mediator, who listens objectively to both sides. Prepare questions to ask both the employee and the employer.

C Hold a discussion. Student C: lead the discussion by asking questions and making sure both employee and employer have enough opportunity to make their case. In the end, decide together who had the stronger argument.

D Choose another situation and swap roles.

VOCABULARY *PLUS*
METAPHORS

6 Read the dictionary entry then underline the metaphors in the advice below. What is the original meaning of the metaphors and which area of life do they come from?

met·a·phor /ˈmetəfə, -fɔː -fɔːr/ ∞ noun [countable, uncountable]
1 a way of describing something by referring to it as something different and suggesting that it has similar qualities to that thing.
Longman Dictionary of Contemporary English online

1 As a new employee it's important to cultivate a good relationship with your colleagues.
2 HR will weed out the CVs of anyone without a good reference from their previous employer.
3 In my first job I felt hedged in by rules and regulations.

7 **A** Read the descriptions of businesses. Work in pairs and discuss. What is the missing name of the company, organisation or place? Would you be interested in working there? Why/Why not?

_____ is a nickname for an area extending from the southern portion of the San Francisco Bay Area. Starting in the 1970s, a large number of trailblazing silicon chip start-ups sprouted all over the area. As technology flourished, the companies branched out into different areas. The area is now home to many of the world's largest high-tech corporations and is the leading start-up ecosystem for high-tech innovation and scientific development.

_____ is a global leader in the food and beverage industry. The Swiss multinational started small, producing condensed milk, but by ploughing profits back into the company, years of entrepreneurship bore fruit. Despite facing some thorny issues over its baby milk products in the 1970s, it blossomed into what is now a global company, operating in almost 200 countries with 2,000 brands of baby food, chocolate, coffee and other foodstuffs.

In 2013, the Swedish branch of _____, which provides long-term humanitarian and development assistance to children in developing countries, realised donations were dropping. The root of the problem was that a 'like' on Facebook is not the same thing as making a monetary donation. In response, they launched a grass-roots campaign which said 'Like us on Facebook and we will vaccinate zero children against polio.' The hard-hitting campaign reaped rewards and as a result enough money was raised to vaccinate 637,324 children.

B Underline four farming/gardening/environmental metaphors in each description above.

C Work in pairs and guess the meanings of the metaphors. Then use a dictionary to check. Do you use the same metaphors in your language?

D Write about a successful company from your country or a brand that you like. Use a minimum of five of the metaphors above. Describe the company/brand to your partner and say what you like about it.

speakout TIP

Metaphors are easy to remember because they link to something concrete, their meaning is guessable and there may be an equivalent metaphor in your own language. Close your book and list as many of the twelve metaphors as you can remember. Then work with another student and check how many meanings you can recall.

8 **A** Underline the correct alternative in these metaphors relating to water. If necessary, use a dictionary to help you.

1 Sometimes I'm so busy I can barely keep my head *above/over* water.
2 Information from the management takes a long time to *surge/trickle down* to us students.
3 I sometimes have to *water down/freeze* my opinions because I can be dominant.
4 I can't stand people around me who are *wet blankets/dripping taps*.
5 Sometimes ideas and creativity just *flow/stream*.
6 When I have to give a talk in public, my mind *freezes/melts* and I can't think.
7 I'm lucky to have a friend who I can *gush/pour* out my frustrations to.
8 When I'm at home I often get *flooded/drowned* with unwanted cold calls.

B Work in pairs. Which sentences reflect your experience?

▷ page 122 **VOCABULARYBANK**

F evading a question
P stress and intonation
V political collocations

SPEAKING

1 Work in groups and discuss.

1 The media devote considerable space to politics. Do you think many people are really interested in politics and politicians?
2 Would you like to be a politician? Why/ Why not?
3 Who should be eligible to vote? Should everyone be legally required to vote?

VOCABULARY

POLITICAL COLLOCATIONS

2 A Complete the sentences with the words in the box.

| allocate   bridge   enforce   promote |
| set   shape   stand up   tackle |

1 The government should _____ more resources to *sport*.
2 The government needs to _____ the development of *scientific research*.
3 The opposition ought to _____ for the rights of *self-employed people*.
4 Governments have a duty to _____ the gap between *urban and rural citizens*.
5 The council should _____ a budget for *parks* and not use it for anything else.
6 Election manifestos always promise to _____ *corruption* but it never happens.
7 When special interest groups manage to _____ policy in *education*, *children* are the ones who suffer.
8 It's not the government's job to _____ regulations for *salary levels* in the private sector.

B Tick any opinions you strongly agree with. Replace any other items in italics with your own ideas. Then work in pairs and discuss your ideas.

▷ page 122 **VOCABULARY**BANK

3 A Do you ever watch interviews with public figures? How do they tend to reply to questions?

B Read the article on advice for politicians and other public figures when answering questions. Which tactic do you think they use most? Which is the most difficult to use effectively?

Politicians these days undertake extensive training to avoid answering tricky questions from journalists and members of the public. Media advisors train them to dodge questions they don't want to answer. Advice can be summed up in six key tactics:

1 **Stall.** Thank the person for the question and say what a great question it is whilst you think of something to say.
2 **Explicitly change the original question** so that it's one you want to answer: 'The question is not what **will** happen but what **should** happen.'
3 **Answer a different but related question**, the one you came prepared to answer. As long as you sound confident, most people won't notice.
4 **Go on the offensive and attack the question** or the questioner: 'That's a hypothetical question' or 'You've taken that quote out of context.'
5 **When you say something that you're comfortable saying, say it again using different words.** It won't sound like repetition, but rather emphasis, and buys you time.
6 **Sound trustworthy.** The easiest way to do this is to quote facts and figures as it's unlikely that these can be verified immediately.

FUNCTION

EVADING A QUESTION

4 A You are going to listen to a politician being interviewed about salary differences between men and women. Is this an issue in your country? If so, why do you think this is? If not, has this always been the case?

B Before you listen, look at the statements. To what extent do you agree with each one?

a) More women are working than before.
b) Women earn less because of the jobs they choose.
c) It's normal that women are paid less.
d) Increasing employment levels overall is a priority.
e) The government can't regulate salary levels.
f) Men are better at asking for higher salaries.
g) Campaign promises can't always be kept.
h) The government is working on the problem.

C ▶ **3.5** Listen and tick the points on the list that the politician mentions.

D Listen again. Which techniques from Exercise 3B do you notice?

5 A ▶ 3.6 Correct the error in each sentence. Then listen and check your ideas.

1 This figure has been taken into context.
2 Let me put it out of perspective.
3 What we're seeing does actually a positive, in that …
4 Well, what we have to take into account that is there can be …
5 I'm glad you've brought up that because there's another point that needs addressing …
6 … let me just add to that what I was saying.
7 Well, what we plan to be is to set up a review …
8 All I'm saying that is the government admits there is a problem.

B Work in pairs and answer the questions.

1 Which two answers in Exercise 5A most obviously avoid directly answering a question?
2 How is the language in answers 3, 4, 7 and 8 similar? What effect does this have?
3 What word does the speaker use twice to start her answer and give herself some time to think?

C Rewrite the sentences starting with the word in brackets.

1 We plan to crack down on drug abuse. (What)
2 It's taking longer for us to fulfil our promises, that's what's happening. (All)
3 The council will promote the development of tourism. (What)
4 I think the facts should be clarified before we hold a vote. (Let me)
5 I just meant that we have kept our manifesto promise. (All)
6 The union will always stand up for its workers' rights. (What)

6 A ▶ 3.7 STRESS AND INTONATION Listen and write the sentences you hear. Mark the main stress in the first half of each sentence. Then listen and check.

speakout TIP

The main stress in the cleft structure falls on the idea that is being emphasised. The intonation often rises slightly at the end to show that the idea is not finished.

B Listen again and say the sentences at the same time as the speaker. Focus on stress and intonation.

▷ page 108 LANGUAGEBANK

LEARN TO

CONTROL THE AGENDA

7 A ▶ 3.8 Complete the phrases that the interviewer uses to control the agenda using the words in the box. Then listen and check.

blunt   due   interrupting (2x) surely   what

1 But _____ that's not the point.
2 Yes, so _____ you're saying is that …
3 Excuse me for _____, but …
4 With all _____ respect …
5 Forgive me for _____, but …
6 I don't wish to be _____, but …

B Work in pairs and follow the instructions.

Student A: ask Student B a question related to: work, study, money, gender roles or any topic of your choice.

Student B: answer but avoid answering the question; just keep talking on the same topic until Student A interrupts you.

Student A: interrupt using a phrase from Exercise 7A, and ask your question again. Each time you interrupt, use a different phrase.

C Swap roles and repeat Exercise 7B with a different topic and question.

SPEAKING

8 A Work with a different student and choose one of the topics below to discuss.

B Student A: turn to page 130. Student B: you are the radio interviewer, and your task is to get Student A to answer the question below. To prepare, memorise and practise the phrases in Exercise 7A, and don't be afraid to repeat the main question!

Are you going to do anything about … ?

the crime problem

public transport problems

the crumbling road system

the lack of sports facilities

the lack of facilities for young people

the need for more public parks and public spaces

DVD PREVIEW

1 A Look at the list of jobs and put them into three categories: a) jobs that have been largely replaced by automation, b) jobs that may be significantly altered or replaced by automation in the future and c) jobs that are safe from automation.

actor	dentist	doctor	estate agent
fast-food cook	hotel maid		HR manager
messenger	school teacher		taxi driver
telemarketer	waiter	writer	

B Compare your ideas with other students. What factors do you think make a job 'safe' from automation?

2 Read the programme information. Which of these statements might be true?

1 The programme synthesises a fantasy and a scientific view of the future.
2 The programme solely looks at the future of work.
3 The programme makes several definite predictions about the future.

◉)) 10 Things You Need to Know About the Future   **BBC**

This programme looks at the issues that will change the way we live our lives in the future. Rather than relying on ideas from science fiction, mathematician Hannah Fry delves into the data available today to provide an evidence-based vision of tomorrow. In this episode, she explores a range of questions including whether a robot will take your job or if, as some believe, we will all one day actually become cyborgs. Hannah's view of the future is something she – and *Horizon* – are confident will definitely happen, and that is to expect the unexpected!

DVD VIEW

3 A Watch the programme. What is Dr William's attitude towards the way that Artificial Intelligence (AI) might affect her job in the future?

B Read and discuss possible answers to the questions below. Then watch the programme again and make notes on the answers.

1 What is the key difference between the workforce pre-1970s and since that time?
2 What examples are given of jobs affected by changes since the 1970s?
3 How can a computer diagnose a person's illness?
4 How does a computer program become better at a job like diagnosing illness?
5 If a computer can diagnose more efficiently than a doctor, is the doctor's job threatened?
6 Where could AI in medicine make the most difference?

C Work in pairs. What word or words could replace the ones in italics?

1 OK, so that's how it *calculates* the probability.
2 It's early days, but the company sees *enormous potential* for their virtual medic.
3 I don't think this is a *race* between machines and humans.
4 It's not just in medicine that software's *becoming more popular*.
5 Many who drive for a living will soon be *replaced*.
6 No job is *invulnerable to* the influence of artificial intelligence.

D Watch the programme from 4:00 and write the words that are used instead of the ones in italics.

4 Work with other students and discuss.

1 How would you feel about being 'seen' by an AI doctor like the one in the programme?
2 What experience do you have with consulting AI or online sources with medical questions? How reliable do you think the sources are?
3 To what extent to you feel AI in medicine is a good thing?

speakout recommending a career

5 A Put the following jobs in order in terms of how likely they are to be significantly altered by automation: musician, financial advisor, tour guide, chef.

B ▶ 3.9 Listen to an interview where a career expert discusses the jobs in Exercise 5A. Make notes on why each job might not be a good choice. Compare these with your ideas.

C Listen again and tick the key phrases you hear.

KEYPHRASES

What *I'm/was* getting at is that …

Those seem to be the most *vulnerable to/threatened by* automation.

A lot of what a *tour guide/musician* does is …/has …

They're supposedly *at least as good as/far more cost-effective than* humans.

You couldn't/I wouldn't call either of them *intellectual/vulnerable/repetitive.*

In reality *the genuinely creative/really lucrative/completely future-proof* jobs are reserved for the *lucky few/few and far between.*

What a human can bring to *guiding a tour/cooking a meal* that a robot can't is …

6 A Work with other students. Choose one person in your group and, all together, decide on a list of five possible jobs that might interest him/her.

B Put the five jobs in order from the most to least likely to be threatened by automation in the future. Use the key phrases to explain your choices.

C Present your final recommendation to the whole class, giving reasons for your choice.

writeback a fact file

7 A Read the fact file on the vulnerability of a particular profession to automation. Do you think the writer's reasoning and conclusion are optimistic or not? Which points do you disagree with?

FutureJob Fact file Hotel maid

How this job is safe from automation

A hotel maid's principle tasks involve cleaning, and the spaces and objects involved are so irregular in shape and positioning that the human maid's ability to physically navigate the space of a room is indispensable. Even in modern hotels the rooms vary in shape, dimension, position of furniture, and while a robot perhaps could be designed to handle the variables, it's unlikely to be worthwhile. Similarly, tasks like stripping sheets off beds, emptying the rubbish and checking nooks and crannies for rubbish that might be overlooked by a robot hoover (if the hotel has one) are incompatible with automation.

How this job is vulnerable to automation

Some tasks can be performed by robots, for example vacuuming, sterilising bathroom surfaces, ordering cleaning supplies, delivering things like an iron to guests' rooms. The tasks of folding linens, inventorying objects in rooms, requesting repair services and handling phone calls could all be at least partially automated. Perhaps though, the efforts on the part of those who design hotels to create spaces that are more easily cleaned are the greatest threat to the profession.

Conclusion

It would seem that the job of hotel maid is likely to be somewhat diminished in the future, since some tasks can be automated (and many have been already). However, the range of types of hotels and motels, including many for whom automation is unlikely for financial reasons, ensures that this is a relatively secure profession.

B Choose a job and brainstorm or research the tasks involved and their potential for being altered or taken over by automation. Write a fact file for the job, using three sections as in the text above (200–250 words).

C Read other students' fact files. Do you agree with their assessments of the various jobs?

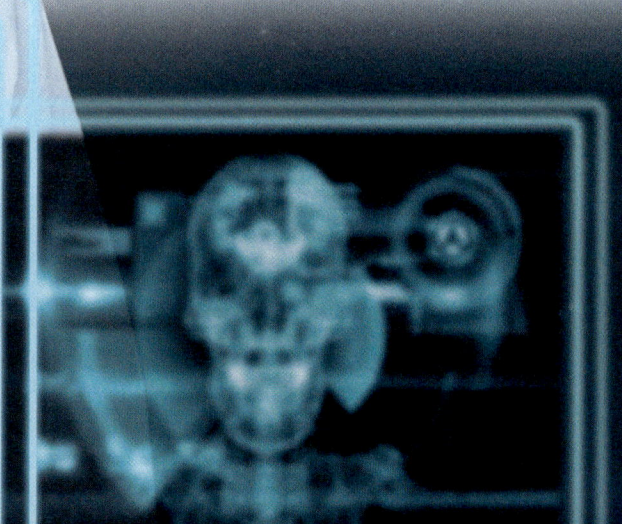

ⓋJOB HUNTING

1 A Complete the job-hunting words in the questionnaire.

> **You're desperate for a job and, qualified or not, have applied for a job in IT.**
>
> **1** Would you need to ¹pl____ up your ²st____ in terms of IT skills just to make your CV ³st____ out?
>
> **2** How can you ⁴co____ the best first impression in the interview?
>
> **3** How might you ⁵je____ your chances?
>
> **4** What's the danger of a ⁶no____ using a lot of ⁷bu____?
>
> **5** How could you demonstrate your ⁸ha____ skills in the area of digital ⁹li____?
>
> **6** If an applicant's biggest ¹⁰se____ points are a proven track ¹¹re____ and a clean digital ¹²fo____, what are your chances of getting the job?

B Work in pairs and discuss each of the questions in the text.

Ⓖ EXPRESSING MODALITY

2 A Rewrite each sentence so that it means the same using the word in brackets.

1 It's crucial that the crew seal the exits first. (obliged)

2 Everyone's supposed to have memorised every word they're going to say. (responsibility)

3 There's a strong likelihood that someone will be in pain. (probably)

4 One would guess that the flames and smoke would be frightening. (must)

5 It's vital that every aspect of service is perfect. (expectation)

6 Being able to work in high places without getting vertigo is important. (capacity)

7 The staff may well know more about the subject than the painters themselves. (imaginable)

8 Most people there are bound to find the motion difficult during a storm. (undoubtedly)

B Work in pairs. What place or job do you think each sentence is about?

Ⓥ HONESTY

3 A Complete the proverbs with the words in the box.

> accurate   candid (x2)   come   gloss
> lose   overstating (x2)   red-handed   true

1 Friends show their _____ colours in times of need.

2 Better to face losing than to _____ face.

3 If you always present a(n) _____ picture of yourself, you'll never have to remember what you lied about.

4 _____ one's wealth is foolish. _____ one's intelligence is for fools.

5 People who _____ over hard truths risk eternal adolescence.

6 It's easier to _____ clean about doing something bad than it is to admit being stupid.

7 _____ comments, like _____ photos, can be as deceptive as a well-crafted lie.

8 When a man caught _____ claims innocence, he's either a fool or a fiend, but never a friend.

B Discuss. Which ones have the most meaning for you?

Ⓖ PASSIVES

4 A Complete the text with the correct form of the verbs in brackets. Sometimes there may be more than one possibility.

You ¹_____ work _____ (do) on your car at the local garage. You ²_____ your car _____ (fix) there in the past, and you've always had the feeling that some of the work ³_____ (do) unnecessarily, or you ⁴_____ (sometimes/charge) for repairs that ⁵_____ actually _____ (not perform), but you don't know a better place. While waiting, you overhear two mechanics talking about how they cheat people, and you start to record the conversation with your smartphone. The trouble is, you ⁶_____ (watch), too – by the boss of the garage – and you realise this. What are your first thoughts?

a) He's unaware and needs ⁷_____ (tell) about what's going on.

b) He can probably ⁸_____ (persuade) to fix your car for free if you say nothing.

c) You're about to lose your smartphone.

B Work with another student and discuss the situation.

Ⓕ EVADING A QUESTION

5 A Work in pairs and list the ways of evading a question.

B Add the missing word to each of the sentences or phrases.

1 All I'm saying that I admit there is a problem.

2 Before I answer that, let me just to what I was saying.

3 I'm glad you've brought that because there's another point that needs addressing.

4 Let me put it perspective.

5 This has been taken of context.

6 Well, what we plan to do is to up a review to look into the issue.

C Write three questions on any topic. Sit in a circle with other students. One student asks another student a question. That student tries NOT to answer it. The other students ask the same student the same question. Each time, he/she tries not to answer it.

4) influence

ROLE MODEL p44   **THINK THIS WAY** p47   **HAVE A GO!** p50   **PERSUASION** p52

SPEAKING   4.1 Discuss role models and other influences in your life 4.2 Talk about breaking out of your 'echo chamber' 4.3 Give a persuasive presentation 4.4 Sell a product

LISTENING   4.2 Listen to a BBC radio programme about the internet 'echo chamber'
4.3 Listen to a presentation about an exciting activity
4.4 Watch people talking about influences when buying things

READING   4.1 Read an amazing story of a role model and her admirer 4.3 Read about 'the elevator pitch'

WRITING   4.2 Write a report about the effects of social media on relationships
4.4 Write a short opinion piece

4.1))) ROLE MODEL

G participle clauses
P word stress in multi-word verbs
V influence; three-part multi-word verbs

VOCABULARY

INFLUENCE

1 A Work in pairs and discuss. Which people have been most influential in your life so far? Think about your beliefs, behaviour, activities, musical tastes, etc.

B Complete the sentences with the phrases in the box which have a similar meaning to the phrases in bold. Make any necessary changes in form.

> an inspiration   be swayed by
> carry a lot of weight
> emulate sb   idolise sb
> pull strings

1 I really respect my older relatives and their views **are highly influential**/_____ in my decision-making.

2 I think it's OK for parents to **influence events from behind the scenes**/_____ to get opportunities for their kids.

3 I **give way to**/_____ people with strong opinions easily because I don't really have strong opinions of my own.

4 When I was younger I had a thing about pop stars; I'd **put them on a pedestal**/_____. I suppose I wanted to **follow in their footsteps**/_____ and be rich and famous.

5 I think it's important for celebrities to remember that they are **a role model** _____ particularly to young people, and to monitor their public behaviour accordingly.

C To what extent do you agree with the sentences? Tick those you agree with and change others to make them true for you. Then discuss with another student.

More than a role model

American gymnast Jennifer Bricker

Jen Bricker is an extraordinary woman with an extraordinary story. <u>Having been adopted at birth</u> after being born with no legs due to a genetic birth defect, from a young age Jen was drawn to physical sports including softball, volleyball and gymnastics.

Raised in Oblong, Illinois, by adoptive parents Sharon and Gerald Bricker, Jen was particularly keen on gymnastics: 'Some of my earliest memories are of watching gymnastics on TV when I was six years old and trying to imitate the moves.' She idolised American Olympic gymnast Dominique Moceanu, whose parents were Romanian immigrants to the USA. Jen watched her and her team win the gold in the 1996 Olympics in Atlanta, transfixed as Dominique became an overnight sensation. 'Dominique was my favourite gymnast. I wouldn't shut up about her. All I knew of my heritage was that I was Romanian and Dominique was also Romanian. We have the same features and spunky personalities. I was just drawn to her.'

READING

2 A Work in pairs and look at the photos of two famous gymnasts. Who do you think was whose role model, and why?

B Read the article and check your ideas. What is the most surprising feature of the story?

C Read the article again. Are the sentences T (true), F (false) or NG (not given)?

1 Jen was adopted because of her disability.

2 Both sisters were immigrants to the USA.

3 Jen took the gold medal in a state-level paralympics competition.

4 It was Jen's initiative to ask her adoptive mother about her background.

5 Jen contacted Dominique right away, but it took Dominique years to reply.

6 Dominique was pregnant when she contacted Jen.

7 Jen resembles her younger sister even more than her older one.

8 Jen regularly tours as a support act with Britney Spears.

D Work with other students and discuss. How do you think you would have acted if you were **a)** Jen **b)** Dominique **c)** Sharon **d)** Jen's biological parents?

Inspired by Dominique's success, Jen entered gymnastics and tumbling competitions and found she had a natural ability. She competed in the Junior Olympics and even won a State Championship in tumbling, competing against able-bodied people.

However, in her teens she began to wonder about her birth family and right before her sixteenth birthday she asked Sharon for more information. Feeling the time had come, her mother handed her a document and said, 'You're never going to believe this, but your biological last name is Moceanu.'

American gymnast Dominique Moceanu

Jen was astounded. She said: 'As soon as the words left her lips, I knew what it meant: my childhood idol was my sister. I remember thinking these kind of things happen in the movies, this is not real life.'

Having found out about her connection to her idol, Jennifer waited four years before writing to Dominique to introduce herself and see whether her biological family knew of her existence. Then she had to wait. 'Just before Christmas 2007, when I was twenty-one, I opened up a letter and it was from Dominique. I saw her signature and it was just the most amazing feeling. Halfway through the letter she said I was about to be an auntie, so I knew that they had accepted me immediately.'

'Four months later I met Dominique and my younger sister, Christina. The similarities were so apparent it was shocking; we sounded alike, our mannerisms were the same and with Christina, especially, it was like looking in the mirror. Since then we've become close and I feel like a piece of the jigsaw of my life has fallen into place.'

Now Jen works as an acrobat, aerialist and motivational speaker and has even toured with Britney Spears, performing acrobat routines.

'Right now I'm living my dream, travelling the world and connecting with people from all walks of life. We are all born with unique gifts and talents and I want to show people we can use them to change lives. Finding out my idol was my long-lost sister was just the beginning, my life has been about making the impossible, possible.'

GRAMMAR

PARTICIPLE CLAUSES

3 A Underline ten participle clauses in the text. The first one is done for you.

B Read the rules and find an example of each in the text.

RULES

1. Participle clauses can begin with:
   a) an *-ing* or the past participle form of the verb
   b) a perfect form using *having* + past participle
2. They can be used to:
   a) describe an action that happens at the same time as the main action.
   b) describe an action that happens before the main action and/or gives background to the main action.
   c) express cause or reason for the main action.
   d) give extra and non-essential information.

speakout TIP

When effectively used, participle clauses help a reader see the connection between and relative importance of events. When writing, look for places to combine sentences using a participle clause.

▷ page 110 **LANGUAGEBANK**

4 A Work in pairs and read other details from Jennifer's story. Which information do you find the most surprising?

1. Jen **was raised** by adoptive parents who didn't allow the word 'can't' to be used, so she believed she could do anything.
2. Jen says she fantasised about being related to Moceanu as early as age six. Perhaps she **sensed** the connection.
3. Jen **grew up** with her three half-brothers. She started playing softball with them when she was seven.
4. When Dominique was seventeen, she sued to become a legal adult. She **accused** her parents of squandering her professional earnings.
5. Jen **assumed** that their biological mother had told Dominique about Jen's physique, and only mentioned off-handedly in their first phone conversation that she didn't have legs.
6. Dominique had no idea what to say, and she was **astonished**.
7. Jen was **amazed** at how many things the three sisters had in common. She said, 'All three of us did gymnastics and Christina loved volleyball, which is my second favourite sport!'
8. Jen **has achieved** amazing success by any standard, but she still has plans. She **says**, 'My real dream would be to perform on a show like *Dancing with the Stars*.'

B Rewrite the sentences in Exercise 4A using a participle clause made from the verbs in bold. For each item make one sentence which includes all the information.

Having been raised by adoptive parents who didn't allow the word 'can't' to be used, Jen believed she could do anything.

SPEAKING

5 A Read these questions and make notes on your answers.

1. Who are seen as role models within your country or globally by: kids, your generation, businesspeople, the older generation? Do you think they are good or poor role models?
2. You have the chance of spending a day with one of your role models to help you in one aspect of your life. Who would you choose and how would you spend the time?

B Work in groups and discuss your ideas.

VOCABULARY *PLUS*

THREE-PART MULTI-WORD VERBS

6 A Replace the phrases in italics with the correct form of the multi-word verbs in the box.

| catch up on | fall back on | feel up to |
| hold off on | make up for | |

1 Jennifer's biological parents didn't *think they had the strength for* the task of raising a child with no legs.

2 Jennifer *delayed* contacting Dominique for four years, and then finally posted the letter.

3 The sisters have to *compensate for* more than twenty years of being separated.

4 They meet once in a while to *exchange* the latest news about each other's lives.

5 Even if she stops gymnastics, Jennifer has her career as an inspirational speaker to *depend on when everything else fails*.

B ▶ 4.1 WORD STRESS

Listen and check your answers. Then listen again and underline the main stress in the multi-word verbs.

C ▶ 4.2 Listen and write the sentence beginnings. Then complete them with your own ideas and compare your ideas with a partner. Stress the correct part of the multi-word verb.

speakout TIP

Some multi-word verbs must always have three parts: *You can't <u>fall back on</u> that excuse again. Who do you <u>look up to</u>?* Other multi-word verbs, when they have no object, lose the final particle: *Let's <u>catch up</u> soon. <u>Hold off</u> until I talk to her.* You can record these types of multi-word verb with a bracket to show the particle can be dropped: *to catch up (with), to hold off (on).* Notice that both types of multi-word verb are inseparable.

▷ page 123 **VOCABULARY**BANK

7 A Discuss. Did you ever have any role models from books or films when you were younger?

B Read about people's ideas of role models from books and films. Do you know the characters mentioned? Why do the speakers admire them?

As a teenager my role model was lawyer Atticus Finch, the hero of *To Kill a Mockingbird*. I read it when I was about thirteen and then I saw the old black and white film on TV with Gregory Peck. Finch was awesome because he confronts racists in his community by defending a black man. Despite [1]_____ resistance and threats, he is a man of principle and doesn't [2]_____ the trial. I wanted to [3]_____ his high ideals.

For young girls, a great role model is Merida in *Brave*, the Pixar animation. She's the one with the red corkscrew hair. Anyway, she wants to [4]_____ a marriage arranged by her mother so she [5]_____ a plan to change her mother's mind. She's the absolute antithesis of the traditional fairytale princess and my daughter, who is ten, really [6]_____ her for doing what she felt was right for her.

For me Holden Caulfield, the main character of *Catcher in the Rye*, was an important role model when I was in my teens and well into my twenties. Holden is a student at a private school who finds it so difficult to cope with the pressures of the 'real world' that he runs off to New York City and gets [7]_____ some scary situations with strange people. I identified with his feelings of alienation and the rejection he experienced time and time again. His adolescent suffering somehow helped me [8]_____ my own issues.

C Work in pairs and guess the meaning of the missing verbs in the descriptions. Do you know any multi-word verbs that fit?

D ▶ 4.3 Listen and write the multi-word verbs.

8 Student A: turn to page 131. Student B: ask Student A the questions below.

Quick quiz!

1 **A friend asks you to make a speech at her wedding. You hate making speeches. Would you**
   a) try to get out of it?
   b) skip the wedding and make up for it later?
   c) fall back on using a ready-made speech from the internet?

2 **Have you ever**
   a) got caught up in something unpleasant that wasn't actually your fault?
   b) held off on making a decision and then found that someone made the decision for you?
   c) come up against an obstacle to pursuing your career or studies?

THINK THIS WAY

G introductory *it* and *there*
P weak form: *there*
V social media

4.2

VOCABULARY

SOCIAL MEDIA

1 A Work in pairs and discuss.

1 How do you access the news? Why?
2 Which, if any, social media sites do you regularly use? Why?
3 How aware are you of the way that social media sites control what you see and don't see?

B Work in pairs and check what you know. Which words in the box refer to:

a) whether something is true or not?
b) something technical related to computers and/or the internet?
c) the separation of people into groups?
d) something that can happen with opinions?

algorithms	bubbles	censored
echo chambers	fake	filtering
hacking	post-truth	reinforced
segregation	trolling	unbiased

C Complete the description of a radio programme below with the words in the box. Two words are not used.

D Discuss. Do you recognise this happening in your own life? If so, give examples. What can you do to counter the effect?

LISTENING

2 A Work in pairs and look at the topics discussed in the radio programme. What do you think might be said about each topic?

a) Differing results from Google searches
b) People's awareness of filtering
c) People's natural biases
d) The consequences of filtering
e) Bubbles are everywhere
f) Facebook in the past and now

B ▶ 4.4 Listen to the programme and number the topics in the order you hear them.

C Work in pairs and make notes of anything you remember about each topic. Then listen again and add to your notes.

3 A Match the excerpts from the programme with the topics in Exercise 2A.

1 Contrary views are going to seem … *incomprehensibly/bizarrely* wrong in the end.
2 I asked a bunch of friends to google the same thing at the same time and send me *images/screenshots* of what they found … people were getting very different results.
3 The searching, the shopping, the information gathering. Bubbles *are present/exist* there, too.
4 The vast majority of Facebook users have no idea that they're seeing a(n) *algorithmically/systematically* filtered feed.
5 We have a tendency anyway to seek out views which *support/reinforce* our own and … to *discount/ignore* evidence which contradicts us.
6 When Facebook first launched, it was … a *sequential/chronological* feed of everything.

B ▶ 4.5 Listen to the excerpts that include the above sentences and underline the words the speaker uses.

C What surprises you (or not) about the statements in Exercise 3A?

BBC presenter Bobby Friction has started to realise that his access to ¹_____ and authoritative news as well as to the full contents of his social network feed are being limited, not by a person but by computer ²_____, basically by sets of mathematical instructions. This method of sorting and ³_____ content has by and large replaced the function of a traditional news editor. The result is increasingly the separation of different online communities into ⁴_____ where someone like Bobby only interacts with people who have the same views as him. In this way his opinions are ⁵_____ and seldom, if ever, challenged. Contradictory views are ⁶_____ completely – he simply never sees them. Recently these social media ⁷_____ have become a big issue, with talk of ⁸_____ news, ⁹_____ politics and the increasing ¹⁰_____ of online communities into groups which share a similar narrow range of views. In this radio programme Bobby investigates the extent of this state of affairs.

GRAMMAR
INTRODUCTORY *IT* AND *THERE*

4 A Check what you know. Complete the comments about the radio programme below with *it* or *there*.

Sid23: ¹_____'s no harm in only communicating with people who feel the same way as me. ²_____ upsets me to read someone's opinion if I can't change it.

BonoV: ³_____ could come a time when, say, homeless people are completely edited out of your feed. ⁴_____'s a mistake to take this whole issue too lightly.

X2Y: Without filtering, I'd be flooded with ads for things I'm not interested in. ⁵_____'s nothing wrong with having ads that are relevant to you.

Deirdre: ⁶_____ seem to be some people who are incapable of thinking for themselves. Why don't they just choose what content they click on more carefully?

Wes: ⁷_____ is a disaster that online filtering is segregating people more and more. People should have more chances to come together.

Fern27: ⁸_____ was Mahatma Gandhi who said 'A small group of determined and like-minded people can change the course of history.' I think ⁹_____'s brilliant how filtering can bring people together. And anyway ¹⁰_____'s impossible to turn the clock back now.

B Tick the comments which support social media echo chambers or don't see a problem with them.

C Work in pairs and check your ideas. Discuss which statements you agree and disagree with, and say why.

5 Look at the comments again and find examples of the following uses of introductory *it* and *there*. Write the number of the example next to the pattern.

RULES

Use *it* as an empty subject to introduce or identify something later in the phrase.
a) + *be* + noun/adjective + *to* infinitive (*It's time/easy to …*)
b) + *be* + noun/adjective + clause (*It's a pity/strange that …*)
c) + verb + object + *to* infinitive (*It hurts me to …*)
d) as part of a cleft structure for emphasis (*It's you I have to thank …*)

Use *there* as an empty subject to show that something exists and to introduce or identify something later in the phrase.
e) + *be* + noun clause (*There's a number of reasons why …*)
f) + verb + *to* infinitive (*There appears to be a …*)
g) + modal verb (*There must be a reason for …*)
h) + something/nothing/someone/no one, etc. (*There's someone to see you.*)

▷ page 110 **LANGUAGEBANK**

6 A ▶ 4.6   **WEAK FORM:** *there* Listen and write the phrases with *there*.

B Listen again and say the phrases at the same time as the speaker. Pay attention to the weak sound of *there* /ðə/.

C Complete the phrases with your own ideas. Tell your partner. Pay attention to the weak sounds.

SPEAKING

7 A Read the list of ways of reducing the echo chamber effect. Put a tick (✓) next to the ones you would be willing to try, and a cross (✗) next to the ones you would rather not try.

GET OUT OF YOUR BUBBLE!

7 ways to reduce the echo chamber effect

1 Click on Facebook links that aren't consistent with your taste or opinion.
2 Engage (constructively!) in forum discussions with people who have opinions that oppose yours.
3 Follow someone who you don't agree with.
4 Subscribe to a newsfeed from a source you don't agree with.
5 Unfollow people whose opinion or taste is the most similar to yours.
6 Whenever you share something with one view, share something with another view.
7 Don't go online for a day, or a week …

B Work with other students. Compare your lists and give reasons for your choices. Which of you seems to be the most open to reducing the echo chamber effect? Did any other ideas come up as to how you might do this?

WRITING

A REPORT: LEARN TO USE USEFUL PHRASES

8 A Work in pairs and check what you know. Make a list of 'Dos and Don'ts' to keep in mind when writing a report. Think about text organisation, style, formatting, inclusion of examples, opinion, etc.

B Check your ideas with the points on page 133.

9 A Read the email request. Then look at the notes compiled from an informal student questionnaire and discuss the questions.

1 What do you understand by each point? Which do you agree with?

2 If you had to omit one point from each section, which do you think is the least relevant?

> Please write a report about the positive and negative effects of social media on interpersonal relationships for the university governing council, which in part supervises student life on campus. Include recommendations as to how to minimise any negative effects. We need about 280–320 words.

+ POSITIVE	– NEGATIVE
• Know what people are up to	• Expectation to always respond
• Easy to touch base daily	• Miscommunication due to short message style
• Closed groups, e.g. classmates	• Insecurity re self-image
• Shared topic, e.g. viral video	• Over-dependence on technology
• Laptop/mobile-friendly	• Loss of ability to interact face-to-face

B Read the first part of the report. Which positive effect from the notes is not included?

Introduction

[1]*The aim of this report* is to summarise the positive and negative effects of social media on interpersonal relationships, based on the findings of a survey of 100 university students. [2]*The final section will* offer recommendations on ways people could change their use of social media [3]*to minimise any negative effects*.

Positive effects

[4]*A significant proportion* of people [5]*interviewed* indicated a positive effect of social media on their relationships. The most [6]*frequently mentioned* reason was that social media makes it easy to keep up to date with people without the need to communicate by email or phone. There was [7]*widespread agreement* that social media apps are convenient tools for making contact with friends on a daily basis and that it was helpful to base exchanges on common topics such as a viral video. [8]*A few people* commented on the advantages of a closed group of friends or colleagues to keep communication private.

C Work in pairs. List two other ways to express each phrase in italics.

D Replace the phrases in italics with the phrases in the box. Three items are not used. Which part of the report could they be used in?

> a clear consensus
> a negligible number
> a substantial percentage
> answering
> commonly cited
> in light of the above
> it will go on to
> this report sets out
> significant disagreement regarding
> this report will present
> to improve the situation

10 A Use the notes in Exercise 9A to write the section on 'Negative effects'. Use phrases from Exercise 9D and write no more than 100 words.

B Work in pairs and read each other's draft. Does the draft

- keep to the word count limit?
- include only the most relevant negative effects?
- use a variety of fixed phrases accurately?

11 A Work in pairs and brainstorm recommendations to deal with the negative effects.

B Work alone and choose the three most useful recommendations. Write the final section of the report. Include a one-sentence introduction, three bullet-pointed recommendations and a closing sentence (70 words maximum).

C Look at the model on page 132 and compare it with your version. Underline three useful phrases for the section.

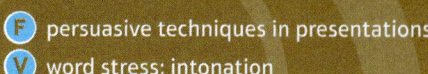

F persuasive techniques in presentations
V word stress; intonation
P persuasion

Are you ready to make your 'elevator pitch'?

The classic scenario that gave birth to the expression 'the elevator pitch' goes like this: You're a newbie working in a big company and you have a great idea, but no way of getting that idea to the people who make decisions. Then one day you step into the elevator and find yourself standing next to the company president. You have about sixty seconds to sell your idea – as long as it takes for the elevator to complete its journey.

VOCABULARY

PERSUASION

1 A Work in pairs. Read the introduction to a short article about 'the elevator pitch' above and answer the questions.

1 In what situation can you imagine yourself making an elevator pitch*?
2 What kind of person do you think is good at it?
3 What qualities do you think the 'pitch' has to have to be effective?

> *****pitch** = the things someone says to persuade someone to buy something, do something or accept an idea
> LDOCE online

B Read the rest of the article and check your ideas.

> So what makes a persuasive elevator pitch? Well, it's got to be succinct – you only have sixty seconds – and compelling, something the listener won't be able to resist. And of course it has to be pertinent to your listener's needs; as they say in advertising, you can't sell dog food to a cat no matter how hungry it is.
>
> And the delivery is just as important, if not more. You need to be enthusiastic, without being too earnest or pushy. You need to be credible, to come across as knowing what you're talking about. And above all, you need to be genuine. Just be yourself.

C Find an adjective in the article that means

a) clearly expressed in few words.
b) convincing.
c) believable.
d) honest, friendly and trustworthy.
e) relevant to the subject.
f) serious and sincere.
g) so interesting that you have to pay attention.
h) too aggressive about one's needs.

D ▶ **4.7** **WORD STRESS** Listen and check your answers. Underline the main stress in each adjective. Then listen again and repeat.

2 A Complete the sentences with the adjectives you found in Exercise 1C.

1 I tend to talk a lot and find it hard to be
_____.
2 I can't say no when someone smiles when asking a favour – it's a _____ technique.
3 Most people are putting on an act and aren't _____, they can't just be themselves.
4 I have a friend who is a(n) _____ storyteller – it's impossible to stop listening to him.
5 If I can't say something _____ to the topic of conversation, I say nothing.
6 Some people get very _____ about sport – I tell them to lighten up. It's just not very important in the grand scheme of things.
7 Sometimes you have to be _____ to get what you want, but it's annoying when someone's like that.
8 People without kids are not very _____ when they give advice on raising children.

B Tick the sentences that are true for you. Then compare and discuss in pairs.

▷ page 123 **VOCABULARY**BANK

FUNCTION

PERSUASIVE TECHNIQUES IN PRESENTATIONS

3 **A** ▶ **4.8** You're going to listen to a presentation about escape rooms. Listen and answer the questions.

1 Would you like to try an escape room?
2 What do you understand about how one works?
3 What sort of person does it suit?

B ▶ **4.9** Work in pairs and complete the sentences with the number of words given. Listen and check.

1 It's _____ this huge 3D puzzle. (1)
2 You've got to communicate a lot with the others, _____ 'Why do you think we got this piece of paper?' (1)
3 But you can't panic, _____ get out, and _____ stop working as a team. (2, 2)
4 If you succeed, it's great, you did it as a team, and you feel really good about it. _____, well that's a shame, but you did it as a team, and you _____ . (3, 5)
5 And who does it suit? Well, it suits people who like doing hands-on work, _____ looking around and taking it all in, trying to connect the dots, and most of all it suits _____ working in a team. (3,3)
6 You have to enjoy the team element, and finding your role in that, whether your role is the foot soldier or the _____ . (1)
7 Not only will you have a unique, exciting experience _____ share an experience with friends that you'll be talking about for years. I guarantee it. (4)

C Look at the sentences in Exercise 3B. How many examples can you find of these persuasive techniques?

a) direct speech: the words of someone speaking
b) simile or metaphor: saying that something is similar to something else or saying it IS that something else
c) negative inversion: a structure that starts with a negation followed by auxiliary + subject (e.g. *No sooner had I found happiness than I lost it again!*)
d) repetition: a phrase or structure is used more than once
e) rhetorical question: a question is asked of the reader that they don't actually answer
f) the rule of 3: saying things in a series of three

D ▶ **4.10** **INTONATION** Listen to sentence 3 in Exercise 3B. Say the sentence with the recording. Copy the rising intonation when something is unfinished and the fall when it is finished.

speakout TIP

Rhetorical devices have been used for centuries. Where might you use them nowadays: selling something online, writing a profile, giving a presentation, other contexts?

▷ page 110 **LANGUAGEBANK**

LEARN TO

USE ADJECTIVE ALLITERATION

4 **A** Look at this sentence from the presentation. Which rhetorical device from Exercise 3C does it use? What do you notice about the adjectives?

The thing is, it's cooperative, it's collaborative, it's <u>not</u> competitive.

B Cover Exercise 2A and complete these sentences with the adjectives there. Think about the sound as well as the spelling.

1 As a speaker I'm self-confident, systematic and _____ .
2 People say I'm generous and _____ although sometimes rather juvenile.
3 Some people are unfocused and too theoretical. I always try to be _____, productive and practical.
4 When I'm trying to make someone change their mind I'm patient and _____ without being _____ .
5 When I talk about my achievements, I think I come across as confident, _____ and _____ .

C Complete the sentences below using alliteration. Then compare your ideas.

1 My favourite city is _____ because it's …
2 My ideal job would be _____ because it's …
3 I'm attracted by people who are …

SPEAKING

A PRESENTATION

5 **A** Choose something – an experience, a product, a computer app – and prepare for a presentation aimed at persuading others to try this thing out. Use the following framework and make notes in your notebook.

Introduce the topic	*I'd like to tell you about …*
Go into a short description.	*So what is … ?*
Include an example or two	*Just to give you an example …*
Wrap up the description	*So that's how X works.*
Give your final pitch	*In short, …*

B Work with another student. Look at each other's notes and find places you can use the persuasive techniques above. Practise giving your presentation to each other.

C Give your presentation to the class and listen to other students' presentations. Which things would you like to try out most?

Michael
Presenter

Sue

Osamah and Amir

Sofia, Matt and Mila

Maria and Kelsie

Simon

Hubert and Kornelia

James and Alex

Hamza

Jeanne

DVD PREVIEW

1 Work in pairs. Think of three things that you've purchased recently and discuss.

1 How did you decide which particular thing to get?
2 Which factors below influenced your decision? Which had no bearing at all?

- Online advertising
- A friend's recommendation
- A celebrity endorsement
- Brand
- Price
- Social media
- Print advertising
- Other factors

3 Generally speaking, which forms of marketing influence you the most?

DVD VIEW

2 A Watch Part 1 of the interviews. Which speakers do you agree with most?

B What three words finish each sentence? Discuss in pairs, then listen and write the words the speakers use.

1 I tend to … look at reviews that are online, and I don't buy anything with less _____.
2 I'll see what my friends are wearing or kind of Instagram and I'll decide _____.
3 Probably, erm, brand, definitely brand. Also, advocacy, so _____ .
4 I'm not too worried about things that look fancy as long as they _____ .
5 … being able to touch and, and, erm, experience a physical object is always a _____ .

C Which of the statements in Exercise 2B do you agree with?

3 Watch Part 2 of the interviews. Which speaker(s) …

1 gives a reason for buying what he/she bought?
2 was the most straightforward in making a decision?
3 was the most systematic?
4 says he/she considered cost?

4 Watch Part 3 of the interviews. Which speakers talk about the following? Make notes on what they say.

- Word of mouth
- Endorsements
- Billboards
- Internet

5 A Work in pairs and discuss. Are you manipulated easily by advertising? Give examples.

B Watch Part 4 of the interviews. How many people say they are truly influenced by adverts? What examples do they give?

C What does the underlined word refer to? Work with another student and try to remember, then watch Part 4 again and check.

1 Other than that I can't say I'm really … er, I wouldn't say myself that I'm easily manipulated.
2 … it looked so good and I actually went looking in the supermarkets …
3 … it's important to actually read erm, customer reviews because they have tried it …
4 I'm a little bit sceptical about it.
5 It doesn't necessarily mean that I will buy if I've seen some, a great ad but I do enjoy watching it.

speakout selling a product

6 A Which of these factors are the most important for making an advertisement effective? Which are the least important? Think of examples of advertisements you know.

> fun honesty illusion memorableness originality simplicity

B Work in pairs and choose one of the products below. How could the manufacturer market it so that you are most likely to choose their version of the product over others? Use the ideas you discussed in Exercise 6A to help.

> headphones trainers a soft drink

C Present your ideas to the rest of the class. Discuss as a class whose ideas are the most persuasive.

writeback a short opinion piece

7 A Work in pairs and discuss. Which of these three bits of advice from marketing experts do you agree with most?

> 'The most powerful element in advertising is the truth.' – Bill Bernbach
>
> 'The more informative your advertising, the more persuasive it will be.' – David Ogilvy
>
> 'Facts are irrelevant. What matters is what the consumer believes.' – Seth Godin

B Read the short opinion piece from a magazine. How does the author argue his/her position? What arguments can you make for the opposite perspective being true?

Truth in advertising: A lost virtue?

I would like to believe that it's right that 'The most powerful element in advertising is the truth,' but life experience tells me otherwise, and in fact I find the statement sadly naive. It's hardly a new concept that advertising is often geared to influence the consumer by manipulating their emotions. I don't think I've ever seen an advertisement that puts truth before this goal; in everything from ads for soft drinks to cars to life insurance, the product is romanticised by associating it with a positive experience, feeling, relationship, etc. Imagine an advert for a soft drink that tells the truth: 'Drink this sugar-filled, artificially flavoured, artificially coloured liquid and you'll feel refreshed, and ruin your teeth in the process!' There, truth would be a powerful element indeed – for ensuring that fewer people buy the product.

Perhaps there was a time when truth was a valued virtue in advertising, when people felt they learnt something when they saw an ad, something that helped them make better-informed choices about what they buy. I would love to experience such an age, as I think that truth in advertising could influence individuals to be more responsible about all their choices, and manufacturers to provide higher-quality, healthier products.

C Choose one of the other two quotations in Exercise 7A and write a short opinion piece. Say whether you agree or not with the quotation and why (200–250 words).

ⓥ INFLUENCE

1 A Correct one word in each sentence to make a phrase connected to influence.

1 My current role modal is X.
2 I am easily swerved by X.
3 X's opinions carry a lot of way with me.
4 X prefers to influence from behind the stage.
5 I'd like to follow in the footprints of X and be …
6 When I was a kid I immortalised X.
7 X's views used to be highly affluential.
8 I never give away to my X in an argument.
9 X is an aspiration to me.
10 X is always pulling ropes to get what he/she wants done.
11 The best way to give a speech is to amulet X.
12 X often puts me on a podium.

B Who for you is X in each sentence? Tell your partner your ideas.

ⓖ PARTICIPLE CLAUSES

2 A Underline the correct alternative.

1 Every summer you can find me *lain/lying* on a beach, *sip/sipping* ice tea, *having watched/watching* the clouds. But I'd rather be …
2 *Having/Having been* studied English for over ten years, I still need to …
3 Every now and then, *being fed/fed* up and *frustrated/frustrating* with life, I feel like moving to …
4 Always *have/having* been shy, sometimes I surprise myself when I …
5 If I want something, I keep pushing till I get it, never *put/putting* off by the negativity of others. People think I'm …

B Change and complete the sentences so that they're true for you.

C Compare your ideas with other students.

ⓥ SOCIAL MEDIA

3 A Add vowels to complete the social media-related expressions.

1 a) c __ ns __ r __ d
   b) __ nb __ __ s __ d
2 a) h __ ck __ ng
   b) tr __ ll __ ng
3 a) b __ bbl __ s
   b) s __ gr __ g __ t __ __ n
4 a) r __ __ __ nf __ rc __
   b) __ ch __ ch __ mb __ rs
5 a) __ lg __ r __ thms
   b) f __ lt __ r __ ng
6 a) f __ k __
   b) p __ st-tr __ th

B How are a) and b) related in each case?

ⓖ INTRODUCTORY *IT* AND *THERE*

4 A Complete the sentences with *It* or *There* and a word or phrase from the box. Add a form of *be* and/or negation if necessary.

> coincidence   doesn't matter
> harm   not likely   a mistake
> nowhere   ~~something~~
> typical of

1 *There's something* _____ to be said for reading news that you don't agree with.
2 _____ to underestimate the importance of a good night's sleep.
3 _____ in sometimes telling a small white lie.
4 _____ to go for a coffee around here.
5 _____ how much salt there is in food. The problem is with sugar.
6 _____ to be another major world war in our lifetime, one would hope.
7 _____ that the gig economy has grown at the same time as the economic downturn.
8 _____ wealthy people to blame the poor for their lack of money.

B Discuss. To what extent do you agree with the statements?

ⓕ PERSUASIVE TECHNIQUES IN PRESENTATIONS

5 A Work in pairs and look at the quotations. What do you think is the source or context of each one?

1 'Government of the people, by the people, for the people.'

2 'So it's time to ask yourself: What will it take to make the big leap? If not now, then when?'

3 'Not only does it last longer but charging time is greatly reduced!'

4 'Elderly American ladies leaning on their canes listed toward me like Towers of Pisa.'

5 'And people come away saying things like, 'That was the most amazing experience of my life.'

6 'All the world's a stage, and all the men and women merely players.'

B Match the persuasive techniques (a–f) with the quotations in Exercise 5A.

a) direct speech   d) repetition
b) simile or metaphor e) rhetorical question
c) negative inversion   f) The rule of 3

C Work in pairs. Choose three rhetorical devices and write a sentence for each, with one coming from an advertisement, one from a speech and one from a literary context.

D Read your sentences to other students. They say what persuasive/rhetorical device each one uses, and what the context is.

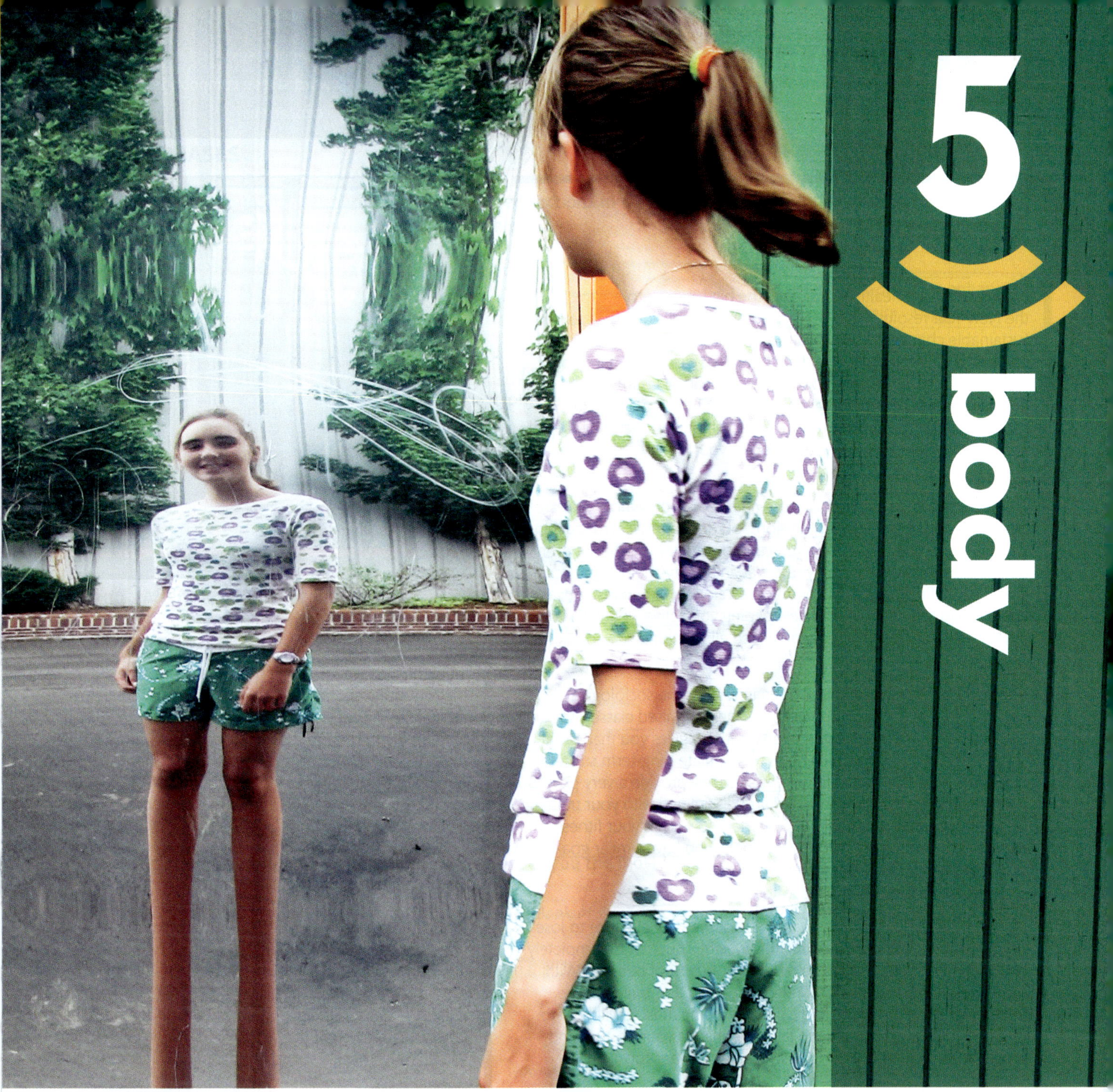

5 body

GOOD FIT p56

THREE APPLES A DAY p59

MAGIC BULLET p62

CULINARY JOURNEY p64

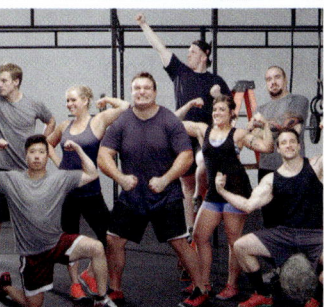

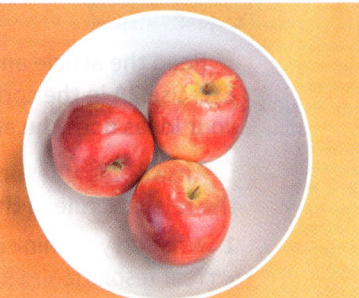

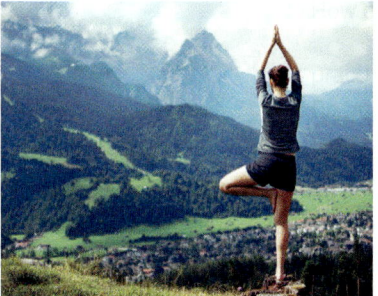

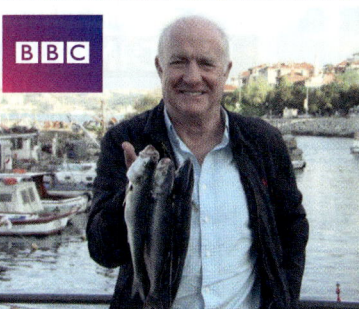

SPEAKING **5.1** Talk about fads in fitness and other fields **5.2** Discuss the pressure to look and dress a certain way **5.3** Suggest ways to make a workplace healthier **5.4** Describe a food memory

LISTENING **5.2** Listen to a woman talk about what it's really like to be a model **5.3** Listen to people discuss their own idea of staying healthy **5.4** Watch an extract from a BBC programme about the feelings food evokes

READING **5.1** Read about secrets of long-term fitness **5.2** Read how looks can be deceiving

WRITING **5.2** Write a description **5.4** Write about a food memory

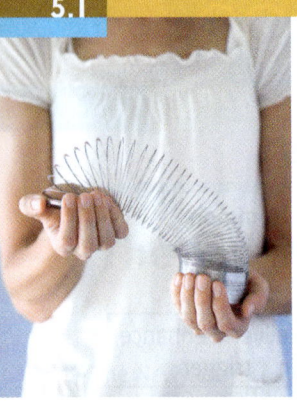

VOCABULARY PLUS

COMPOUNDS

6 A Check what you know. Complete the compound adjectives.

The problem with quick fixes for exercise or diet are that they are ¹_____-lived. ²_____-term solutions take more time and effort. ³_____-intensity sessions can be effective and can be ⁴_____-cost. But you need motivation and a lot of ⁵_____-discipline to sustain your programme.

B Work in pairs. Which words in the box can be added to the adjectives in the table to make compounds? Use a dictionary to check your ideas. Note useful examples for items that are new to you.

> awaited   end   grade   haul   key   lost   maintenance   powered   profile   range   risk   staffed   suffering   tech   tempered   winded

Student A:	Student B:
high-_____	low-_____
long-_____	short-_____

C Explain the meaning of any new compounds to your partner. Write down the new ones in your notebook.

D ▶ 5.1   WORD STRESS: compounds Listen to some of the compounds. Which word is usually stressed? The first or the second? Listen again and repeat.

7 A Answer the questions using a compound adjective from Exercise 6B.

1 Why did the gym hire more people?
2 Why did the trainer go on an anger-management course?
3 What sort of equipment is best to have on a desert island?
4 For which type of flight is it particularly worth travelling in business class?
5 How would you describe a hairstyle which takes an hour to get right?
6 How should someone behave if they don't want to be noticed?

B Work in pairs and write at least three questions using the compounds. Add a follow-up question to each.

Do you have a high-maintenance friend? What's he/she like?

C Work with other students. Ask and answer the questions.

speakout TIP

Compound words are high frequency in English. You can enrich your vocabulary by investigating and noting compounds with common compound 'starters', e.g. *good* (*good-hearted*, *good-looking*, *good-natured*). Find six compounds in your dictionary with *self-* that are new to you.

▷ page 124 **VOCABULARY**BANK

SPEAKING

5 A Work in pairs and look at the photos. What, if anything, do you know about these fads?

B Work alone. Which fads did you experience when you were younger? Choose three categories from the list below and prepare to describe a particular example. Say who it was popular with and why.

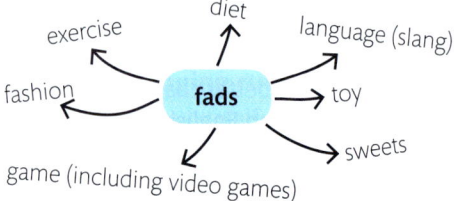

diet
exercise
language (slang)
fashion
fads
toy
game (including video games)
sweets

C Work with other students and tell them about your experience. How many of the fads do other people recognise?

THREE APPLES A DAY

G fronting, headers and tails
P chunking
V fashion and looks

((5.2

VOCABULARY

FASHION AND LOOKS

1 A Work in pairs and discuss the questions.

1 Are you interested in fashion? If so, how do you find out about it? If not, why not?

2 Do you have a favourite item of clothing that you wear time and again?

3 What colours or fabrics would you never wear? Why not?

4 When you were a child, what was the worst item of clothing you were made to wear?

B In sentences 1–8 cross out the alternatives that are not possible. In many cases both alternatives are possible. If so, is there any difference in meaning?

1 One hundred percent of magazine photos are *photo-shopped/retouched* after the fashion *shoot/filming*.

2 Fashion *victims/martyrs*, or people who try to *follow/keep up with* the *last/latest* fashion, are as likely to be men as women.

3 The average *catwalk/runway* model is 1.77m tall and weighs about 49kg.

4 Even five-year-olds these days are fashion *conscious/aware*, and that's a matter of concern.

5 Male models are catching up with female models in terms of *eating disorders/ailments* such as anorexia.

6 Looks can be *deceiving/deceptive*; often a model isn't more beautiful than the average person, but more *photogenic/photographable*.

7 The sixties look is *back in fashion/fashionable again*. In fact it's never *gone out of fashion/been unfashionable*.

8 The media is solely to blame for *distorting/contorting* people's idea of beauty, and leading young people to *regard/view* looking good as equivalent to being healthy.

C Work in pairs and look at the sentences in Exercise 1B. Which are presented as fact and which as opinion? If opinion, do you agree? Which of the supposed factual statements surprises you the most?

LISTENING

2 A Compare the two photos of French model Victoire Dauxerre.

B ▶ 5.2 Listen to part of a BBC radio interview with Dauxerre and tick the things she talks about.

early childhood	being discovered	taking pills
diet	illness	the industry
travel	recovery	a law*

*Dauxerre has a French accent and pronounces 'law' as /ləʊ/.

C Listen again and take brief notes under the relevant headings in Exercise 2B. Compare your notes with another student.

D ▶ 5.3 Read the sentences. Can you guess or remember which words are different from what Dauxerre actually says? Listen and correct the sentences. One sentence is already correct.

1 You have an incredible face. It will take the light perfectly …

2 … I couldn't eat anything, because you have to be so thin, you know, to fit into these clothes.

3 So, I ate three apples a day, and I couldn't eat anything else, or I was going to gain weight, and that's why I fell into illness.

4 … you know I fainted all the time, I fell down in the street, and my agent actually only gave me a piece of sugar …

5 I took laxatives, and then my body was used to it, so I took two pills, and four, and five, then I had to go to the hospital.

6 I actually had the body of, I mean the skin of a seventy-year-old woman when I was nineteen.

3 Discuss the questions.

1 Which part of the interview did you find the most disturbing?

2 Who do you think bears the greatest responsibility for what happened to Victoire?

3 If you were the parent of a child who wanted to be a model, what would you do to minimise the chance of your child having a similar experience to Victoire?

SPEAKING

4 Work with other students. Look at the photos and discuss the questions.

1 How much do you think people are influenced by images, for example of famous people?

2 Do you think the representation of males and females in toys and videos aimed at children should be regulated?

3 How much does a pressure to conform/peer pressure influence how you dress or have your hair cut?

4 Which is more important, how comfortable you are, or how you look?

5 Is it reasonable for an employer to set an appearance and dress-code policy for their employees?

GRAMMAR

FRONTING, HEADERS AND TAILS

5 A Work in pairs and match the sentences with the discussion topics in Exercise 4. Which sentences do you identify with?

1 'This shirt I bought because my girlfriend said it looks good on me.'

2 'I had my hair cut this way after I saw them, those photos of Emma Watson.'

3 'Dress codes I think are a good idea in some jobs because of the impression you make on customers.'

4 'In some jobs, like working in a restaurant, it affects the customers, how you look.'

5 'A mirror, I don't even have one, I don't care how I look, I just want to feel relaxed.'

6 'My boss, if he tried to tell me how to cut my hair or dress, I'd quit in an instant.'

B Look at the sentences above and answer the questions.

1 Which start with a phrase that usually comes later?

2 Which end with a phrase that usually comes earlier?

3 What reasons can you think of for changing the phrase order?

4 Are they spoken or written, formal or informal?

C Match the rules below with the sentences in Exercise 5A.

> **RULES**
>
> **Fronting**
>
> Fronting is used in informal spoken English to put the focus on something important. A phrase can:
>
> **a)** move and start a sentence with no other changes.
>
> **b)** move and start a sentence, and a pronoun is added later to refer to it. This is a **header** and if written down is normally followed by a comma.
>
> **Tailing**
>
> **c)** A **tail** is used in informal spoken English to help the listener understand what is being discussed. The topic comes after the main clause and a pronoun in the main clause refers to it. When written, a tail is normally preceded by a comma.

▷ page 112 **LANGUAGE**BANK

6 A Rewrite each sentence. Move the position of the underlined phrase and use a fronter with no extra pronoun (F), a header (H) or a tail (T). Make all other necessary changes (to punctuation, etc.).

1 I'll never understand <u>some things</u>. (F)

2 Would you mind lending me <u>your phone</u> just for tonight? (H)

3 <u>That friend of yours</u> has just come in. (T)

4 Have you finished <u>that book I lent you</u>? (H)

5 I really don't know <u>why he married her</u>. (F)

6 A: Why is he here? **B:** I couldn't tell you <u>that</u>. (F)

7 I don't think <u>working as a model</u> is the right job for you. (T)

8 I forget the name of <u>that actor</u> but he was in *Thor*. (H)

B ▷ 5.4 **CHUNKING** Listen and tick the sentences where you hear a pause. Listen again and say the sentences with the speaker, focusing on whether to pause or not.

7 ▷ 5.5 Listen and rewrite each sentence in a more neutral, written style.

1 The idea that big companies can make rules about what you can and can't wear is ridiculous.

WRITING

A DESCRIPTION; LEARN TO USE FRONTING

8 A Read the first part of the description and answer the questions.

1 Where do you think the narrator is?
2 What is his or her relationship with the old man?
3 What feelings does the narrator have towards him?

The whittler

He crouched down close to the ground, huddled over as if to protect the small animal in his hands from the driving rainstorm that battered his back and ran in rivulets off of the rim of his hat. Carefully, gingerly, I moved closer to take a look at what he was holding, and saw that it was indeed an animal, a bird, but not alive – nor was it ever alive, for the man was the whittler and the bird his latest creation. On the ground next to him lay several such birds, unfinished or perhaps discarded. He held a small knife to the throat of the creature in his hand, not to slash it but to further shape it, to whittle it down to the perfect proportions that only he could see in his mind's eye.

I longed to ask him how he did it, how his hands and his surprisingly small (but no doubt razor-sharp) jack-knife found their way to move in concert with the block of wood so as to create a flawless shape that exactly matched his vision, like a pianist weaving a quiet melody from the black dots on the musical score; but I knew I would receive no answer, not because the old man would withhold his secrets but because his concentration was clearly impenetrable.

B Read the rest of the description. What changes in the image that the writer has created so far? If this is the beginning of a story, what might happen next?

At last I moved on, but before I did I rubbed my hands over the shiny bronze of the man's spindly fingers, just as so many had done before me. Like a vision, an image flashed through my mind, that one day this statue of bronze, larger than life and so imposing on its pedestal, would be melted down and returned to the earth where it came from. Ahead of me lay the path back to my car. Mindless of the rain, I walked slowly back, smiling weakly at the figure slumped over the steering wheel.

C Work in pairs and answer the questions.

1 What is the function (or focus?) of each of the three paragraphs?
2 Which message best fits the story? Why?
   Beauty is ageless
   Looks can be deceiving
   Truth is subjective
3 The writer uses carefully chosen adjective + noun combinations to enrich the description, e.g. *driving rainstorm*. Find other examples of this.
4 Sometimes the writer puts an adverb or adverbial phrase or a prepositional phrase at the beginning of the sentence. Find five examples of this.

speakout TIP

Even though fronting is common in spoken English, the same structure is used in literary contexts to change emphasis/focus. An adverb might be moved from the end of a clause to the beginning of the sentence:
Warily, she opened the door and peeked around it.
Sometimes when a prepositional phrase is moved to the front, the subject and verb are inverted. *From the top of the building came a loud cry.* (Instead of *A loud cry came from the top of the building.*) As with all stylistic devices, these should not be overused!

D Use fronting in the following sentences to create a more dramatic, literary effect.

1 A tiny cabin lay in the centre of the forest.
2 She slammed the door angrily and stormed out of the room.
3 An enormous river flowed through the valley beneath us.
4 A parrot perched on his shoulder, tilting his head as if trying to understand something.
5 Greta climbed out onto the top of the cable car ignoring the temptation to look down.
6 A huge black leopard snarled from the corner of its cage.

9 A Write a description of a person, place or animal using the theme 'Looks can be deceiving'. Your audience is the readership of a university creative writing magazine (220–280 words).

B Work in pairs and help each other improve the descriptions by:
- using fronting in at least three places to create a more literary style.
- modifying some of the nouns with carefully chosen adjectives. Use a thesaurus to help.

C Read other students' descriptions. How are looks deceiving in their texts?

5.3)) MAGIC BULLET

F informal turn-taking
P intonation: gaining a turn
V well-being

VOCABULARY

WELL-BEING

1 Look at the photos and discuss.

1 Have you or anyone you know done any of these activities? How did you/they get on?

2 Can you think of other activities that are good for the body and mind?

3 What do you do to lower stress and maintain a sense of well-being?

2 A Read the article below. Which activity do you find most appealing. Why?

WHAT'S YOUR MAGIC BULLET?

We're all looking for that <u>magic bullet</u> to ensure we have a healthy body and mind, and strenuous physical exercise isn't the only way. Studies show that <u>getting engrossed in an activity</u> is highly beneficial to mental health. Here are some activities which have health benefits that you may never have considered.

Painting landscapes
You don't need to be an artist, but the hours spent staring at the canvas, playing with the oils, coaxing an image from the different colours is the perfect <u>panacea</u> for everyday stress. Anytime you're feeling a bit <u>out of sync with yourself</u>, just pick up the brush …

Group cooking
Don't like to go solo? Cooking a meal in a group is <u>a cure-all</u> for what ails you, pressing all the buttons of well-being by promoting a sense of community and of working towards a common goal … and you can eat the results! This is perhaps the easiest to <u>incorporate into your daily routine</u>, since you need to eat anyway!

Fishing
In fact you do <u>exert yourself physically</u> when you carry your equipment to some isolated spot. Then you spend the day in the fresh air, in nature. And the activity itself is meditative – perfect for <u>restoring one's peace of mind</u>.

B Complete each sentence with the correct form of the underlined phrase in the article that has the closest meaning to the words in bold. Make any other necessary changes, for example, to pronouns.

1 Pouring out my problems to other people is not **something that solves everything**. It's not a _panacea._

2 I like activities that don't require **using the body**, **or sweating**. I don't like to _____.

3 There are few things that I can really **focus on for long**. But there is one thing I can always _____.

4 I'll only do something regularly if I can **make it part of my day**, for example, like going to a class. So it's important that I can _____.

5 Sometimes **things just don't feel right inside**. I'm simply _____.

6 I don't really believe there's **one single easy solution** to make problems disappear. There is no _____.

7 Though I have a fair bit of stress in my life, I know how to **get myself back to a calm state**. I have a way of _____.

8 For me a long walk is **a solution to every possible problem**. It's a general _____.

C ▶ 5.6 Work in pairs and decide how to pronounce the second sentences in 1–8 in Exercise 2B. Then listen and check your ideas.

D Discuss with other students. To what extent do you agree with the statements above? Give examples from your life.

FUNCTION

INFORMAL TURN-TAKING

3 A Three friends are having a conversation about what they do to maintain their well-being: a diet programme (5:2), a kind of yoga (bikram) and singing. Have you ever done any of these things or know anyone who has?

B Which of the points below could relate to each activity, dieting (D), yoga (Y) or singing (S)?

	D	Y	S
a) burning calories			
b) feeling very good at the end			
c) a sense of community			
d) how it fits into their daily routine			
e) doing it at home			
f) health benefits			

C ▶ 5.7   Listen and check your ideas.

4 A Read the phrases for informal turn-taking. Listen again and tick the ones the speakers use.

Anyway …

Anyway, what was I saying?

Anyway, where was I?

As I was saying, …

To get back to (what I was saying before …)

Going back to …

Like I said, …

That reminds me of …

Actually, that's like …

And speaking/talking of …

Funny you should mention that …

I feel the same way about …

I just want to add …

Oh, I meant to add/say …

Before I forget …

B ▶ 5.8   **INTONATION** Listen to two extracts from the conversation. In which one does the person interrupt by using a) a more forceful tone of voice b) a higher intonation?

speakout TIP

When a listener wants to interrupt, get the topic back or keep the topic, they can use a more forceful tone of voice or start with a higher pitch. Using a high pitch can feel strange if this doesn't happen in your own language but is a useful technique for gaining attention.

C Work in groups. Each student chooses a different activity from Exercise 1. Have a conversation and try to keep the conversation focused on your topic. Choose six expressions from Exercise 4A and try to include them in your discussion.

▷ page 112 **LANGUAGEBANK**

LEARN TO

JUSTIFY YOUR POSITION

5 A ▶ 5.9   Look at the expressions the speakers use for justifying their position. Do you remember which speaker used the expression? Work in pairs and write D, Y or S. Then listen and check.

1 What I've found really works for health for me …

2 (I) don't know if you've tried it but …

3 The advantage of something like that is …

4 Apart from the weight loss, it does have proven benefits of …

5 It's not just about …

6 I do think … is the way forward.

B Work alone and write down at least three ways you can think of for relieving stress in one's daily life. Consider ideas that will appeal to other students, and think about how you might use the expressions in Exercise 5A.

C Work with other students and share your ideas, using phrases from Exercise 5A to justify your own. At the end, try to agree on the three most convincing ideas.

SPEAKING

6 A How do you think a company can create a healthier workplace? Read the ideas and tick three that you think are the best.

10 Steps towards a healthier workplace

☐ Have a trainer teach workers 'deskercise' – exercises they can do while sitting at their desks.

☐ Provide free fruit in the company kitchen, all the time.

☐ Have compulsory walk-around breaks every hour.

☐ Build a gym in the workplace, available to all employees.

☐ Offer a vegetarian lunch option at the company canteen, and price it below the meat options.

☐ Hold company outings once a month.

☐ Remove high-calorie food, like doughnuts, from the vending machines.

☐ Give time off during the work day to participate in company-sponsored exercise classes.

☐ Offer an incentive (money, time off) for achieving fitness goals.

☐ Provide a shower/changing room so employees can jog or bike to work.

B Work with other students. Student A: turn to page 129. Student B: turn to page 131. Student C: turn to page 132.

C You have exactly five minutes to decide which five ideas to implement. Three other students should watch, listen and keep the time. At the end, the three students will say which arguments were most convincing and why.

DVD PREVIEW

1 Work in pairs and discuss the questions.

1 When you travel, how important is it for you to try the local food?

2 Have you ever had a meal prepared by a local when you were travelling? What was it? What was special about it?

3 What is particular about food in the region you come from? What is your favourite food region?

2 Read the programme information. What countries might Rick Stein have visited in the series? What do you know about the food in those countries?

◁)) Rick Stein: From Venice to Istanbul

BBC

Rick Stein embarks on a new gastronomic road trip from Venice to Istanbul through the countries of the former Byzantine Empire – a melting pot of East and West. In this episode, Rick's culinary odyssey has brought him to the legendary city of Istanbul, where he arrives in time for the bluefish season and catches a few himself while fishing on the Bosphorus. Finally, a local fisherman named Mesut shows Rick how to make Turkish fish stew in the same way a boat captain makes it.

DVD VIEW

3 A Watch the programme and choose the statement that is most true for you as a viewer.

The programme makes me want to
* travel to Turkey.
* taste the fish stew.
* try making that dish.
* buy one of Stein's cookbooks.
* do something else?

B Watch the extract about cooking fish stew again and answer the questions.

1 What does Stein mention as being special about Mesut's dish in relation to
   a) cooking on a boat?
   b) seasonal ingredients?
   c) how fresh the fish is?
   d) the surroundings?

2 What joke does he make about the cats?

3 What specific cooking technique does Stein learn from watching the fisherman?

C Watch the extract again from 3:40 and complete the sentences. Four words are missing from each.

1 That's Mesut's fisherman's stew. That's how they do it here, and this is _____.

2 I think I've only had a fish stew cooked by a fisherman _____, so um, it's a bit of a rare occasion really, and I'm very much looking _____.

3 What I really like about this is all that large quantity of green chillies in there. It's going to make it very hot on _____.

4 Ah! Wow! What a lovely fish!
   This bluefish is just perfect. It's got this _____ because it's so fresh.

speakout describe a food memory

4 A Read an invitation from a website. What can you tell about the person who wrote it? Think about the content and the style.

> I'm about to start a series about food memories from around the world. Maybe you could tell me about a particular type of food/meal that you had when you were younger, or you had once and you particularly liked. It would be great to get your videos or descriptions for us to upload to the website. If you send a description, perhaps you could include a photo of the dish.
>
> **NEW TODAY**   GET IN TOUCH

B Think of a food memory and make notes on these points.

- The name of the food
- The context you had it in
- Who made it
- What's in it
- Why it was special

C ▶ 5.10 Listen to someone describing their memory of a dish called 'Coquilles Saint-Jacques' for the website and make notes on the points above.

D Listen again and underline the alternatives you hear.

> **KEYPHRASES**
>
> I can just *taste/smell* it now.
> *She'd/She used to* make this amazing sauce …
> It's coming back to me now, how it *tasted/smelled* …
> What really made it was the *presentation/freshness of the ingredients.*
> My mouth waters *just thinking/whenever I think* about it.
> It's *incredibly succulent/impossibly light,* decadently rich.
> When *I used to/I'd* smell this cooking, *I knew/I'd know* it was a special occasion.
> *I'll always associate this dish with/This dish always reminds me of* home.
> I've sometimes tried making it but it never *comes out/turns out* the same.

5 Work in small groups. Use the notes you made in Exercise 4B and the key phrases to tell each other about your food memory.

writeback a food memory

6 A Read the food memory for the blog. To what extent does it reflect the situation in homes in your country?

MOST RECENT POST   💬 23

My mum's Chinese and she comes from quite a well-to-do home so when she left China she didn't know how to cook anything and she made up a lot of things to replicate what she was used to eating at home. One thing she did, which I do now, was her own version of Chinese dumplings. I remember a Chinese friend once berating her because she'd cook the meat and vegetables before wrapping up the dumplings, unlike the authentic Chinese dish where raw meat is used, so the inside cooks at the same time as the dumplings steam or boil.

Anyway, as far as we were concerned, it's what my mum used to cook and we had it at Chinese New Year and so it became a family tradition. It's got minced pork, beef, white cabbage, tomatoes, mushrooms and dried shrimps and some secret ingredients I won't share as it's a family recipe. My mouth is watering now even as I think of it! The dumplings taste fabulous, really rich and spicy, but the whole thing is ridiculously labour-intensive. My mum and I, and later my daughters, would spend hours, rolling and wrapping and steaming. We used to make 300 or so and then everyone would compete as to how many they could eat. The men and boys would all be sitting in the other room while the women were in the kitchen. That was the way my mother liked it, and somehow my (very feminist) daughters and I still do that. It's a very communal activity and it's to do with bonding and family and catching up with each other as much as enjoying the actual taste of the dish.

B Write a description of your food memory for the website (250–300 words).

Ⓖ NOUN PHRASES

1 A Add the phrases from the box to the description underneath. Make any other necessary changes or additions to the texts. The phrases are given in order.

> ~~martial~~   China   worldwide   calmness   outdoors   like-minded

                                    martial
Tai Chi is a traditional /art. It has a following and its practice can lead to a focused state. In China it's often practised somewhere with other people.

> plant-based food   loss   proven   follow this diet   have a reluctance

It is claimed that a **vegan diet** increases weight and has health benefits. People often started as vegetarians and say they harm or eat animals.

B Work in pairs and take turns. Extend the descriptions of a noun in the box by adding one extra piece of information each time.

> a class   a gym   a sport
> a swimming pool   a trainer

A: a cookery class
B: a cookery class for kids

Ⓥ COLLOCATIONS

2 A Work in pairs and remember at least two nouns that can come after:

1 sustain   3 enhance
2 trigger   4 deliver

and at least two verbs that can go before:

5 success
6 an aspect of sth

B Write questions using at least five of the collocations in Exercise 2A.

C Work with other students. Ask and answer each other's questions.

Ⓥ FASHION AND LOOKS

3 A Complete the words in bold by adding the missing letters.

1 I think it's fine when someone has their wedding photos **re_ _ _ _ _ed**. Some people aren't particularly **ph_ _ _ _ _ _ic** and they should have photos they feel proud of.

2 I would want my child to be **fashion co_ _ _ _ _us** and to **k_ _ _** up with the latest styles; people who dress well are **re_ _ _ _ed** as having greater potential in social and professional contexts, and it's never too early to start learning.

3 **Eating di_ _ _ _ _ _s** will end when being thin goes **out of fa_ _ _ _n**, and I think that's the direction we're going in anyway.

4 **C_ _ _ _ _k models** also contribute greatly to **di_ _ _ _ _ _ng** notions of beauty, since most of them choose to profit from whatever is **_ _ fashion** at the moment.

5 If everyone knows that looks are **de_ _ _ _ing**, why do we still consider them to be important?

6 The term '**fashion vi_ _ _m**' is a bit misleading, since it implies that the person has no choice but to invest all their resources in whatever is **fa_ _ _ _ _ _le** at the moment.

B Work in pairs and discuss. Which of the statements in Exercise 3A do you agree with? Why?

Ⓖ FRONTING, HEADERS AND TAILS

4 A Expand the sentences with an appropriate fronter (F), header (H) or tail (T) and your own ideas.

1 Do you ever let anyone borrow it? (T)
2 Have you seen it yet? (H)
3 Sometimes I wonder if it's the best thing for me. (T)
4 Can you remember where you got it? (H)
5 Have you noticed it? (T)
6 I just can't stand, for example … (F)

B Share your ideas with other students and respond to theirs.

FUNCTION
INFORMAL TURN-TAKING

5 A Which one or two words can be removed from each phrase without much change to the meaning?

1 That sort of reminds me of when …
2 Actually, that's something like the time …
3 Funny thing you should say that, the same thing happened …
4 I just wanted to quickly add …
5 Going back to what I was just saying about …
6 I also meant to say …
7 Anyway, so what was I saying?
8 To get back briefly to what I was saying before …
9 Then, as I was saying, …
10 I do feel exactly the same way about …

B Write down a good

1 hobby for a child.
2 place to go on holiday.
3 way to get a good night's sleep.

C Work in groups and discuss the first topic above. Use the phrases in Exercise 5A to get a turn. Whoever uses a phrase <u>first</u> ticks that phrase, and when all 10 phrases are ticked, the student with the most ticks wins. Move on to the next topic.

Hubert and Kornelia

Priscilla

Praneet

Hamza

Ewan

Sami

speakout examining beliefs

5 A Read these quotations about culture, habits and tradition and make notes of examples to support or contradict the idea behind each quotation.

> 'Habit is necessary; it is the habit of having habits, of turning a trail into a rut that must be incessantly fought against if one is to remain alive.' (Edith Wharton)

> 'Traditions are the guideposts driven deep in our subconscious minds. The most powerful ones are those we can't even describe, aren't even aware of.' (Ellen Goodman)

> 'No culture can live if it attempts to be exclusive.' (Mahatma Gandhi)

> 'Tradition is a guide and not a jailer.' (W. Somerset Maugham)

B Work with other students and discuss each quotation.

C Choose the quotation that elicited the most interesting discussion and tell the rest of the class about your group's response.

writeback an article

6 A Read the article below. How would you describe its tone, for example serious, humorous, satirical? Why? Do you think any parts of it are offensive?

How to blend in: Techies

It's not everyone's goal in life to blend in with techies, but if you find yourself sitting amongst a group of them, there are a few things you should know.

Attire: The important thing is not to draw attention to yourself – that's the key to blending in in any situation – and the key concept here is 'underdressing'. Dress is informal, but not without its unwritten code: Think jeans, sneakers and a Mark Zuckerberg hooded sweatshirt ... though by the time you're reading this that may have become passé.

Behaviour and conversation: The first thing you should know is that techies hate to be called techies, so just don't use that word. Like any group of people these days, you'll notice that everyone has a mobile device in their hands and is constantly clicking away, but in the case of a techie there will be a lot of commenting on what they're doing, on how a particular app is responding, wifi speed, etc. So be prepared to make a few comments along these lines if you don't want people to notice that you're NOT one of THEM.

Language: Memorise a handful of up-to-date computer terms. Don't say 'terrabytes', say 'terra'. Beware of terms that have gone out of style (e.g. DON'T refer to your laptop as 'a lapper' – that's so uncool now!).

Interests: Well, it's obvious, isn't it? Software (say 'app'), hardware, gizmos, gadgets, gaming, VPNs, the darknet, hacking – but stick to what you know, and if you don't know anything, just listen and soak it up.

Other things: Remember, techies are people, not members of a tribe. You'll click with some and not with others – and that won't depend on how many terra you've got on your lapper ...

B Choose a group that you identify with, using the list in Exercise 1A for ideas if necessary, and write a similar article to the one above. Pay particular attention to not being offensive (250–300 words).

V CITIES

1 A Complete the city words.

TIPS for moving to a big city

At first everyone feels ¹**out of p**_____ and it can be ²**inti**_____, but these tips will help:

- First, find a ³**sanc**_____, somewhere quiet for when the ⁴**hust**_____ **and b**_____ is too much.
- Safety first! Find and avoid any ⁵**no-**_____ areas.
- Find out what places are ⁶**on your** _____. Find a local shop and make it your regular.
- Explore public transport at the weekend when it's not so ⁷**hec**_____ and the roads aren't so ⁸**con**_____.
- Give yourself time – most people find change ⁹**alie**_____ at first. Embrace the ¹⁰**bu**_____ – that's what makes cities so alive!

B Which are the best tips? What tips would you add?

G CONCESSION CLAUSES

2 A Complete each concession clause with ONE word.

Introverted ¹_____ I am, I love it when people around me speak a language I don't understand well, ²_____ this does mean lots of time understanding little. ³_____, if several people are chatting, I don't have to take part, and I understand more this way, ⁴_____ nowhere near 100 percent. ⁵_____ fast people may speak, I can usually guess the meaning. And even ⁶_____ I'm wrong, what's at stake? OK, sometimes I'm asked a question, and avid amateur linguist ⁷_____ I am, I hate being put on the spot. I've found the solution ⁸_____: I know 'Sorry, my phone's ringing!' in a dozen languages.

B Discuss. To what extent do you agree with the writer?

V SUMMARISING VERBS

3 A Add vowels to complete the summarising verbs.

1 __ ckn __ wl __ dg __
2 __ ll __ g __
3 c __ ll f __ r
4 __ ch __
5 __ ll __ str __ t __
6 m __ __ nt __ __ n
7 pl __ __ d
8 r __ l __ t __
9 r __ pr __ m __ nd
10 r __ p __ d __ __ t __
11 v __ __ c __
12 v __ w

B Summarise the sentences using reported speech and an appropriate verb.

1 'As my opponent has also said, education is the key.'
2 'My position is unchanged.'
3 'I will never, ever betray the public's trust.'
4 'I ask that the public remain calm pending an investigation.'
5 'The opposition's use of immoral tactics is abominable!'

C For at least three other verbs in Exercise 3A, write a sentence in direct speech that can be summarised using the verb.

D Work in pairs. Student A: read a sentence out. Student B: summarise it using one of the verbs.

G INDIRECT SPEECH

4 A Read one side of a phone conversation. Who is speaking to whom? What's the topic? Write A's side of the conversation.

1 **A:** … **B:** No, he says he didn't see anything. He must have fallen asleep. Let's check the security camera footage.
2 **A:** … **B:** We'll usually keep everything for one week before the footage is deleted.
3 **A:** … **B:** Yes of course. I'll email them over straightaway.

B Write A's written report of the conversation. Do not repeat the same verb.

I phoned Mrs Jones because I wanted to know …

F TALK ABOUT CUSTOMS

5 A Correct the expressions for talking about customs. One is already correct.

I found it difficult to ¹accustom to the constant movement. But when we eventually returned to port, ²I so used the rocking that the ground seemed to move all the time. And it took forever to wash the smell off my hands.

Most people ³find the weightlessness complete alienation, but I found it easy ⁴to get used to, perhaps because as a child I did so much swimming and diving; water and space feel similar to me.

⁵It's given that you won't see your family for months at a time, but that's one reason it pays so well. I think that ⁶a normal is to hire single people for the long-term stints. The heights, though – ⁷if you can't be used to those, you can't do the job.

B Discuss in pairs. What job do you think each person is talking about?

C Choose another job and write at least three sentences about it, each using an expression to talk about customs. Don't make it too obvious what the job is.

D Read your sentences to other students and see if they can guess the job.

7)) classics

HAPPY ENDING? p80   **MORE THAN WORDS** p83   **CLASSIC JOURNEYS** p86   **GREAT EXPECTATIONS** p88

SPEAKING **7.1** Talk about alternate endings to your favourite film or novel **7.2** Discuss two poems; Talk about song lyrics and poems **7.3** Tell travel anecdotes in an informal style **7.4** Tell a story about a strange event

LISTENING **7.1** Listen to an editor advising a writer **7.2** Listen to two poems and to people saying why they like them **7.3** Listen to someone's experience on a classic rail journey **7.4** Watch a BBC classic drama: *Great Expectations*

READING **7.1** Read about how sad endings to films become happy ones **7.2** Read two poems **7.3** Read about classic journeys

WRITING **7.1** Write a review; Edit a complex text **7.4** Describe a strange event

Happy ending, at all costs

Hollywood movies appear to be obsessed with 'the happy ending', with the belief [1]it is essential that the audience leave the cinema on a high. So even when the script is otherwise perfect, the studios will try to find a way to turn a downbeat ending into an uplifting finale, since [2]it is in their interest that the film be a financial success.

A classic example is the movie *Pretty Woman*, one of the most successful romantic comedies of all time. A quintessential Cinderella story, it's about a prostitute and a businessman falling in love and essentially saving each other. Or rather it is about Julia Roberts and Richard Gere falling in love, and audiences falling in love with them. So, how popular would the film be [3]if it ended with Julia Roberts' character returning to the streets, rejected by the businessman? And then dying of a drug overdose? Well, that was the original idea, and it was only after much deliberation that the producers went ahead with the happy ending.

Even the Star Wars movies did not escape this treatment. One version of the script of *Return of the Jedi* had the Harrison Ford character getting killed about halfway through the film. Apparently [4]director George Lucas insisted that Han Solo not die, that he be kept alive, in part because the death of the character would have a negative impact on merchandising. Evidently, it is harder to sell Han Solo dolls if he's dead! And harder to make a sequel. Sometimes the death of the hero seems inevitable, but in order to ensure that audiences are not left with too negative a feeling, the filmmakers are careful about how they handle the scene. Take *Thelma and Louise*, the classic road film. (Don't EVER let anyone call it a chick flick – its universal appeal keeps it out of that cubby hole.) After days on the run from the law, our heroines decide to go out gloriously by driving their car off a cliff. In the version of the film that was NOT released, the car is seen falling downward, plummeting horribly into the canyon. However, the final image that made it to the screen is of the two women in the car, frozen in the air and in time, [5]as if the duo were to live forever. There is seemingly something about the freeze-frame that immortalises whoever is caught in its eternal grip, and [6]it's not surprising that it should now have become something of a cinematic cliché.

But not every American film conveys this message of hope and immortality. Viewers of *Se7en* will be forever haunted by the dark and gruesome ending. Avoiding spoilers for those who haven't seen the film (Don't ask what's in the box – [7]you will wish you didn't know!), the film's creators contemplated a whole range of endings before settling on the final one. The variables don't just involve that box, but who shoots whom and why. With a cast of A-listers – Pitt, Paltrow and Freeman – to play with, the filmmakers had a handful of combinations to consider, choosing to go with perhaps the most desolate of options. Yet dark as the ending is, [8]the studio thought it was crucial that a tiny message of hope be slipped in, which is why there is an epilogue complete with a quote from Ernest Hemingway: 'The world is fine place, and worth fighting for …' And perhaps so is the happy ending.

VOCABULARY

FILM

1 A Work in pairs and check what you know. Which word(s) in the box is/are

1 a type of film?
2 something a film might have?
3 derogatory?

| A-lister   chick flick   female protagonist |
| flashback   formulaic plotline |
| heist movie   indie film   plot twist |
| road movie   spaghetti western |
| supporting cast   universal appeal |

B ▶ **7.1** WORD STRESS Listen and underline the stressed syllables.

C Work in pairs and discuss.

1 Of the five types of films, which do you like best and least? Which other genres do you enjoy?
2 Who are your favourite A-listers?
3 Is a formulaic plotline necessarily a bad thing?
4 Are you good at working out a plot twist before it happens?
5 What factors contribute to the universal appeal of a film? A star-studded cast, a strong plotline, a memorable soundtrack? Others?

READING

2 A Look at the stills from four classic films. What do you know about the plots and actors involved?

B Read the article. What choice did the creators of each of the four films make about the ending?

C Read the article again. Are the statements true (T) or false (F)? Underline the part of the article that helps you decide.

1 The article blames directors for changing sad endings to happy ones.
2 The decision to change the ending of *Pretty Woman* was a difficult one.
3 George Lucas wanted Han Solo to die at the end of the film, not in the middle.
4 Filmmakers use the freeze-frame because they can't think of how else to end a film.
5 The makers of *Se7en* considered many other endings to the film.
6 Hemingway appears at the end of the film.

D Discuss.

1 Which film versions would you prefer to see? Why?
2 Why do people often feel the need for a happy ending? Do you? Give examples from films you've seen.

Return of the Jedi

Pretty Woman

Se7en (Seven)

Thelma and Louise

GRAMMAR

SUBJUNCTIVE

3 Match examples 1–8 in the text with the rules below.

RULES

The present subjunctive (the infinitive without *to*, e.g. *he go*) is used mostly in formal written contexts. Sometimes *should* is used before the verb.

Use the present subjunctive after:
a) reporting verbs, e.g. *We recommend/suggest/insist that she leave now.*
b) adjectives and nouns with the idea that something is desirable or important, e.g. *It's vital/ crucial that the president agree. Our advice is that she sign now.*
c) expressions of annoyance, regret, surprise, inevitability, using *should* + verb, e.g. *It's odd/ understandable that you should say that.*

The past subjunctive (*were* or the past simple or continuous form) is used to talk about hypothetical situations in the present.

Use the past subjunctive after:
d) *if, supposing, if only, wish, as if, it's time, would rather*, e.g. *I wish I were taller. I'd rather you went now.*

▷ page 116 **LANGUAGE**BANK

4 A Complete the article with the correct form of the words in the box. Use the subjunctive to make the article sound formal.

> adapt be change distribute exist
> familiarise matter satisfy see cut

The 'real' version?

To the average person it may seem odd that so many versions of classic films [1]_____ but the realities of distribution often demand that a film [2]_____ for a local market. If, for example, Kurosawa's *Seven Samurai* [3]_____ abroad in its original 207-minute length, fewer people would watch it. When it was originally distributed abroad, commercial forces required that fifty minutes [4]_____ for international distribution, which upset Kurosawa (perhaps it is best that a director [5]_____ the altered version of their work!). The classic spaghetti western *Once Upon a Time in the West* started at 171 minutes and was cut to 140 for the U.S. market. It is hardly surprising that all this editing [6]_____ the storyline, and some versions even omit the death of a key character near the end; the version that runs in Hungary simply stops ten minutes before the end, as if the final sequence [7]_____ irrelevant. When re-cutting a film, the aim is not always that it be shorter, but also that it [8]_____ certain artistic demands. The sci-fi thriller *Blade Runner* has at least seven versions, but all about the same length. Perhaps for the average moviegoer, it is strange that the differences [9]_____ so much, but the controversy over which is the 'real' version is the stuff of movie legend. We suggest that a serious film buff [10]_____ themselves with all seven, so that they can let us know which indeed is the definitive version.

B Which of the two reasons for changing a film that the article mentions seems more reasonable to you?

SPEAKING

5 A Work with other students. Choose a film that all of you are familiar with. List the main characters and the main events of the story.

B Discuss how the story could unfold differently. Make at least three changes to the plot. How would your version affect a viewer differently compared to the original version?

C Tell other students about your story and why you made the changes. Do you like any of the ideas better than the original stories?

Paterson ★★★★☆

Indie movies have always occupied a comfortable niche at film festivals and in art cinemas, and yet most movie-viewers – and I say 'viewers', as who <u>goes</u> to the movies anymore anyway? – associate indie films with low budgets and slow, artsy stories. Meanwhile, relatively few independent film directors have achieved the kind of success that American director Jim Jarmusch has, going back to his early successes *Stranger than Paradise* and *Down by Law*. And with *Paterson*, Jarmusch has added a masterpiece to what is already an impressive body of work.

Richard Driver plays Paterson, a bus driver in a New Jersey (USA) town by the same name. In his working hours, Paterson observes the interaction of passengers, and uses idle moments to compose poetry in his 'secret notebook'. He writes on the bus when parked, on his lunch break, in his basement at home; composing poetry is in a sense his refuge from an ordinary life which in fact he seems entirely content with. His modest yet powerful poems are woven through the film and convey the beauty of his mind, and one begins to see Paterson as a poet who drives a bus rather than the other way around. Paterson's deeply devoted partner Laura, played by the exquisite Golshifteh Farahani, is a keen supporter of his artistic pursuits and spends most of her time pursuing her own, each more whimsical than the one before.

While there is a storyline to *Paterson*, it is not a plot-driven film. Like many of Jarmusch's films, its style might best be described as unhurried. I was particularly struck by the way he creates a lyrical and separate world that seduces us with its stark imagery, and interlaces images of Paterson's

environment with the simple yet imposing voice of the protagonist sharing his musings on life. His world is populated by characters no less entrapped by their daily lives, and it is a tribute to the casting director and Jarmusch himself that each character comes across with a realism that creates a sense of intimacy with the audience. Driver's performance as Paterson is extraordinary in the way he draws us into his world such that we understand his every reaction, and after a time it's as if we know what he's thinking.

Even for the moviegoer who rarely ventures into the indie film world, *Paterson* will surprise and reward you. It is, as one reviewer has already said, a film for everyone.

WRITING

A REVIEW; LEARN TO EDIT A COMPLEX TEXT

6 Read the review of the film *Paterson* and answer the questions.

1 Who is the review written for? Why do you think that?
2 Does it keep your attention? Does it make you interested in seeing the film?
3 Which of these elements does the reviewer comment on, and in which paragraph: acting, directing, music, editing, casting, plot, who the film would appeal to?
4 Find at least five words or phrases which are
   a) related to cinema in general. b) evaluative.
   c) descriptive.
5 What is the main focus of each paragraph? Are the ideas cohesive (do they hang together well)?

7 **A** ▶ 7.2 Listen to an editor giving the writer feedback on the review. Make notes on a) the strengths b) the weaknesses c) what to change.

B Work in pairs. Make the changes to the first paragraph suggested by the editor.

C In the second and third paragraphs, find a sentence that you can omit without losing the overall coherence of the paragraph.

speakout TIP

Text length and respecting word limits are important factors both in exams and in real-life writing. When reducing your draft, go through each paragraph and a) number the sentences in order of importance; then b) simply omit the ones that you have 'ranked' the lowest. In writing as in many things, less is more!

8 **A** You have been asked to write a film review for a media arts magazine. Choose a film you have seen recently. What particularly struck you about it? Who might it appeal to and who not? Draft your review. Write at least 380 words.

B Swap your draft with another student. Read his/her review and make notes using the questions in Exercise 6. Check the word count and find out how many words the student needs to cut to reduce the word count to 280–320.

C Work with the other student and share your ideas on each other's draft. Make suggestions as to how to adjust the text to meet the word count requirements.

VOCABULARY

RELATIONSHIPS

1 A Change the sentences so they have the opposite meaning by replacing the underlined words with a word or phrase from the box. Make any necessary changes to the form.

> be on friendly terms   bear a grudge
> click straightaway   dislike
> meet people halfway
> put a strain on   rocky   working

1 I often find myself taking an instant <u>liking</u> to someone.
2 I'm the sort of person who <u>forgives easily</u>.
3 There are a number of things I do which <u>enhance</u> my relationships.
4 I <u>never compromise</u> in relationships.
5 I <u>don't get on</u> with my manager.
6 I have a <u>stable</u> relationship with my ex.
7 The first time I met my best friend we <u>didn't take to each other</u>.
8 I have a good <u>personal</u> relationship with my colleagues.

B Rewrite at least five of the sentences to reflect your experience. Then compare your ideas with a partner. Give examples.

Occasionally I find myself taking an instant dislike to someone. For example, my sister once brought a new boyfriend home and …

SPEAKING

> I explain quietly. You hear me shouting.

> I have spread my dreams under your feet

2 A Work in pairs and look at the short extracts above from two classic poems. What does each express about the relationship?

B Student A: look at page 84. Student B: follow the tasks below.

Student B

1 Read the poem on this page. Check any new phrases in a dictionary. What is it about? Try to summarise the poem in one sentence.
2 Work with other students who have read the poem and compare your summaries.
3 Discuss the questions.
   a) How old do you think the 'I' in the poem is? Is the 'I' a man or a woman, do you think?
   b) What do you notice in the poem about a) the arrangement of lines b) the use of contrast?
   c) You are going to put this poem up on YouTube. What images would you put behind the words as they are read out?
4 Turn to page 84, Exercise 3.

You and I

I explain quietly. You
hear me shouting. You
try a new tack. I
feel old wounds reopen.

You see both sides. I
see your blinkers*. I
am placatory.** You
sense a new selfishness.

I am a dove. You
recognise the hawk. You
offer an olive branch. I
feel the thorns.

You bleed. I
see crocodile tears. I
withdraw. You
reel from the impact.

Roger McGough (1937–)

> *blinkers = leather put beside a horse's eyes to prevent it seeing on both sides
> **placatory = trying to calm someone down

Student A

1 Read the poem on this page. Check any new phrases in a dictionary. What is it about? Try to summarise the poem in one sentence.
2 Work with other students who have read the poem and compare your summaries.
3 Discuss the questions.
   a) How old do you think the 'I' in the poem is? Could the 'I' equally well be a woman?
   b) What do you notice in the poem about a) the use of repetition, b) the use of rhymes c) the use of contrast?
   c) You are going to put this poem up on YouTube. What images would you put behind the words as they are read out?

He Wishes for the Cloths of Heaven

Had I the heavens' embroidered cloths,
Enwrought with golden and silver light,
The blue and the dim and the dark cloths
Of night and light and the half-light,
I would spread the cloths under your feet:
But I, being poor, have only my dreams;
I have spread my dreams under your feet;
Tread softly because you tread on my dreams.

W. B. Yeats (1865–1939)

*enwrought = an archaic way to say 'made/crafted in a special way', and often used with metals

3 ▶ 7.3 Read and listen to the two poems. Work with a student who read the other poem and discuss your ideas.

LISTENING

4 A You're going to hear two people talk about the poems. Which poem do you think each of these ideas is connected with? Write Y (Yeats) or M (McGough) next to each.
• a breakdown in communication • repetition
• direct and simple everyday language
• elegant style • paradox • rich imagery
• seeing the relationship from outside • trust

B ▶ 7.4 Listen and check your ideas.

C Listen again and note the example or exact phrase from the poem that the speaker gives for each of the ideas listed.

GRAMMAR

ADVERBIALS

5 A Check what you know. Underline the correct alternative in each sentence.
1 I first read it when I was *thoroughly/fairly* young, about fifteen.
2 We have such high hopes that the smallest hint of a criticism can seem … *utterly/somewhat* devastating.
3 It's *quite/absolutely* simple language really – lots of conversational phrases.
4 And I think the very simple title is *quite/very* perfect, too.
5 And if you examine it *sincerely/closely*, you see it's impossible to read it fast.
6 We're all *badly/painfully* aware of how easy it is for a loved one to hurt us.
7 *Sad to say/To his sadness*, Yeats himself was deeply in love with a woman who did not return his love.
8 *Unsurprisingly/Genuinely*, it's a classic and often features in people's top ten poems.

B Add examples from Exercise 5A to the rules.

RULES

1 Sentence adverbials often come at the beginning of a sentence and show the speaker's attitude to a statement. They can be connected to:
   a) surprise, e.g. *difficult as it is to believe*,
   _____
   b) other emotions, e.g. *to my amusement*,
   _____
2 Adverbs can intensify (strengthen) or modify (weaken) meaning:
   a) Ungradable adjectives use a strong intensifier, e.g. *totally inadequate*,
   _____
   b) Gradable adjectives can be intensified, e.g. *relatively quiet*, _____
   or modified e.g. *terribly happy*,
   _____
   c) *Quite* has different uses:
   quite + gradable adjective = modifies, e.g. *quite energetic*, _____
   quite + ungradable adjective = intensifies, e.g. *quite astonishing*, _____
3 Many adverbs collocate strongly:
   a) with adjectives, e.g. *highly successful, painfully aware, utterly devastating*
   b) with verbs, e.g. *thoroughly recommend*,
   _____

▷ page 116 **LANGUAGE**BANK

6 A Read the comments. Which are in favour (✓) and which are against (✗) the award and why?

In 2016 the Swedish Academy awarded the Nobel prize for excellence in the field of literature to songwriter Bob Dylan. The move divided opinion. What do you think?

Comments

1 **PoetLover22:** His lyrics are poetry, though I was *somewhat* ⟨ surprised by the choice of songwriter; there are contenders with a better claim. I remember reading that 60 percent of songs are about love and relationships and I think that's the same in poetry.

2 **MexIkal7:** I have to say that actually what we have here is a brilliant musician but his writing is linked to his music and I think that the award should honour a genuine writer.

3 **MCStar28:** As a rap-artist I sometimes get asked about whether my work is poetry. On balance, I'd say not and so I query the award. Some rap themes are similar but most are associated with politics and the backing track dictates the rhythm. You can tell the difference between poetry and rap.

4 **NoorAlfaaz7:** People don't realise that poetry is a performance art, just like singing. You only have to think of great poets like Homer or Faiz or Maya Angelou to realise this. And Poetry Slams are all over YouTube these days. So it's a reasonable choice.

B Add the adverbials to the relevant comments above. You do not need one of the adverbials in each set.
1 vaguely, far, widely, ~~somewhat~~, roughly
2 exclusively, inextricably, with some reluctance, relatively, quite
3 nearly, totally, instantly, closely, quite
4 perfectly, fully, deeply, truly, obvious as it is

SPEAKING

7 Work with other students and discuss.
1 To what extent do you agree with the comments in Exercise 6A? Give examples from songs you know.
2 What is one poem that everyone in your country knows? In school did you have to memorise poems? Can you remember any now?
3 Do you have any favourite poems or song lyrics? Why do you like them?

VOCABULARY *PLUS*
ADVERB-ADJECTIVE COLLOCATIONS

speakout TIP
Many intensifying adverbs collocate strongly with a number of adjectives e.g. *highly*: *complex, effective, successful, significant, unlikely, competitive*, etc. A good collocations dictionary or website will help with this. Other intensifying adverbs have strong collocations with only a few adjectives, e.g. *painfully*: *aware, shy, slow, obvious, thin*.

8 A Work in pairs. Cover Exercise 8B and look at the list of adverbs below. Brainstorm any adjectives you think collocate strongly with them.

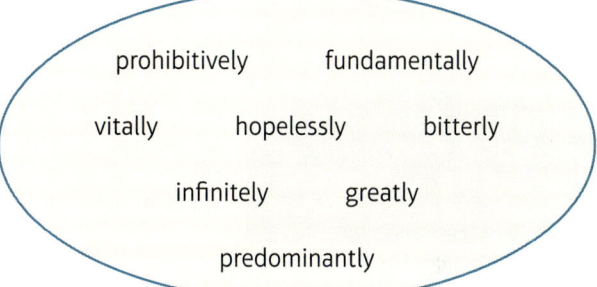

prohibitively   fundamentally

vitally   hopelessly   bitterly

infinitely   greatly

predominantly

B Match the adverbs above with the adjectives below. Choose strong collocations.

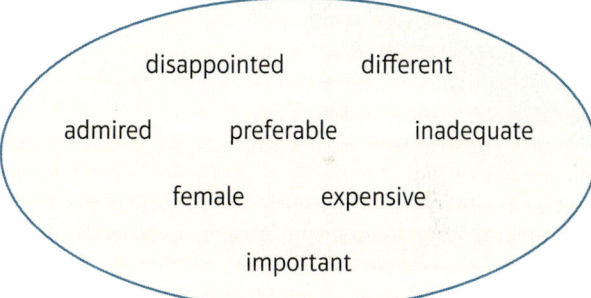

disappointed   different

admired   preferable   inadequate

female   expensive

important

C ▶ 7.5   **STRESS AND INTONATION** Listen and agree with the comments using one of the strong collocations above. Pay attention to the intonation and stress in the adverb. Then listen to the suggested answer.
A: *I think poetry and song have very little in common.*
B: *I agree. They're fundamentally different.*

D Work in pairs and look at these extracts from eight different conversations. What are the people talking about? Which collocation could they use?
1 Not cut out for the job. Not even close.
2 They'll never see eye to eye.
3 Way beyond our means.
4 A legend among mortals.
5 Nursing, speech therapy, social work …
6 You're the air that I breathe.
7 A humiliating defeat.
8 Nothing comes close.

▷ page 126 **VOCABULARYBANK**

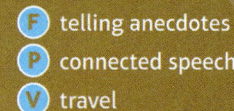

F telling anecdotes
P connected speech
V travel

List | Map | Sort by Recommended ⬍ | Filter

Walk the Camino de Santiago

This legendary journey across Spain is 790 km and will take you one month.

What makes it special: the fellow walkers you meet, the scenery on the way and the chance to take time out from your everyday life. Pass rocky hillsides, soaring mountains and panoramic views on your way to the pilgrimage centre of Santiago de Compostella. Spend the nights in hostels sharing tales of your journey with other travellers, or in a *parador*, a hotel built in a historic building. It's the epitome of walking holidays.

Take a road trip on Route 66

A 2,450-mile three-week car ride from Chicago to Los Angeles, USA. The original road no longer exists in its entirety, but highways link the remaining parts.

What makes it special: the wide open road, the quintessential small town diners with their original jukeboxes intact, the authentic cuisine featuring the eclectic mix of Deep South Cajun and Mexican dishes, museums in towns en route celebrating the indigenous culture, the amazing diversity of people and places, all ending up with a couple of nights in Los Angeles to unwind at the end of this road trip to end all roadtrips.

Take the Trans-Siberian Railway

A six-night rail journey from Moscow through Siberia, Mongolia and on to Beijing.

What makes it special: the vast open spaces of Eastern Siberia, the stories of your fellow travellers and the opulent dining (depending on which company you travel with). Wonder at Lake Baikal, a contender for one of the most beautiful and tranquil lakes in the world. Learn about the turbulent history of Kazan, the Tartar capital, and enjoy the hustle and bustle of Beijing. If you love train journeys, it's the trip of a lifetime.

VOCABULARY

TRAVEL

1 A Work in pairs and discuss.

1 Compare the photos. Why might people choose to take this kind of journey? What difficulties could they encounter?

2 Have you ever been on a long journey by bike, train, boat or hiking? How was it?

3 Which well-known journeys would you like to go on?

4 Have you ever seen any road movies that made you want to take a similar journey?

B Read about three classic journeys. Which appeals to you the most and which the least? Why?

2 A Cover the text and work in pairs. Which adjectives described the words in the box?

> journey mountains views cuisine culture
> dining lakes history

B Check in the texts. Underline the adjective–noun collocations.

C Replace the underlined words below with an adjective from Exercise 2B.

1 From the top of the Burj Khalifa you can see <u>wide and impressive</u> views of Dubai.

2 The 1790s were a <u>chaotic and conflict-filled</u> time for France.

3 We like staying with locals to experience <u>genuine, traditional</u> Thai cooking.

4 Che Guevara is a <u>famous and admired, almost mythical</u> figure in Cuba.

5 I love the <u>peaceful</u> countryside in Tuscany, Italy.

6 The <u>original native</u> people in parts of New Zealand have significant land rights.

7 You can see the <u>tall and impressive</u> cliffs of Moher as you approach Ireland from the Atlantic.

8 A visitor must see the <u>luxurious</u> Hermitage Museum in St Petersburg.

D Change six of the sentences above. Keep the adjectives and provide your own examples. Add any extra suitable adverbs and adjectives.

From Picnic Point, there are absolutely breathtaking panoramic views of the Lockyer Valley.

▷ page 126 **VOCABULARY**BANK

FUNCTION

TELLING ANECDOTES

3 A Work in pairs. You are going to listen to someone talking about his Trans-Siberian railway journey. How do you think the items below are linked to his story?

Student A: instant noodles   no lingua franca
drawing pictures   a bunch of kids

Student B: fellow travellers   roast chicken
chewing gum   a kid on his own

B ▶ 7.6 Listen and make notes on your topics. Were your predictions correct? Then work together and reconstruct the story.

4 A ▶ 7.7 Work in pairs and try to complete these extracts. The number of words is in brackets. Then listen and check.

1 Some friends who had done it _____ 'yeah, it's amazing but it's actually quite tedious.' (2)

2 There were two young Chinese guys and _____ Russian guy, a really nice guy, more on him in a minute. (1)

3 Fairly typical situation for a traveller in an exotic context, you know _____? (3)

4 … It was really nice, _____ relaxed, like 'we're all in this together and let's just enjoy it'. (2)

5 Funny, I don't remember much about him now but I remember understanding quite a lot about his family, his kids, his house, job, _____. (3)

6 … for example on the second day I think _____, he pulled out a whole roast chicken, still warm … (2)

7 I had brought stuff with me like chocolate and chewing gum, _____ guy I met in Beijing told me it's a good idea to have stuff to give to kids or even sell. (1)

8 Then I spotted _____ kid on his own. (1)

9 Stupid thing to do, maybe, but _____ moments when you realise you're so out of your element that you have to just let go. (5)

B Use the examples in Exercise 4A to complete the categories.

Informal reported speech:

a) Use _____ instead of 'says/said' when reporting direct speech.

Informal use of determiners:

b) Use _____ instead of 'a/an' in a neutral way.

c) Use _____ instead of 'a/an', meaning 'of no importance.'

Vague language:

d) Use expressions such as: _____ *like that, I think* _____ or _____ + adjective

Other informal expressions to involve the listener:

e) Use adjectives such as *Strange* or _____ at the beginning of a sentence.

f) Use expressions such as *You know what* _____ and *It was one of* _____ to show shared experience.

▷ page 116 **LANGUAGEBANK**

5 Work in pairs. Student A: turn to page 131. Student B: turn to page 129.

LEARN TO

USE ELLIPSIS

6 A Which words can be left out in these sentences? Cross out the number of words in brackets.

I got up when I felt like it, I went to the loo, I made some tea and noodles, and I stood at the window staring outside. (4)

No one spoke any English. It was a fairly typical situation for a traveller in an exotic context. (3)

B ▶ 7.8 Listen and check.

speakout TIP

Ellipsis, or the omission of (superfluous) words from a sentence, is often used in anecdotes. Omit a) the subject and/or verb if they are obvious from the context (e.g. *he pulled out a whole roast chicken, ~~I was~~ not sure where he got it*) and b) introductory phrases using *It* (*~~It was a~~ stupid thing to do*).

7 A Which words have been left out in the conversation below?

A: Ever been to Turkey?

B: Yes, several times. Brilliant beaches and fabulous old ruins.

A: Sounds great.

B: Thinking of going there?

A: Yes, maybe next year.

B ▶ 7.9 **CONNECTED SPEECH** In the conversation above, underline the main stressed words and circle any weak forms with /ə/ or /ɪ/. Listen and check.

C Work in pairs. Change the conversation to talk about a place you've been to.

SPEAKING

8 A Think of something that happened to you or a friend whilst travelling. Make notes. Use the prompts to help.

Where? When? Who with? What happened? What did people say? How did you feel? Include interesting/memorable details.

B Find places in your notes for items from Exercise 4B and two examples of ellipsis. Write the first few words of those sentences.

C Work in pairs. Practise telling your story using your notes.

D Tell your story to a new partner with no notes.

DVD PREVIEW

1 Read the programme information. Who or what do you think the adjectives in the box refer to?

| cold | decaying | dilapidated | eccentric |
| naive | overawed | poor | scornful | wealthy |

◀)) **Great Expectations** **BBC**

Great Expectations is a classic BBC drama based on a novel by Charles Dickens and set in the southeast of England in the early nineteenth century. The novel tells the story of an orphan, Pip, and the way his life is profoundly changed by two separate encounters he has as a boy. In this episode Pip has been summoned to the house of a mysterious woman, Miss Havisham, and her adopted daughter Estella.

DVD VIEW

2 Watch the programme to check your ideas from Exercise 1. What other adjectives could you use to describe the house and the people?

3 A Check what you remember. Complete Miss Havisham's comments and questions.

1 He went to the furthest _____ of the earth in his quest for the purest _____ of beauty and when he found it he _____ a pin through its heart.

2 He's dead now. Cholera. In the tropics. Struck down in his relentless _____ of beauty. Perhaps it was beauty's _____, to stop his heart when he had stopped so many others.

3 Do you think beauty is a _____ of men, Pip?

4 Everything that was certain can change, in a _____.

5 Perhaps you were _____ for something special? Perhaps it is intended that you, like Estella, will be different and _____.

B Watch the programme again and check your answers.

C What, if anything, do you learn about Miss Havisham's personality and preoccupations from the comments in Exercise 3A?

D Work in pairs and discuss the questions.

1 What thoughts and feelings went through your mind as you watched the scene?

2 Why do you think Miss Havisham has invited Pip to the house?

3 How do you think this encounter might change Pip's life?

speakout a strange event

4 A Read about a competition. Who is it for? What criteria would you use to judge the winner? List at least three things.

We are looking for your audio and written submissions for a story which begins:

A strange thing happened to …

The story can be about yourself or someone you know.
Or it can be imaginary.

Go to our website for more information.

B ▶ **7.10** Listen to two speakers telling stories about something strange that happened to them. Which one meets your criteria in Exercise 4A better?

C Listen to the first story again and underline the alternatives you hear in the key phrases.

KEY PHRASES

You'd think I'd have been *annoyed/upset* but to the contrary …

This was one of those *times/situations* where you feel …

It was as if I was in a(n) *heightened/altered* state of mind.

The whole thing had an aura of *destiny/inevitability* about it.

Anyway *what was I saying/where was I?*

I thought *no/nothing* more of it.

Talk about *an unexpected turn of events/coincidences!*

5 A Work in pairs. Remember or make up your own entry to the competition described in Exercise 4A. You can each develop a story or share the same one. Practise telling the story using some of the key phrases above.

B Work with a new partner. Tell each other your stories. How well does each of your stories meet the criteria you developed in Exercise 4A?

writeback describe a strange event

6 A Read this version of the second story you listened to. In what ways is it different from the spoken version as you remember it? In which sentences does the writer foreshadow, or signal, an event to come?

I'm not one for believing in mystical powers, but sometimes something happens that makes you wonder. In this case it was several years ago, and I was in Scotland for a conference. At some point during dinner on the first night, I realised I didn't have my wallet, which sent me into a mild panic because it had all my credit cards and cash in it. The guy I was having dinner with, Rob, saw me patting my pockets and looking worried, and he asked me why. Looking back now, there was something in the way he listened that gave me a strange feeling.

First we worked out that it must be in my room, so I excused myself, and pretty much turned my room upside-down looking. I looked everywhere, through all the drawers, the wardrobe, under the bed, in all my pockets but to no avail. I returned to the dining room and Rob said 'I guess you didn't find it.' 'No,' I answered dejectedly. Then he said, 'Give me your key and I'll be back in five minutes with your wallet.'

I handed over my key and was sitting reading the hotel brochure (ironically, the lost-and-found information) when Rob sauntered back, smiling, and handed me my wallet. I was gobsmacked. Of course I asked him where he'd found it, and he said 'In the secret lining of your suitcase, right where you hid it.' Then I remembered I'd put it there for safe-keeping, and had completely forgotten. For the rest of the evening Rob told me about the many times he'd found lost things. He called it his 'object radar', the key being not to think too much when doing it. However it works, I know who to call next time I lose something.

B Write the description of the strange event you talked about in Exercise 5A. Use foreshadowing where appropriate (250–300 words).

VOCABULARY
FILM

1 A Correct two errors in each sentence.

1 I prefer an inky film with unknown actors rather than something with A-lasters.

2 Plenty of films offensively labelled as 'chicken flicks' by some critics have universal peel.

3 I'd rather see a host movie than a pasta western.

4 The key to a really good ride movie is the sporting cast.

5 My favourite films either have female pronarcissists, flushbacks, or both.

6 Formative plotlines are inevitable since there are no more original stories to write; even plot switches have become predictable.

B Which statements do you agree with?

GRAMMAR
SUBJUNCTIVE

2 A Read the text. Where is the person from?

If someone ¹visited my hometown, I suggest that he or she ²reads up on *the history of the country*, and ³keeps an open mind. It's inevitable that a visitor ⁴asks about *the townships, if they're safe or not*. I usually recommend that *a guide* ⁵shows them around. Also, my main desire is that *he or she* ⁶sees the positive side of *the place and the people, and that can be tricky*. I mean it's understandable that *someone is curious about the darker side*, but I find it annoying that anyone ⁷goes away with a negative impression. *It's almost as if apartheid* ⁸was the only thing that ever happened there.

B Use the subjunctive with the numbered verbs to make the text sound formal. Use *should* where appropriate.

C Rewrite the text about your hometown or any place you choose. Replace all the sections in italics.

VOCABULARY
RELATIONSHIPS

3 A Complete the expressions.

I have a problem with a colleague. When we first met we ¹cl_____ straightaway, and started dating. Then she got the promotion I wanted. That put a ²st_____ on our relationship. I just felt like we couldn't ³me_____ ha_____ on anything we disagreed about – in our private life. After a while the ⁴ro_____ times became too frequent, so we split up. I admit I'm ⁵be_____ a gru_____ about that promotion and I've taken a ⁶dis_____ to her personally as a result. But I'd like to find ways to stay on ⁷fri_____ te_____ so that we can have a good ⁸wo_____ relationship. Is that possible?

B Work in pairs. What advice would you give?

GRAMMAR
ADVERBIALS

4 A Read the poem and the readers' comments. Which comments do you identify with most?

> To move, to breathe, to fly, to float,
> To gain all while you give,
> To roam the roads of lands remote,
> To travel is to live.
>
> *(Hans Christian Anderson)*

1 I love the way he conveys the basic and important notion that giving is receiving, all in a short turn of words. This poem captures my feelings.

2 I remember my mum reading this to me when I was young, so I get a feeling of nostalgia reading it that is connected to my past.

3 The first line evokes a sense of liberation that I once felt when I travelled, when I was younger. Perhaps I find it hard to see all the waiting in lines at airports and sitting in seats with no knee-room as even resembling that sort of travel.

4 I don't have the life experience to understand this poem. I've never really travelled, and I feel aware that I am ill-equipped to respond to it in any positive way.

B Add the adverbials to the comments above. You need to use all three in each set.

1 utterly, vitally, perfectly

2 inextricably, distinctly, quite

3 unsurprisingly, instantly, vaguely

4 totally, painfully, sad to say

FUNCTION
TELLING ANECDOTES

5 A Cross out seven of the words in italics which are not needed.

Friday, *when I think it was*, and I was at the checkout and I *was like* 'Where's my wallet?' Panic stations! And *some of* woman in the queue behind me started *sort of* sighing. So rude, *you know what do I mean*? And *there it was one of those moments* when you really don't need *the stuff like that*. Then *this the* guy comes over waving my wallet! *Funny experience*, how finding something you've lost is the best kind of feeling.

B Work in pairs and tell each other a story about when you lost and found something. Aim to use at least four ways of making your story informal.

8 choice

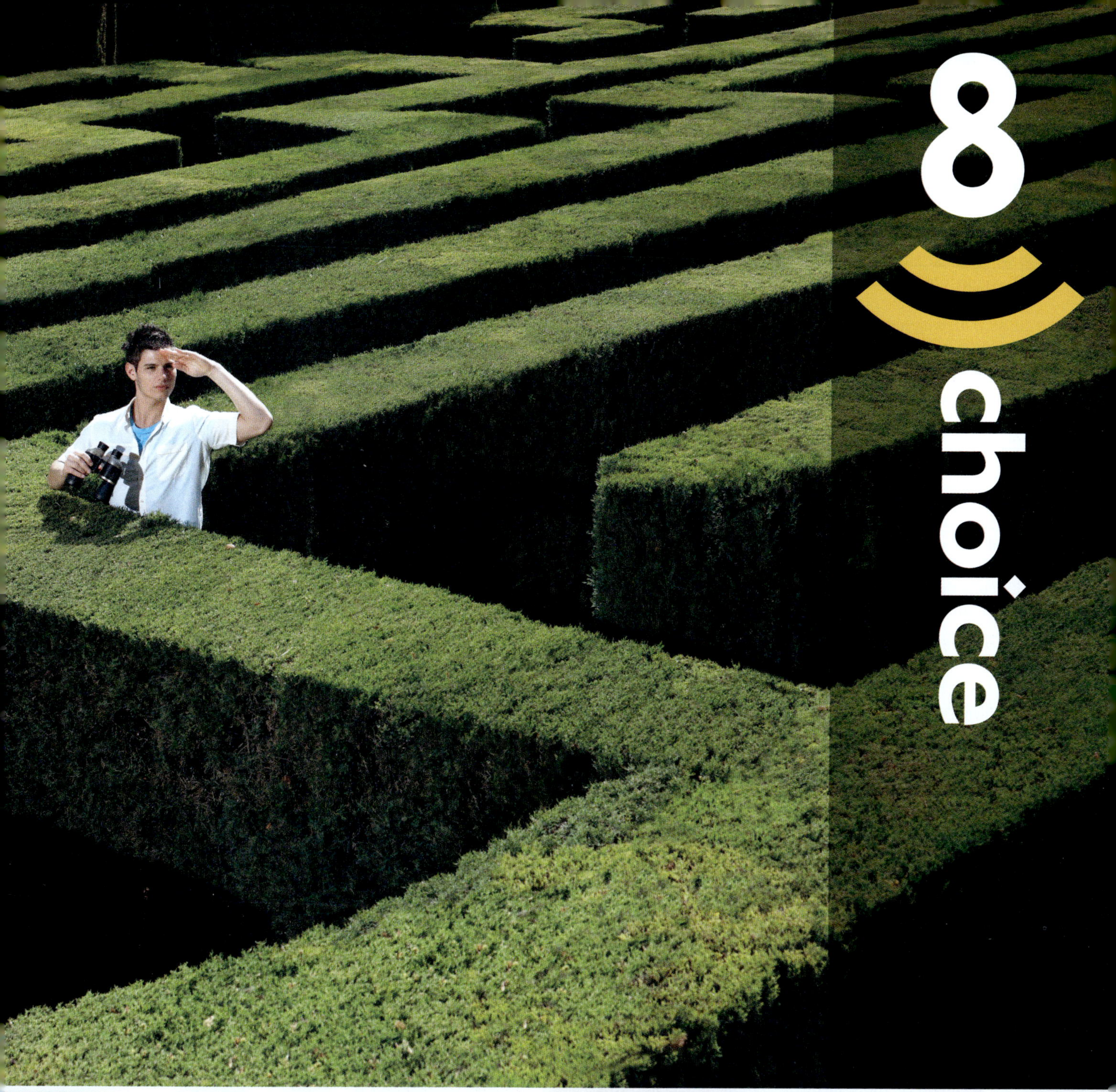

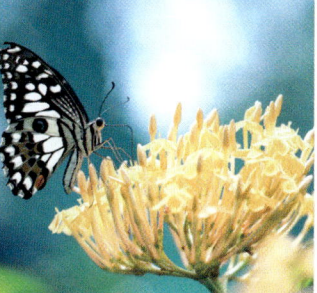

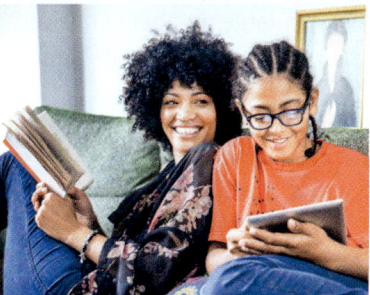

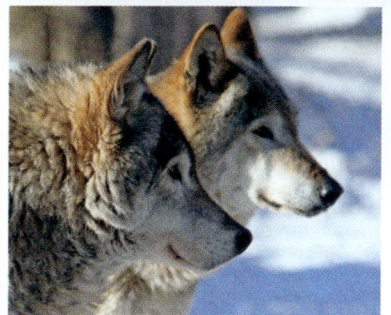

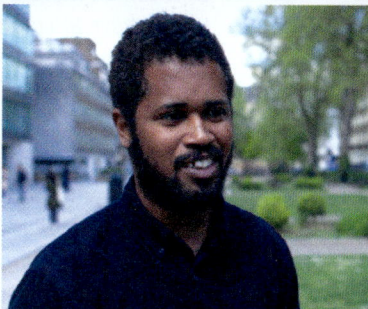

'S THE LITTLE THINGS p92

OUT OF PRINT? p95

THEM OR US? p98

DECISIONS p100

SPEAKING **8.1** Talk about the little choices that change your life **8.2** Discuss the impact of digital technology on our reading habits **8.3** Discuss wildlife dilemmas
8.4 Do a personality quiz; Discover what you are like

LISTENING **8.2** Listen to a programme about how digital texts change the way we read
8.3 Listen to two people discuss the return of wild animals to civilised areas
8.4 Watch people talking about different choices

READING **8.1** Read about a book that can change how we make decisions
8.3 Read about the problem of wolves 'invading' Europe

WRITING **8.2** Write a for and against, essay; Improve your introduction and conclusion
8.4 Write a key for a personality quiz

8.1)) IT'S THE LITTLE THINGS

G understanding complex sentences
P word stress
V idioms for choices

Review: Discover your 100 Most Important Life Choices

How many choices do you make in a day? Dozens? Hundreds? Thousands? The figure bandied about on the internet as 'the real number' puts it at 35,000, which presumably defines 'choice' pretty broadly; but once we consider the decisions we make on a daily basis – what to wear, eat, say, how to get to work, whether or not to talk to the interesting-looking guy/girl sitting near you – the number is hardly surprising, but no less overwhelming, and anyone with difficulty making decisions might find themselves literally paralysed. And ironically, it seems that [1]the decisions people have the most difficulty dealing with are often the smaller ones.

Nearly three decades ago [2]the immensely successful self-help author and social psychologist Dr Shad Helmstetter in his book *Choices: Discover your 100 Most Important Life Choices* invited us to reflect on the decisions we make, drawing our attention to the way everyday choices are the ones that have the greatest impact on our lives and indeed on who we are, rather than the 'biggies' such as career/partner/home-related ones. [3]Helmstetter's list, which ranges from decisions about 'Your posture' to 'Who you spend most of your time with' or 'How you spend your holidays', comes as good news for those who agonise over the decisions they make. [4]People judged negatively for their reluctance to make simple decisions may find some validation in Helmstetter's book. Since each decision has significance, then it is totally reasonable to approach each one seriously.

Perhaps Helmstetter's greatest contribution is the way he empowers readers to create a framework for their decision-making. However, his list is engaging in itself. [5]By exploring so many disparate examples of everyday decisions which have consequences of greater significance than one might think at the time, he reminds us that in fact we are the ones in control of our destinies. [6]It's not only actions such as what time we go to bed or how often we lie that are under our control, but also how much patience we have, what makes us angry and even how happy we are.

Given the degree to which self-reflection has become the norm these days, Helmstetter has to be seen as

VOCABULARY

IDIOMS FOR CHOICES

1 A Work in pairs and check what you know. Write the letter of the expression a)–h) that can replace the words in italics.

1 It's better to be decisive than *refuse to decide or give your opinion*.
2 It can be more difficult to make a decision when you *have too many options*.
3 When both of the two possible options are bad, best to choose *the best from the bad choices*.
4 In a group decision, I tend to *avoid conflict in a decision* and go with the majority.
5 If I'm really *unable to decide* about something, I *give myself more time to think about it*.
6 Then if I'm still *unable to decide*, I flip a coin. In the end it's often *all the same either way*.

a) take the path of least resistance
b) six of one, half a dozen of the other
c) (be) spoilt for choice
d) sleep on it
e) sit on the fence
f) torn
g) the lesser of two evils
h) in a quandary

B Tick (✓) the sentences in Exercise 1A that you agree with, and put a cross (✗) next to the ones you disagree with. Then compare your ideas with other students.

READING

2 A Discuss. Do you find it easier to make big decisions or smaller everyday decisions? Give examples.

B Read the review and tick the statements that are an accurate summary. Bracket the section of the text that supports your answer.

1 It's surprising that modern life involves such a large number of choices.
2 Small choices are often as important as big ones, if not more.
3 Maybe it's a good thing to have difficulty with minor decisions.
4 The list of choices is not the best thing about Dr Helmstetter's book.
5 The book is somewhat dated and therefore has lost some of its relevance.

C Read the text again and answer the questions.

1 How many specific examples of decisions does the author refer to?
2 Where does the author make <u>overtly</u> positive comments about the book? In which paragraphs?
3 To what extent does this review make you want to read the book, or not? Why/How?

D Look at the choices at the end of the text and put them in order of importance for you. What might each decision say about you?

something of a prophet in making the notion of 'it's the little things that matter' so fashionable. Perhaps associating this book with fashion is unfair as, unlike so many books of its genre, *Choices* has stood the test of time, and remains a go-to title for those looking for focus and motivation. This is all the more remarkable given that it was published in 1990 and hasn't been updated since; you may not even have been born at that time, and the internet was only in its infancy. Helmstetter's list therefore is (refreshingly, it has to be said) devoid of references to technology and both the nature and process of decision-making in the internet age.

16 – Which telephone calls you return

17 – The appearance of your home

18 – How long something stays broken before you fix it

19 – How late you stay up at night

20 – What time you get up in the morning

21 – How well you listen to others

GRAMMAR
UNDERSTANDING COMPLEX SENTENCES

3 A Work in pairs and discuss.

1 Which numbered sentences in the first two paragraphs of the review could be difficult to understand? Why?

2 In each numbered sentence:

a) underline the subject (sometimes this is very long)

b) circle the verb which goes with this subject

c) add any relative pronouns (*who, which, that*, etc.) and/or verbs to make the sentences clearer.

B Look at the rules and match them with the numbered sentences in the review. Some sentences match more than one rule.

RULES

Some texts, (articles, academic texts and other formal texts) use long, complex sentences which are challenging because:

a) a relative clause is used without a relative pronoun, and this puts two nouns side-by-side.

b) a past participle clause is used, and this looks like the past tense so can be misread as the main verb.

c) the subject is extremely long and often includes one or more subordinate clauses so it is difficult to identify the main verb.

d) a string of examples are included mid-sentence.

e) a long adverbial clause comes before the main clause.

SIX THINGS ABOUT DECISION-MAKING YOU MIGHT NOT KNOW

1 The choices made when you're in your teens are the ones that will have the most impact on your life.

2 The time of day a person makes a decision matters, and morning is considered best for most people because mental energy is highest.

3 People who can't make small decisions let alone big ones often leave decisions to others.

4 By developing daily routines in connection with predictable activities like eating, working and getting around, good decision-makers preserve mental energy.

5 Decisions like which dish to choose at a restaurant or whether to buy the blue or red socks can cause some people greater stress than choosing a partner.

6 People put into groups to make decisions generally do worse than individuals working on their own.

4 A In the sentences above

a) underline the whole of the subject.

b) circle the main verb that goes with the subject.

c) within the subject, bracket any subordinate clauses.

d) add any relative pronouns (*who, which*, etc.) and/or verbs which would make the sentences clearer.

B Discuss in pairs. To what extent do you agree with the points about decision-making? Which are worth taking into account in your own life?

5 A Read the summary of some research related to decisiveness. Do the results surprise you? Do you think they are valid?

Numerous studies looked at what rich and successful people have in common.
The studies zeroed in on decisive people, i.e. people who:
- are equipped with the capacity to make quick and determined decisions.
- make these decisions without hesitation.
- aren't put off by the degree of risk.
These studies showed that decisive people:
- tend to go further in a range of fields (e.g. business, politics and the arts).
- are more likely to accumulate wealth.
- are in a better position to fulfil their dreams.

B Write the above information into <u>one</u> sentence, using everything you know about building complex sentences, but <u>don't</u> use relative pronouns. Start with 'According to …'.

▷ page 118 **LANGUAGE**BANK

SPEAKING

62 – How you look at problems in the past

63 – How you treat or relate to members of the opposite sex

64 – How often you feel sorry for yourself

65 – Who upsets you the most

66 – Whether you like a challenge

67 – Who controls the conversation

68 – How you feel about world problems

69 – What you think about while you're getting ready in the morning

70 – How much you worry

71 – How much patience you have

72 – How many compliments you give

6 A Look at the extract from the list in the book and make notes on your answers to the questions.

1 Which of the items on the list do you think you <u>can</u> make a choice about? Which do you think are not really within your control?

2 Which are the most relevant to your life?

3 Choose three that are relevant to you. What choice do you actually make in connection to these points? How could you change that choice, and what would be the effect?

B Discuss your ideas with other students. Then choose one of your choices and tell the whole class about it.

VOCABULARY *PLUS*

CONNOTATION

7 A Work in pairs and complete the sentence with the most appropriate word or phrase.

1 'Liz and me, we had a huge row about where to go on holiday – the beach or the mountains – in the end I just _____.'
   a) acquiesced   **b)** buckled   **c)** capitulated
   d) gave in

2 'Some people say I'm choosy, but I prefer to think of myself as _____.'
   a) discerning   **b)** finicky   **c)** fussy
   d) picky

B Student A: look at page 131. Student B: look at page 133. Read the information and then check your answers above. Without looking back at the information, explain the differences between the words to your partner.

C Work in pairs. Read the Speakout tip. Discuss how you could record any words from Exercise 7A which are new to you.

speakout TIP

Words which are similar in meaning often have different connotations or shades of meaning. Also they can be formal (f) or informal (inf), particularly positive (pos) or negative (neg), be more used in British (BrE), American (AmE) or another form of English, or not polite, old-fashioned, literary, etc. A good dictionary will give you information about this and some dictionaries have a thesaurus section to help. You can record relevant information in your notebook.

e.g. futz around (inf, AmE) to waste time, especially by doing small jobs slowly. I spent the whole day just futzing around and got absolutely nothing done. A typical Saturday.

8 A Complete the questionnaire. Use a dictionary and a thesaurus to help.

CHOOSE YOUR WORDS WISELY!

1 You overhear some friends talking about you. Which word(s) in each group would hurt your feelings the most?
   a) articulate, garrulous, chatty
   b) determined, headstrong, resolute
   c) proud, self-assured, conceited

2 You're listening to an American and an English friend talking about a mutual acquaintance, and occasionally they misunderstand each other. Which word in each group might cause a problem, and why?
   a) intelligent, smart, well-dressed
   b) mean, nasty, stingy
   c) gifted, excellent, brilliant

3 Which alternative is the most offensive?
   a) Your report is *meticulous/nit-picking/systematic*.
   b) That class is for *disabled/special needs/handicapped* students.
   c) He is *famous/celebrated/notorious* for his work in providing loans to small start-ups.

B ▶ 8.1 WORD STRESS How many words or phrases in the questionnaire have the stress on the first syllable? Mark the stress. Then listen and check.

C Work in pairs and discuss your answers to the questionnaire.

▷ page 127 VOCABULARYBANK

OUT OF PRINT?

G prepositional phrases
P connected speech
V ways of reading

8.2

VOCABULARY

WAYS OF READING

1 A Complete the quiz and check the key on page 133. Compare your results with another student. Do you think the quiz is accurate?

HOW YOU READ: Deep, shallow or not at all?

1 Before I go on holiday, I …
  a) **pore over** maps and guidebooks, learning everything I can about the place.
  b) **flick through** a guidebook to check out the highlights.
  c) pack my clothes and toothbrush. Why would I read anything?

2 When I write something for school or work, before I hand it in I …
  a) **scrutinise** it for errors, checking down to the last letter and punctuation.
  b) get someone to **cast an eye over** it to make sure things are more or less alright.
  c) press 'send'. I'm not preoccupied with perfection.

3 If I were to have a job interview with a company, beforehand I would …
  a) **read up on** the company to show that I know all about their operations.
  b) **dip into** any literature I can find about the company, just to catch key bits.
  c) practise the company jingle and hum it during the interview.

4 When I get a new computer or phone, first I …
  a) **plough through** the manual so that I understand everything there is to know, dull as a manual can be.
  b) **peruse** every word of the quick start guide so I am confident with the basics.
  c) turn the device on and figure things out for myself.

B Look at the words in bold. Which refer to a) quick or shallow reading b) slow, careful or deep reading?

C Work in pairs. For each verb in bold, think of one more thing that you read in the way the word describes.

LISTENING

2 Work in pairs and discuss.
  1 What sort of things do you read in a typical week? What are your reasons for reading?
  2 What proportion of your reading is on screen versus print? What is your preference? Why?
  3 Do you read the two media, print and screen, differently?

3 A You are going to listen to a BBC radio interview discussing the pros and cons of reading print books and e-books. Before you listen, discuss and make notes on the following.
  1 Which is best, print or e-books, for a) concentration, b) comprehension, c) emotional involvement?
  2 Why, in each case?

B ▶ 8.2 Listen to the programme. Were your answers to question 1 similar to the professor's? Does the professor give the same reasons as you for question 2?

C Read the questions and make notes on anything you remember. Listen again and check. Add any information missing from your notes.
  1 What are the pros and cons of print books from the millennials' point of view?
  2 Which reading skills do e-books promote?
  3 What was the Israeli experiment?
  4 How did the results differ from other similar experiments?
  5 How does the professor see the difference between 'getting involved in' and 'being emotionally drawn into' a book?
  6 Why do some people think they are more emotionally involved when reading a print book?

D Read the extracts from the interview and discuss the questions.
  1 'It's real reading.' Why do you think the millennials said this about print books?
  2 'They're not designed for concentrated reading.' In what ways do you think this is true about digital media?
  3 'How many people today will ever cry over a book?' Have you ever been emotionally invested in a book? How does this compare with a movie version of a book?

GRAMMAR

PREPOSITIONAL PHRASES

4 A Read the comments about the programme. Which comments express a preference for print (P), digital (D) or neither (N)?

Chilled: [1]I wasn't aware that e-book sales were declining. [2]So there's less likelihood that my local bookshop will have to close. Hurrah!

MikiOg: I have to confess that I don't possess any books. [3]The reasons that people read print seem so twentieth century!

Rav: By 2025 print books will be a thing of the past. [4]I have no regrets that they are disappearing.

Avid: [5]I'm confident that print books will continue to be popular. And I say that even though e-books are more convenient.

Browse: [6]We should insist that online sites charge the same for e-books and print versions.

AliB: I didn't agree with a few points. [7]For example, I believe that a book can involve me emotionally, whether it's in print or online.

ReBoot: [8]The constant need for stimulation is an indication that people increasingly rely on digital input. I find that disappointing.

B Check what you know. Complete each sentence below with a preposition in the first gap and a noun/gerund in the second so that it means the same as the sentences above.

1 I was unaware ___*of*___ the ___*decline*___ in e-books.

2 So, there's less likelihood _____ my local bookshop _____.

3 People's reasons_____ _____ print seem so twentieth century!

4 I, for one, shall have no regrets _____ their _____.

5 I'm confident _____ the continuing _____ of print books.

6 We should insist _____ online sites _____ the same price for e-books and print versions.

7 For example, I believe _____ a book's _____ to involve me, whether it's in print or online.

8 The constant need for stimulation is indicative _____ people's increasing _____ on digital reading.

5 A ▶ 8.3 **CONNECTED SPEECH** Listen and write down the five sentences.

B Listen again. Underline the main stressed syllables, write /ə/ over any weak sounds and draw links between final consonants and initial vowels.

C Listen again and practise saying the sentences at the same time as the speaker.

▷ page 118 **LANGUAGE**BANK

My life as a digital immigrant

I am <u>conscious that</u> I'm not a digital 'native', and you probably find it ridiculous that I'm <u>amazed that</u> people are addicted to texting in restaurants. Yes, I get deeply <u>upset that</u> people sit together but read or watch different things on their tablets and phones. And I love reading, so the <u>thought that</u> the number of libraries is decreasing depresses me. My <u>anger that</u> people download pirated books for their e-readers is intense. But even I am not resistant to change. Last year I <u>decided that</u> I wouldn't take novels on holiday and bought an e-reader instead. It's now <u>normal that</u> I listen to an audiobook while driving to work. And while I used to get <u>annoyed that</u> my kids were on their computer all the time, now I'm actually <u>convinced that</u> YouTube is important in encouraging kids' creativity. Still, part of me is <u>terrified that</u> I'll be replaced by an app, which is probably silly since I'm a chef in a five-star restaurant.

6 A Read the blog above. How well do you identify with the writer? Do you know anyone who has gone through a similar change?

B Change the underlined items to a prepositional phrase and make any other necessary changes.

I am conscious of not being a digital 'native' …

SPEAKING

7 A Work in groups and choose three of the statements to discuss.

1 All types of texts are better in print.

2 Students' textbooks should be replaced by notebook computers or tablets.

3 Students should be allowed to use the internet when doing exams.

4 It is environmentally irresponsible to read print newspapers and books.

5 Modern schools rely too much on technology.

6 Print advertising is obsolete.

B While your group discusses, take turns taking notes for each statement. After the discussion, each note-taker gives a short summary of his/her statement to the rest of the class.

University students are increasingly seeking out study areas which are non-internet enabled. This seems counter-intuitive for today's millennials who are more dependent than any previous generation on 'being connected'. So, should students and workers learn to concentrate despite distractions or should they admit that doing so is damaging to their productivity?

On the one hand, a desire to work undisturbed is understandable. It is extremely difficult to resist distractions, especially when these distractions meet deep-seated psychological needs such as the urge to connect with other people. Also, the myth that people can multitask with ease has been well and truly discredited. Our brains can switch between tasks with astonishing speed, yet this switching has been shown to decrease mental performance significantly. A third point is that studying a web-based text filled with hyperlinks is extremely inefficient. Such hyperlinks may point us in worthwhile directions but the result is that our reading becomes fragmentary, and we find it difficult to remember anything.

Conversely, it can be argued that people in the twenty-first century need to become used to handling distractions as these are a feature of everyday life. It is unrealistic and indeed unproductive to expect people to concentrate for extended periods. A quick check of our emails or social networking accounts can provide a welcome break and means we can return to work refreshed. Finally, access to the internet enables us to research quickly and efficiently information that may be necessary to our studies or work and can thus be said to enhance our productivity.

In conclusion, the importance of having uninterrupted periods of sustained concentration in work and study far outweighs any arguments for maintaining access to the internet. It is my opinion, then, that everyone would benefit from working and/or studying in an internet-free zone as part of their daily routine.

WRITING

FOR AND AGAINST ESSAY; LEARN TO WRITE AN INTRODUCTION AND CONCLUSION

8 A Work in pairs and make notes. Give a minimum of three reasons in support of the statement and three reasons against it.

The only way to get any serious work or study done is to work somewhere with no access to the internet.

B Read the essay. Which of your points does the writer mention?

C Work in pairs and do the tasks together.

1 What is the purpose of each paragraph?

2 In an opinion essay, the writer states his/her position at the start. Where does this happen in a 'for and against' essay?

3 Underline the linkers used in the two main paragraphs. How many different types of linkers can you identify for each of these categories: contrastive, additive, exemplifying, cause-effect, other?

4 List the main ideas of the second and third paragraphs as concisely as possible. Then look at page 133 and compare your notes with the writer's pre-draft outline.

9 Work in pairs and look at the introduction and conclusion. Note the function of each sentence. Then check your ideas on page 133.

speakout TIP

Introductions and conclusions are challenging to write and it is important to keep your purpose in mind. The main goal of the introduction is to engage the reader with something relevant and to make the focus of the essay explicit; the purpose of the conclusion is to give the reader a clear sense of the writer's position, and a sense of the whole argument 'adding up'. Good writers often develop the content of the main body of their essay first, before writing the introduction and conclusion. In this way, they have a better idea of how to focus each part.

10 A Work in pairs and look at the essay topics below. Discuss them briefly, and decide if you agree with each statement or not.

- Texting and tweeting helps language learners' reading and writing skills.
- Everyone should have a microchip embedded in them with personal information (to reduce kidnapping and identity theft).
- Innovation ultimately frees people up so that they are more active and creative, and lead healthier lives.

B As a class, choose one of the essay topics. Brainstorm content for the two main paragraphs of the essay. Reduce your list to three or four points for each paragraph.

C With the main content in mind, write an introductory paragraph. Follow the framework that you looked at in Exercise 9.

D Compare your introduction with other students' work. Give each other feedback on how well the introduction a) gets the reader's attention, b) makes the main dilemma clear and c) avoids hinting at the writer's opinion.

11 A Draft a conclusion for the essay. Remember to state your opinion and use the framework in Exercise 9 to help.

B Compare your conclusion with another student's work. Does the conclusion give a clear view of the writer's opinion and supporting reasons for this?

12 Choose one of the other topics in Exercise 10A and write a full essay.

A WOLF AT MY BACK DOOR

When she looked out her kitchen window and saw a lone wolf rummaging through the rubbish bin just outside her back door, Camila Soto did a double-take and then a quick mental check. 'Where are the kids? That was my first thought.'

Once she realised her son and daughter were upstairs playing, she quickly phoned the police. 'They were like, "Oh, another one, OK just stay inside". I had no idea that this was actually so common.'

Wolves, which flourish in times of political and economic crisis, are back in force, roaming through populated areas of Europe in packs, igniting a fierce debate: should the wolves be protected, or should their numbers be controlled through culling? Their return to Europe in the past twenty years is thought to be linked to causes such as people migrating from rural areas, the reduction in state-organised culling and less money available for protection. According to some sources, there may now be 25,000 of these animals, some of which are within less than 50 kilometres of major cities. And one problem is that the wolf has no predators in Europe.

To the farmers who work the land, this is a worrying comeback of their ancient foe whose activities threaten their livestock. They also find the response of conservationists and animal lovers naive; in the words of one farmer, 'Protecting the wolves is insane. The first time one kills a kid there's going to be a lot of finger pointing.'

To people like Camila Soto, it's just one more thing to be vigilant about when considering the welfare of her children. 'But I have mixed feelings,' Soto says. 'I don't feel it's right to kill off these animals and I wish we as human beings could find a way to live in greater harmony with nature.'

VOCABULARY
WILDLIFE

1 A Look at the photos and discuss the questions.

1 How would you feel about having these animals living wild near where you live?
2 What might be some reasons for an increase in wild animal populations in urban areas?
3 If you had to choose between using public funds to protect the animals or to cull them, which would you choose?

B Read the article and check your ideas for question 3 above. Who in the article do you most agree with?

C Check what you know. How are the following pairs of words and phrases similar in meaning, and how are they different?

1 hunt/cull   4 predator/prey
2 lone wolf/pack   5 livestock/animals
3 roam/migrate   6 conservationist/animal lover

▷ page 127 **VOCABULARY**BANK

FUNCTION
GIVING OPINIONS

2 A ▶ 8.4 Listen to a man and woman talking about the article. Whose opinion is similar to Camila Soto's? Which person gives more convincing arguments, in your opinion? Give reasons for your answers.

B Work in pairs and look at the phrases below. Think of a word that could complete each one.

Asking for an opinion
What's your [1]_____ on this?
How do you see this?

Giving/Justifying an opinion
I'm really against any [2]_____ of …
Why should it be any different with … ?

Agreeing
In that [3]_____ I'm with you.
No one [4]_____ disagree with that.

Expressing disbelief or belief
I'd be surprised if that was the [5]_____.
That doesn't surprise me in the least.

Prioritising facts over supposition
On the [6]_____ of it, it seems … but actually …
Well supposedly so, but look at the facts.

C Listen to the conversation again and complete the phrases with the words the speakers use.

D ▶ 8.5 INTONATION: VOICE RANGE
Underline the main stressed words in the expressions in Exercise 2B. Work in pairs and say the expressions, using a high pitch on the main stressed words. Then listen and say each expression with the speaker.

▷ page 118 **LANGUAGE**BANK

LEARN TO

HEDGE AN OPINION

4 A Work in pairs and look at the sentences from the conversation. What phrases could you add before each sentence to make them sound less direct?

1 The danger is always exaggerated.
2 It's important that the risk is properly assessed.
3 That could cause you a real problem.
4 Tourists bring money to places and it's actually a plus to have wolves.

B ▶ 8.6 Listen to excerpts from the conversation and write the phrases the speakers use.

speakout TIP

A simple statement of opinion can sound too direct or even aggressive, and hedging phrases can lessen this effect. The speaker is acknowledging that what he/she is saying is an opinion rather than a fact. Hedging is more appropriate in some cultural and social contexts than others. Would it be appropriate in the context(s) where you use English?

C Work in pairs and cover the phrases you wrote down in Exercise 4B. Use the prompts below to remember each one. Then take turns saying each sentence in Exercise 4A using any one of the hedging devices.

a) guess
b) just me but
c) some things, agree
d) no expert

3 A Work in pairs and look at the headline. Discuss briefly whether it's a good idea. List at least three reasons for and against the idea.

> ## Zoos to be closed, declared cruel to animals and of no benefit to society

B Roleplay the situation with each of you taking opposite sides of the argument. Use the flow chart to help and phrases from Exercise 2B.

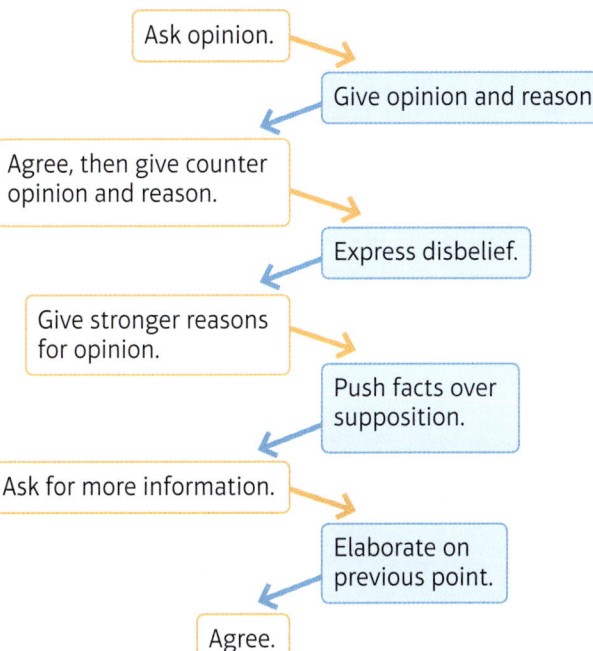

Ask opinion. → Give opinion and reason.

Agree, then give counter opinion and reason. → Express disbelief.

Give stronger reasons for opinion. → Push facts over supposition.

Ask for more information. → Elaborate on previous point.

Agree.

SPEAKING

5 A Look at the statements below. Which of them would you approve of being made into a law? Make notes on your opinion, and for each one list some of the consequences of your choice.

- Ecotourism should be heavily subsidised.
- Hunters should only be allowed to use a bow and arrow.
- Plastic bags should be banned.
- Meat should be phased out as a food.
- Health insurance should cover household pets.
- Tap water should be taxed at a higher rate so that people waste less.
- Keeping pets in apartments shouldn't be permitted.

B Work with other students and discuss each topic for two minutes. Give your opinion and reasons for feeling the way you do, and add examples to justify your point of view. Pay attention to the language you use to express your opinion, including responding and hedging.

C Report back on your group's consensus on each topic. Who made the best arguments against the majority point of view?

DVD PREVIEW

1 A Work alone and note your answers to these two questions.

1 If you could live in a different country, where would it be? Why?

2 If you could change one thing about your lifestyle, what would it be?

B Work with other students and compare your answers. How many of you

- gave similar responses?
- chose countries based on climate, food or people?
- are drawn to a lifestyle that is simpler, healthier or materially more secure?

DVD VIEW

2 A Watch Part 1 of the interviews and write the country each person chooses.

B Work in pairs. What do you remember? List the reason the person gave for their choice. Then watch again and check.

3 A Read the excerpts from Part 2 of the interview. What animal might the person be referring to?

1 … just fly in the sky, somewhere warm …

2 Like generally all herbivores it's a lot of just eating … over and over again.

3 … have a nectar, go to the next flower, chill out, go out, party.

4 … they are incredibly cute and have fun all the time.

5 Don't they have three brains and seven hearts … ?

6 … he doesn't have to do any work, he plays, eats all day …

7 … they seem to bounce back after any experience of adversity.

8 … an animal that lived a long time so it would be a …

B Watch Part 2 of the interviews and check your ideas.

C There are 1–3 words missing from each excerpt in Exercise 3A. Watch again and add the words.

4 A Look at the adjectives in the box. What is the noun form of each?

Michael Presenter

Agnes

Ewan

> attractive   enthusiastic   innocent
> naive   optimistic   loyal

B Where can each word in either adjective or noun form fit in the sentence below? Work with a partner, then watch Simon (from 01:37) and check.

'Dogs have a lot of fun, and dogs seem to be relentlessly _____ and very _____ to their owners, to the other members of their pack, and dogs have an _____ and a _____ and an _____ which is very _____.'

5 A Watch Part 3 of the interviews. Who thinks he/she

1 doesn't move enough?

2 moves around too much?

3 has a nasty habit?

4 needs to follow a more rigid routine?

B Work in pairs. The following sentences were cut from the interviews. Who said which sentence, do you think?

1 Then perhaps I can blossom!

2 I wish I could take my own advice.

3 I feel trapped between the four walls.

4 We complement each other!

5 I have to stop putting off what I need to do.

6 I mean lose out, you know, miss out on stuff.

C Watch again to help you decide.

Sofia, Matt and Mila

Tricia and Jack

Praneet

Simon

Michael

Sami

James and Alex

Peter

speakout a personality quiz

6 A Work in pairs and follow the instructions.

1 Choose a category from the box and list five items for each.

> animals   forms of transport   fruit
> furniture   vegetables

2 Write one or two adjectives next to each of your five items.

B Work with a new partner and ask the questions.

1 If you were one of these five (animals), which would you be?

2 What characteristics do you think you have in common?

C Discuss. Do the adjectives you wrote in Exercise 6A fit your partner?

writeback a quiz key

7 A Which appliance do you most resemble or identify with: fridge, microwave, kettle, electric toothbrush or sewing machine? Tell another student which you chose and why.

B Read the quiz key. Does the description for the appliance you chose fit you? Do you disagree with any of the characteristics described by the writer?

ANSWERS

Fridge – You like stability and function over appearance. You're a practical person, down to earth, but with a cool heart and an inner world that is sometimes rather cluttered. You don't like to move around too much and are happiest just sitting in one place, humming away.

Microwave – You're slick in appearance, you enjoy it when people notice that, but you don't like to stand out too much. You have a lot of confidence because you know how important you are; friends call on you for help at the most surprising times, out of the blue, and you're always ready to help. Sometimes you surprise people by how much power you have.

Kettle – In groups, you prefer not to be noticed too much – you'll find an unobtrusive place to sit and are happy to just listen to others. You still thrive on attention, and experience almost disproportionate gratification when someone calls on you to give your opinion or chip into the conversation. Quiet as you usually are, there are moments when you become extremely passionate about things.

Electric toothbrush – You're the jump-in-and-get-your-hands-dirty type, ready to solve a problem not by talking about it but simply by getting on with the solution (in fact the all-talk-no-action type of person annoys you no end). You're not afraid to get close to others, to share your own secrets and to listen to theirs.

Sewing machine – People admire you for your practicality. You're good with your hands and that shows in your ability to fix just about anything and to cook a great meal out of whatever you find in the fridge. You're a bit of a loner but a content one, as you thrive on having periods of contemplation and solitude in your everyday life.

C Choose a category from Exercise 6A or your own idea, and list five items. Write a quiz key including the personality and behaviour associated with each item (250–300 words).

D Work with other students and do your quiz with them.

Ⓥ IDIOMS FOR CHOICES

1 A Complete the idioms for choices.

1 If you always vote for the l_____ of two e_____, you will always have evil, and you will always have less. (Ralph Nader)

2 The p_____ of least r_____ leads to crooked rivers and crooked men. (Henry David Thoreau)

3 To lose a friend, either lend him money, or refuse to lend him money. It is six of o_____ and half a d_____ of the other. (George Jean Nathan, paraphrased)

4 All you'll ever get from s_____ on the f_____ is splinters. (Anonymous)

5 Surely if we have learnt anything from the history of morals it is that the thing to do with a moral q_____ is not to hide it. (H. L. A. Hart)

6 I arise in the morning t_____ between a desire to improve the world and a desire to enjoy the world. That makes it hard to plan the day. (E. B. White)

7 I couldn't decide whether to take medication to help my insomnia. So my doctor told me to s_____ on it. (Anonymous)

8 The shopper who is s_____ for c_____ may in the end choose nothing. That's not good for business. (Anonymous)

B Work in pairs and discuss.

1 Which of the sayings tries to use humour to make its point?

2 Which sayings are the most relevant to you, and why? Which have no relevance to you?

Ⓖ UNDERSTANDING COMPLEX SENTENCES

2 A Read the text below. What context do you think it appeared in, i.e. what sort of publication and what country?

> **After a frantic 36-hour search** involving 150 local volunteers and a family pushed to breaking point with panic, blonde-haired, blue-eyed little Lucy Reed, who disappeared early Saturday morning, was found safe and sound at the water's edge yesterday by an off-duty patrolman vacationing in Rye Beach out for a morning jog.

B Work with a partner and make a list of all the facts that make up the story in your notebook.

36-hour search, 150 volunteers, family panicking …

C Close your book and write the information into a single sentence. Then open your book and compare it to the original.

Ⓥ WAYS OF READING

3 A Add vowels to complete the words for ways of reading. Then answer the questions.

Why might you … ?

1) p __ r __ over a map?

2) p __ r __ s __ a tabloid newspaper?

3) pl __ __ gh through a chemistry textbook?

4) d __ p into a book on architecture?

5) r __ __ d __ p on famous Australians?

6) c __ st __ n __ y __ over an email from your boss?

7) scr __ t __ n __ s __ a contract?

8) fl __ ck thr __ __ gh someone's passport?

B For each type of text, what reasons can you think of for reading it differently from the way given?

Ⓖ PREPOSITIONAL PHRASES

4 A Write the preposition that comes next.

1 There's no chance _____ …

2 Listening to music is conducive _____ …

3 I'm eligible _____ …

4 It's astounding, the increase _____ …

5 I struggle _____ …

6 It's always important to be mindful _____ …

7 I'd love to do a course _____ …

8 There's no justification _____ …

B Work in pairs and complete each sentence above with an idea you both agree on.

Ⓕ GIVING OPINIONS

5 A Add a missing word to each expression. Then find pairs of expressions that have a similar meaning or function.

1 I'd be surprised that was the case.

2 I'm really against form of exploitation, but …

3 In respect I'm with you.

4 No one disagree with that.

5 On the face it, it seems … but actually …

6 That doesn't surprise me the least.

7 How do you see?

8 Well so, but look at the facts.

9 What's your take this?

10 Why it be any different with … ?

B Discuss with other students. One student reads out a statement below and adds a reason to support this opinion. Other students give their opinions. Use the expressions in Exercise 5A.

1 Human beings' use of animals for entertainment is cruel.

2 Ecotourism may seem well intentioned but it's actually damaging to the environment.

3 Hunting for sport, when used as a way of culling, is beneficial to the community.

IRREGULAR VERBS

Verb	Past simple	Past participle
be	was	been
beat	beat	beaten
become	became	become
begin	began	begun
bend	bent	bent
bet	bet	bet
bite	bit	bitten
bleed	bled	bled
blow	blew	blown
break	broke	broken
bring	brought	brought
broadcast	broadcast	broadcast
build	built	built
burn	burned/burnt	burned/burnt
burst	burst	burst
buy	bought	bought
catch	caught	caught
choose	chose	chosen
come	came	come
cost	cost	cost
cut	cut	cut
deal	dealt	dealt
dig	dig	dug
do	did	done
draw	drew	drawn
dream	dreamed/dreamt	dreamed/dreamt
drink	drank	drunk
drive	drove	driven
eat	ate	eaten
fall	fell	fallen
feel	felt	felt
feed	fed	fed
fight	fought	fought
find	found	found
fly	flew	flown
forbid	forbade	forbidden
forget	forgot	forgotten
forgive	forgave	forgiven
freeze	froze	frozen
get	got	got
give	gave	given
go	went	gone
grow	grew	grown
hang	hung	hung
have	had	had
hear	heard	heard
hide	hid	hidden
hit	hit	hit
hold	held	held
hurt	hurt	hurt
keep	kept	kept
know	knew	known
lay	laid	laid
lead	led	led
leap	leapt	leapt
lean	leaned/leant	leaned/leant
learn	learned/learnt	learned/learnt

Verb	Past simple	Past participle
leave	left	left
lend	lent	lent
let	let	let
lie	lay	lain
light	lit	lit
lose	lost	lost
make	made	made
mean	meant	meant
meet	met	met
mistake	mistook	mistaken
pay	paid	paid
put	put	put
read	read	read
ride	rode	ridden
ring	rang	rung
rise	rose	risen
run	ran	run
say	said	said
see	saw	seen
sell	sold	sold
send	sent	sent
set	set	set
shake	shook	shaken
shine	shone	shone
shoot	shot	shot
show	showed	shown
shrink	shrank	shrunk
shut	shut	shut
sing	sang	sung
sink	sank	sunk
sit	sat	sat
sleep	slept	slept
slide	slid	slid
smell	smelled/smelt	smelled/smelt
speak	spoke	spoken
spell	spelt	spelt
spend	spent	spent
spill	spilled/spilt	spilled/spilt
split	split	split
spread	spread	spread
stand	stood	stood
steal	stole	stolen
stick	stuck	stuck
sting	stung	stung
swim	swam	swum
take	took	taken
teach	taught	taught
tear	tore	torn
tell	told	told
think	thought	thought
throw	threw	thrown
understand	understood	understood
wake	woke	woken
wear	wore	worn
win	won	won
write	wrote	written

GRAMMAR

1.1 verb patterns

verb + -ing

Use an -ing form after prepositions. *It's for making bread. She left without paying.*

This includes prepositions after certain:

- adjectives. *committed to, justified in, meticulous about, renowned for*
- nouns/noun phrases. *thanks for, in addition to, with a view to, the idea of, the purpose of, devotion to*
- verbs/verb and object combinations. *specialise in, feel like, admire sb for, compliment sb on*

-ing forms also follow:

- many verbs. *involve, imagine, can't help, suggest, bother*
- multi-word verbs. *end up, put off, give up, take up, burst out, look forward to*
- a few adjectives. *(not) worth, hopeless*, pointless**
- time linkers. *when, before, since, on, upon, until, while, whilst*

Kit broke his arm whilst skiing.

-ing forms when functioning as nouns (gerunds) are often the subject of a sentence.

Overfishing is depleting the cod species.

-ing forms can also function as adjectives (participles). *satisfying results, a mystifying problem, participating countries.*

*can also be followed by the infinitive with *to*

infinitive with *to*

Use an infinitive with *to* after:

- certain verbs/verb and object combinations/verb phrases. *arrange, manage, fail, prepare, persuade sb, allow sb, want sb, occur to sb*

It didn't occur to me to resign.

- adjectives. *ready, inclined, reluctant, willing, liable, bound*

The road is liable to flood. Ann's bound to be late.

- nouns/noun phrases. *a (long) way, (it's her) ambition, (go to) great lengths, (there's) no need, (the) aim/motive is*

Kate has gone to great lengths to find an answer.

Use an infinitive with *to*:

- after *too* + adjective/quantifier. *It's too heavy to lift. There's too much to see.*
- to express purpose. *He's saving to buy a house.*

-ing form or infinitive with *to*

Some verbs can take the -ing form or infinitive with *to* but there is a difference in meaning.

go on, remember, forget, start, regret, try, stop

I remember locking the door but I can't find the key.

Remember to lock the door before going out.

With other verbs there is little or no difference.

start, begin, like, bother

Use the perfect infinitive or -ing form to emphasise the order of activities.

I would love to have met Michael Jackson.

Henson admitted having started the fire.

1.2 continuous and perfect aspect

The continuous aspect

The continuous aspect focuses on an action/activity and its duration rather than its result. It is used to describe:

- a temporary activity with a limited duration.

The train was nearing Paris. I'm trying to sleep.

Ben will be waiting to pick you up outside.

- a repeated action or a state.

We were conducting a series of pilot studies at that time.

The team is currently enjoying a week's holiday.

The perfect aspect

The perfect aspect links two time frames. It is used:

- to emphasise that an action is completed before another time.

I realised I'd sent the wrong email.

By 2040, electric cars will have replaced petrol models.

- when the exact time is unimportant or unknown.

Has anyone seen my glasses?

She's been to Morocco a couple of times.

- to emphasise the result rather than the process.

I've already eaten, thanks.

The company has made a huge investment in the country.

- when the event is incomplete, in an unfinished period up to another point in time.

I'd lived there for six years before I met him.

Continuous and perfect together

Both aspects can occur, showing the linking of two times and the duration or temporariness of an activity.

The CEO had been planning the merger for months before he made the announcement.

By next June I'll have been working here for a year.

1.3 presenting survey results

Generalising	Exemplifying	Hedging/Speculation
On the whole, … tended (to be …) Generally speaking though,	To cite one example, Another illustration of this is …	Our impression was simply that … (Their interest) presumably (reflected …) One might speculate that … The consensus seems to be that …

PRACTICE

1.1

A Correct the mistakes in sentences 1–8. Each sentence contains one or two mistakes.

1 Sonya's renowned not for answering her emails in addition to never check her phone.
2 I was reluctant to acknowledging that I was saving up for buying a second car.
3 Since see the film, Ron bursts out cry every time he sees a cat.
4 I'm not looking forward to be forty, so there's no need to organise a party.
5 The judge decided they were justified in having leave the restaurant without paying while running from the fire.
6 It's worth remembering packing your case the night before so you don't forget taking everything.
7 It was great to have visit so many countries but pointless trying picking which was the best.
8 When Dan was complimented on having prepared such a good meal, he admitted to have ordered it from a caterer.

B Complete the text. For each verb, write *to* or – before the verb, and add *-ing* or – after the verb. Make any spelling changes necessary.

Trailblazers?

A team of volunteers committed ¹_to_ extinguish_ing_ forest fires have taken their organisation's name too literally and will end up ²____ spend____ some time behind bars. All nine members of the volunteer firefighting unit The Trailblazers initially denied ³____ start____ the fires they were putting out, but after police went to great lengths ⁴____ collect____ the evidence, they admitted their crime. 'I've always admired firefighters for their devotion ⁵____ protect____ the community,' said the mayor, 'and I will go on ⁶____ do____ so – this is a situation where one or two bad apples persuaded a group ⁷____ carry____ out an activity that they will later regret ⁸____ have____ got involved in.' A police spokesperson said their motive seemed to be ⁹____ make____ heroes out of themselves. 'We noticed the Trailblazers were remarkable at ¹⁰____ put____ out fires quickly, as if they knew where one was liable ¹¹____ start____. The admiration made it simply too rewarding ¹²____ give____ up their behaviour.

1.2

A Underline the correct alternative.

1 We *were/'d been* approaching the border when we realised our papers *were/had been* stolen.
2 Once you*'d/'ve* had enough, text me and I*'m/'ll be* waiting for you in the car park.
3 *Didn't you find/Haven't you found* the book you *were/'d been* looking for yet?
4 The letter said *he'd missed/he missed* the payment but he was sure he *hadn't/didn't*.
5 By midnight they*'d been/were* on the road too long and *were needing/needed* a bed for the night.
6 I *was/'ve been* having problems with my phone since I *downloaded/'ve downloaded* that new app.
7 *I've been meaning/I've meant* to change my email for ages but I *haven't had/didn't have* the time yet.
8 They *do/'re doing* some repairs here, but they *finish/'ll have finished* by tomorrow.

B Complete the story with the verb in brackets in the perfect, continuous or a combination of forms.

This happened last year. I ¹_____ (take) part in lots of ventriloquist competitions before but I ²_____ (never feel) so nervous, and while I ³_____ (wait) to be called I had this sensation that I ⁴_____ (lose) my voice. But I ⁵_____ (work) far too hard to mess this one up, so I told myself, 'If you don't win, then next year you ⁶_____ (flip) burgers again.' Finally, my name was called and while I ⁷_____ (walk) on stage the oddest thing happened. Nino, my dummy, suddenly said, 'Hey, Pat, you're the best. See, even now your lips ⁸_____ (not move).' Of course they ⁹_____ (not move), I was petrified! As Nino ¹⁰_____ (give) me his pep talk I realised the performance ¹¹_____ (start) and I ¹²_____ (stand) on stage with my dummy talking to me. Then he stopped, lifeless, as if he ¹³_____ (not say) a word, and I got massive applause. I ¹⁴_____ (never hear) an audience clap so loud before or since.

1.3

A Complete the presentation with the words in the box.

| ~~speaking~~ tended consensus cite illustration reflects whole impression speculate |

speaking
Generally ⋀, a majority of respondents to feel that while a shortened (four-day) working week is an appealing idea, it would be too problematic in practice. The seems to be that the resulting complications for human resources and management and the decline in productivity wouldn't be worth the benefits. To one example, a factory manager indicated that going to four days would require increasing his workforce by 20 percent. Another of this is that many people said they would have to work at home to make sure their tasks got done anyway. This view presumably the degree of inflexibility of many companies. On the our was simply that people in fact like their routine, and one might that they identify so much with their work that they can't imagine life with less of it.

GRAMMAR

10.3 *if and related expressions*

Use:

- *if so/not (if this is/isn't the case), if in doubt (if it's unsure)* at the beginning of sentences or clauses to refer back to a previous idea.

*Start exercising slowly. **If in doubt**, consult your doctor.*

- *if any* to emphasise a small number or amount, after a quantifier or at the end of a clause.

*Few, **if any**, people knew Jo's background.*

*There is **little, if any**, difference. There is little difference, **if any**.*

- *if anything/anyone* to emphasise that there are limited possibilities.

*What can we do to help, **if anything**?*

***If anyone** can solve this problem, Jackie can.*

- *if ever* to show infrequency, often with *seldom* or *rarely*.

*The staff here **seldom, if ever**, miss a day's work.*

- *as if* to express similarities after verbs such as *look, act, behave, talk, (would) seem/appear*, etc.

*It **would seem as if** we have underestimated the risk.*

*They **acted as if** they had all the time in the world.*

- *if* + past participle or adjective with no subject or *be*.

***If completed** by March, the bridge would open in June. (it were)*

***If necessary**, I'll drive you. (it is)*

Alternatives to *if*

Use:

- *provided/providing (that), on condition (that)* and, less formally, *as long as* to mean *if and only if*, often when the speaker has serious reservations.

*You can hire a car **provided that** you have a valid licence.*

- *otherwise* in real and hypothetical situations to mean *if this doesn't happen/if this were not the case*.

*You need a ticket. **Otherwise**, you won't get in.*

- *unless* in real conditional sentences to mean *if not*.

***Unless** you have a ticket, you won't get into the party.*

- *unless* used formally with a past participle, or to express an afterthought.

*Do not touch this switch **unless authorised** to do so.*

*Let's see a movie – **unless** you want to stay at home.*

- *without* + noun or *-ing* form to replace *unless* + verb.

***Without** a boarding card you won't get on the plane.*

- *whether or not* or *even if* to show something will still be true if another thing happens.

*We would always go for a walk **whether or not** it rained.*

- *but for* in written and more formal situations to mean if something hadn't happened.

***But for** her mother's support, Lena would have given up.*

2.2 nominal relative clauses

A nominal relative clause is a type of noun clause and is used to express ideas more concisely.

In a nominal relative clause a noun/pronoun and another pronoun are 'fused' together into one relative pronoun. Typical relative pronouns are: *what, who, when, where, how, why, whatever, whoever, whichever*.

*I know ~~the things which~~ **what** I like.*

*~~The person who~~ **Whoever** is elected will serve five years.*

Some nominal relative pronouns can be followed by *to* + infinitive.

*I considered **what to say**.*

*The manual illustrates **how to troubleshoot** problems.*

A nominal relative clause can be a subject or object. As a subject, it can function as a cleft structure to add emphasis.

***What other people think** is irrelevant.*

*Did you tell them **where we're meeting**?*

Use nominal relative clauses after the expressions *This/That/It + be + just, exactly, precisely*.

***This is precisely** what I feared would happen.*

***That's exactly** when we're away.*

***It's just** what I wanted!*

Don't use *what* in a normal relative clause.

*It's a video ~~what~~ I made. Use **that**/**which** or nothing (if the relative pronoun is the object of the verb).*

Whoever, whichever, whatever, whenever, wherever, however

Use *whoever, whichever*, etc. in nominal relative clauses to replace *anyone who, anything which/that, any time that, any place where, any way that/which*.

*I'll do **whatever** you want.*

***Whoever** wins goes forward to the next stage.*

Note the difference with *who*.

***Who** we're looking for is a genuine entrepreneur. = the specific person who*

2.3 leading a discussion

Initiating a discussion or a topic	Getting others to clarify ideas
So our task today is to … What I'd like to do I think, is start with … Who would like to kick this one off?	Could you elaborate on that? Could you run that past us again? Could you explore that further? Can I just check where you're coming from? Correct me if I'm wrong, but what you're saying is that …
Giving feedback/Evaluating	
That's an interesting perspective. I can imagine that working. That's certainly worth considering.	

PRACTICE

2.1

A Underline the correct alternative.

The wisdom of deliberate mistakes

[1]*Rarely, if ever/If in doubt*, will you find errors on the best maps, but [2]*without/otherwise* a few embedded errors – fictional towns, for example – mapmakers would have no way of catching out plagiarisers. [3]*If necessary/If anything*, it might inconvenience a few unwitting travellers, but [4]*without/otherwise* all a mapmaker's work could easily be stolen by others.

Hopefully [5]*little/few*, if any, of us will find ourselves lost in the woods with nothing but a compass and map, but [6]*if so/if not*, what, [7]*if any/if anything*, can you do to get yourself 'unlost'? Well, [8]*provided that/unless* you know roughly the direction and distance of the point you want to reach, aim 10 degrees to the right – yes, get it a bit wrong on purpose – and [9]*as long as/if in doubt* you have an idea of how far to walk, you'll know in which direction to head once you walk that distance … [10]*providing/unless*, of course, you've misjudged the direction of the destination entirely.

B Rewrite the second sentence so that it means the same as the first.

1 If the doctor hadn't intervened quickly, he would be dead.
But for _____.

2 I'd still love you even if you didn't love me.
Whether you _____.

3 He can't go to the dance if he doesn't have a partner.
Without _____.

4 Let him sleep late unless there's an emergency.
Let him sleep late as long _____.

5 Stay in your seat except if the crew instructs you otherwise.
Unless instructed _____.

6 You don't agree? Say yes anyway.
Say yes whether _____.

7 I'll attend the meeting unless I'm obliged to speak.
I'll attend the meeting provided _____.

8 You can't use a TV without a licence.
Unless _____.

2.2

A In each sentence find a noun + pronoun or a pronoun + pronoun combination and replace it with a single pronoun.

1 I remember the time that we actually enjoyed weekends.

2 Anyone who thinks writing a book is easy should try it for themselves.

3 If you don't like the way that she treats you, tell her.

4 I'll have my eggs any way that you want to make them.

5 Don't forget the thing that is important to you and you can't go wrong.

6 There are two routes, so you can choose the one that you prefer.

7 The person who I like best is best kept a secret.

8 You can have anything that you want, just name it.

B Complete each of the replies with a pronoun.

1 I meant your cousin Susan, not your classmate Susan.
a) That's exactly _____ I was talking about.
b) _____ you meant, I don't think either of them is unlucky.

2 We got them some champagne glasses.
a) That's just _____ *we* wanted to get them!
b) We're giving cash, then they can get _____ they want.

3 The first week of October works for me.
a) That's exactly _____ we were planning to be away.
b) OK, _____'s good for you.

4 Pizza for dinner?
a) That's precisely _____ I was thinking!
b) _____ you want is fine by me.

2.3

A Correct the error in each underlined sentence or phrase. One is correct.

A: [1]<u>What I'd like to do I think start with</u> the point about getting students to memorise poems. [2]<u>Who would like to kick one off this?</u>

B: Well, to me it's clearly good for them, so I'm for it. It's good for brain development, isn't it?

A: [3]<u>Can I just check from where you're coming?</u> You think we should promote memorisation, have them do more, not less?

B: That's right.

A: [4]<u>That's an interesting perspective.</u> I would have thought the opposite.

C: Me too. [5]<u>Correct me if you're wrong, but what you're saying is that</u> rote learning by itself is good for cognitive development, and we should build it into the curriculum?

A: [6]<u>That's certainly worthy considering.</u>

B: Yes, we could have competitions, a sort of Poetry Memorisation Olympics.

A: [7]<u>I can imagine working that.</u>

C: Seriously? I'm not convinced.

GRAMMAR

3.1 expressing modality

Use **modal verbs** to express probability or likelihood. These include *will, must, might, may, could, can't*.

That'll be Dave at the door. (certainty/logical deduction)

*We **might** be seeing Rosa at the weekend.* (possibility)

*I'm sorry, it **can't** be done by then.* (impossibility)

Use **other expressions** to express:

• certainty.

*She's **bound** to have prepared carefully.*

*It's **guaranteed** to save you money.*

*The economy **is undoubtedly** in trouble.*

*The decision **will inevitably** lead to tensions.*

• probability/possibility.

*You **may well** be right.*

*He's **most probably** lost his mobile signal.*

It could be that robots will replace most jobs.

*I **would guess that** she earns about a million.*

• improbability.

It seems totally unimaginable that they'll lose.

It's highly unlikely that we'll get any news before tomorrow.

Other uses

Use **modal verbs** to express necessity, desirability, obligation, permission, ability and their opposites. These include: *must, have to, should, ought to, may, can*.

*Hard hats **have to** be worn in this area.* (obligation)

*I **ought to** have known better.* (desirability)

***May** I leave my coat here?* (permission: polite)

Use **other expressions** to express:

• necessity.

*It's (absolutely) **crucial/vital/essential that** we win.*

*We **need to** discuss this further.*

• obligation.

*We're **expected to** do two hours' homework.*

*It's (my) **responsibility to** welcome new trainees.*

*Students **are supposed to** leave their mobiles at home.*

• ability.

*Do you think he's **capable of** managing a team?*

*The robot **has the capacity to** interact with patients.*

• permission/prohibition.

*We **weren't allowed to** ask questions during the talk.*

*You're **permitted to** use the facilities from 9a.m. to 5p.m.*

3.2 passives

Use passive structures in a text:

• to keep the focus on a particular subject.

*Robert left the house at 6a.m. He **was never seen** again.*

• when the agent is unimportant, obvious or unknown.

*The meeting's **been cancelled**. Your room **is being cleaned**.*

• in formal writing and speaking.

*Taking photographs **is prohibited**.*

Use *get* in informal spoken English or in situations where things happen outside our control.

*I **got paid** yesterday.*

*Emma's hat **got knocked off** by a branch.*

Use passive infinitives and *-ing* forms in subject or object position in a sentence. Note the position of *not*.

Being 'liked' on Facebook is addictive.

Not to have been consulted is unforgivable.

*I hate **not being believed**.*

*He expects **to be promoted** soon.*

Use modal passives to express necessity, possibility, etc.

*Something **must be done**.*

*The play **could have been written** earlier than 1620.*

Use *There is everything/a great deal/a lot/much/not much/ very little/nothing* + infinitive with *to* to talk about amount, often in a slightly formal way.

There's a great deal to be gained by talking.

There's nothing further to be said.

Causative passive

Use *have* + object + past participle for a (usually paid) service.

*I'm **having my car checked** today.*

*Have you **had your hair straightened**?*

Got is used more informally.

*I **got my teeth fixed** last year.*

The structure can also be used for a negative experience.

*She **had her bike stolen**. = Her bike was stolen.*

Note: in the causative there is an emphasis on the person rather than the situation.

3.3 evading a question

Obvious avoidance	Cleft structures
This figure has been taken out of context. I'm glad you've brought that up because there's another point that needs addressing. Before I answer that, let me just add to what I was saying.	What we're seeing is actually a positive, in that … What we have to take into account is that there can be many reasons … What we plan to do is to … All I'm saying is that …
Giving yourself time to think	
Well, … Let me see, … Let's see, … That's a very good/an interesting question.	

PRACTICE

3.1

A Correct the following sentences from a tourist brochure. Two sentences are correct.

1 You probably will most see wildlife that you've never seen before.

2 Could be that some parts of the park are closed during the wet season.

3 We should guess that most people come via personal recommendation.

4 It seems totally unimaginable that a visitor wouldn't find this exhilarating.

5 This will doubtedly be the most memorable experience of your life.

6 Visitors are not suppose to tip their guides, but the practice is not overtly discouraged.

7 It's essentially absolute that you keep your car windows closed.

8 Elephants are capacity of speeds of 40 kph.

9 So no, even the fastest human is not capable of outrunning one.

10 You guarantee of having a great time!

B Complete the text with the words in the box.

| bound   capable   capacity   expected   inevitably   likelihood |
| not allowed   permitted   responsibility   unlikely   vital   well |

Young as I am, I'm a realist, and I know it's absolutely ¹_____ to have humility when starting out in the working world. I knew my first job after university was ²_____ to be neither easy nor personally rewarding. I knew that it may ³_____ be my ⁴_____ to carry out menial tasks. But it's worse than I foresaw. First of all, we're ⁵_____ to work 12-hour shifts; at the interview they said this was highly ⁶_____ except during holiday periods. Physically, I don't have the ⁷_____ to work 60-hour weeks. Secondly, I'm translating documents from English to French, Spanish and Japanese – and the only one of those I am ⁸_____ of translating into competently is Japanese. Finally, we're ⁹_____ to take a lunch break away from the premises, we are only ¹⁰_____ to eat outside in the courtyard. All this will ¹¹_____ lead to me quitting. I think there's a strong ¹²_____ that it will affect my long-term health. Frankly, I'm not willing to risk that.

3.2

A Choose the best option for continuing the sentences.

1 Did you see the story about world famine on TV?
   a) Something has to be done.
   b) Somebody has to do something.

2 The company's relocating. It upsets me
   a) that someone didn't ask me how I feel about it.
   b) not to have been asked how I feel about it.

3 I was at the hairdresser's and
   a) I had my hair completely messed up.
   b) she completely messed up my hair.

4 Excuse me, Madam. Would you please turn off your recording device?
   a) Recording this concert is not permitted.
   b) You're not supposed to record this concert.

5 Oh no, my laptop's crashed again.
   a) I should get it repaired by someone different.
   b) It should be repaired by someone different.

6 I'm glad I brought my raincoat.
   a) There's a lot that I might say about being prepared!
   b) There's a lot to be said for being prepared!

B Complete the text with the correct form of the verb in brackets. Use the active or passive voice as appropriate.

It's not just employees who ¹_____ (catch out) on Facebook and find their jobs in peril. Company managers need to be wary of how their postings ²_____ (might interpret). Managers ³_____ (expose) boasting about underpaying workers and competing with other managers for who ⁴_____ (spend) the fewest number of hours in the office. In one example, a department store manager ⁵_____ (video) himself posing as a shoplifter in the very store he worked in, and ⁶_____ (make) it into a 'how-to' video uploaded for public view online. The security department of the store ⁷_____ (inform) and used the content of the video to ⁸_____ (improve) their anti-theft measures. The store's owner was appreciative – a thank-you note to the manager ⁹_____ (include) along with the notice informing him that his employment ¹⁰_____ (terminate), effective immediately. There's a great deal ¹¹_____ (gain) by thinking twice before pressing the 'upload' button. ¹²_____ (sack) for something so obviously irresponsible is perhaps not too high a price to pay.

3.3

A Read what an interviewee is really thinking and use the prompts to complete what he/she actually says.

1 I hate that question, but I can easily change the subject.
   glad / bring up / another point / need / address

2 That's another tough question, so I'll simply continue what I was saying before.
   Before / answer / let / add / I / say

3 I don't know what to say, so I'll make a comment to buy time.
   Let / see/ That / very interesting / question

4 I can twist the interpretation of those statistics in my favour if I change the context.
   figure / take / context

5 I'm going to pretend my point is simple and obvious.
   All / say / be

6 True, that's a negative, but let me twist it by telling you that in fact it's positive.
   What / see / actually / positive

GRAMMAR

4.1 participle clauses

Participle clauses tend to be used in more formal speaking and writing to make texts more succinct and sophisticated.

Past participle clauses are passive while **present participle clauses** are active.

Derided by all, she nevertheless became a renowned scientist.

Having a fertile imagination, he opened the door slowly.

The perfect form can be active or passive.

Having considered the problem, we propose the following.

Liz still had an accent, having been brought up in Ireland.

Use participle clauses:

- to describe something happening before the main action. Where necessary, the perfect form can emphasise this.

Created by IBM, the first smartphone from Apple wasn't produced until fifteen years later.

Diving over the side of the boat, she swam for the shore.

Having been warned about the risks, he still continued smoking.

- to describe simultaneous actions.

Tom ran towards his father, laughing.

Caught in the headlights, the deer stood frozen.

- to show the cause or reason for the main action, replacing *as* or *because*.

Motivated by a desire to help, Ana became a doctor.

Ed was the obvious choice for the job, having a proven track record in sales.

Having lost his wallet, Stefan had to walk home.

- to give essential information or extra descriptive detail, often replacing relative clauses.

The soldiers sent by the king were too few too late.

It was a luxurious house, not overlooked by any others.

The train approaching platform six is the 1.15 to Paris.

- to express a condition, replacing *if* (usually with the past participle).

Barbecued over a low heat, the fish tastes great.

4.2 introductory *it* and *there*

It and *there* sometimes act as the subject of a sentence.

It

Use *it* as an empty subject to introduce or identify something later in the clause or sentence.

It's a pity that I can't make Sundays. It will be June before I'm free.

Use *It + be +*

- noun + *to* + infinitive: *It's time*/a relief*/(our) hope*/a mistake/(my) job to …*
- adjective + *to* + infinitive: *It's easy/hard/possible/ essential/pointless to … It's typical of (her) to …*
- noun + clause: *It's a pity/a disaster/a shame that … It's no coincidence/wonder that …*
- adjective + clause: *It's brilliant/strange/amazing/ odd/obvious/extraordinary that/how …*

Use *It + verb +*

- object + *to* + infinitive: *It hurts*/upsets*/bothers* me/makes me laugh* to …*
- clause: *It doesn't matter that/if … It looks as if/ though … It appears/seems as if/though/that …*
- past participle to report something: *It is said/ reported/claimed/thought that …*

*these can also be followed by a 'that' clause

Use *It* as part of a cleft structure for emphasis.

It's you I have to thank … It was Eleanor Roosevelt who said …

It was my sister you saw, not me.

Use *It* as an empty object after certain verbs to introduce a clause or infinitive:

I'd appreciate it if … I could hardly believe it when …

I'll leave it to you to decide. I find it hard to think.

There

Use *there* as an empty subject to show that something exists and to introduce or identify something later in the phrase.

Use *there +*

- be + noun + clause: *There's an advantage to … no harm/point/ use/sense in … There's no doubt/likelihood/possibility that … There's a number of reasons why …*
- verb + *to* + infinitive: *There appears/seems to be a …*
- modal verb: *There could/might/may come a time when … There have to be four crew members before the plane can take off.*
- be + something/nothing/anything/someone/no one/nowhere, etc.

There's someone here to see Jacques.

There's nothing wrong with the waiter.

Is there anyone who doesn't like … ?

There's nowhere to hide.

Use *there* as an empty object.

I'd like there to be round tables.

What's the chance of there being a storm?

4.3 persuasive techniques in presentations

The following techniques can be used in presentations.
Direct speech:

And they'll say things like 'You look fantastic.'

Simile and metaphor:

Your friends will follow you like sheep and show the loyalty of a spaniel.

Negative inversion:

At no time in your life will you feel so empowered.

Repetition:

It can be seen as a huge opportunity and a huge breakthrough.

Rhetorical question:

What have you been waiting for?

The rule of 3:

You'll feel confident, composed and courageous.

PRACTICE

4.1

A Underline the correct alternative. In two cases both alternatives are correct.

¹*Blessed/Having blessed* with an amazing family, I've always been inspired by my mum. ²*Crippled/Having been crippled* by polio, she literally couldn't stand up on her own, but ³*confronted/confronting* with any injustice, she always stood up for her principles. Once, when a poor family knocked on our door, ⁴*having had/having* their electricity cut off, my mum got on the phone, ⁵*having persuaded/persuading* the electric company to restore the family's electricity.

⁶*Having seen/Seeing* many of her own dreams destroyed by her illness, she taught me to believe in my own. I remember when at four I ran into her room, ⁷*buzzed/buzzing* with excitement about my idea of organising a school party, she sat down, ⁸*planned/planning* the event with me down to the last detail. At seventeen, ⁹*having learnt/learning* English and ¹⁰*obsessed/obsessing* with going to England but ¹¹*having not/not having* the resources to do so, I asked her for help. ¹²*Handing/Having handed* me a pen and paper she said 'Write a letter to the Queen.' So I did.

B Replace the phrase in italics with a participle clause. Where possible, start the sentence with the clause and make any other necessary changes.

1 It can survive for hundreds of years *if you keep it away* from direct sunlight.
   Kept away from direct sunlight, it can survive for hundreds of years.

2 They decided to leave the shelter *after they had eaten* all their food.

3 *Resources which are allocated* to the health service have been reduced each year.

4 We had to phone for directions *as we didn't have* any idea how to get there.

5 Ed decided to quit *because he had jeopardised* his chances of a promotion.

6 *The people who lived* in the flats didn't stand a chance.

7 Julia saw no point in denying taking the bribes *once she was caught* red-handed.

8 *The kids emulated* their favourite pop star and all wore torn black T-shirts.

4.2

A In each online advert, add *it* and *there* three times each.

> ▶ **Digital image advice**
>
>   *there*
> Is / anyone who thinks is no unwanted content about them on the web? is my job to advise people on how to modify their digital image – doesn't matter if you haven't posted it yourself, is no doubt that a time will come when you'll want to get something deleted. Don't leave too late.
>
>   Contact us on …

> ▶ **Editing support**
>
> is claimed that more than 500 children's books are sent to publishers every month so is no wonder that are a lot of disappointed would-be writers out there. As an author, is an advantage to having a fertile imagination but is obvious that something special is needed and is nothing wrong with getting some extra help from our experienced editors.
>
>   Contact us on …

B Write the first part of each sentence using *It* or *There* and a phrase using words from the box. Add *be* in the correct form where necessary.

may come	no likelihood	you	odd
seems	nothing	typical	bothers

1 of large corporations to take a profit-driven approach.

2 you can do to bridge the gap between management and workers.

3 how few role models come from academia.

4 to be a tendency for people working in the marketing team to steer clear of conflict.

5 me to see how little is done to tackle bribery.

6 a moment when you look back at your childhood with fondness instead of regret.

7 that he'll come clean about what he's done.

8 who said that everything would be OK, not me!

4.3

A Complete the presentation excerpt with the phrases (a–f).

Are you fed up with your job? ¹__ Do you know about the three-step programme? ²__ you need to turn your life around. You'll be ³__ with your new life, ⁴__. ⁵__ find yourself sitting at a desk, stuck in a rut. Your friends will marvel at the new you and ask, 'How did you do it?', ⁶__ It's no secret, it's no mystery, it's the three-step programme. And here's how it works …

a) 'What's your secret?'
b) happy as a pig in mud
c) It's easy, it's exciting and it's everything
d) Do you want the career of your dreams?
e) on cloud nine
f) Never again will you

B Write the the persuasive technique next to each item in A.

C What other examples of persuasive techniques are there?

GRAMMAR

5.1 noun phrases

A noun or pronoun can be pre-modified (have words before it) or post-modified (have words after it) to make a noun phrase. Noun phrases make writing and speaking more succinct and sophisticated. More complex noun phrases are often found in news, academic and descriptive texts.

Pre-modification
Before a noun use:
- simple or compound adjectives.

a vulnerable person, mutual respect, a persuasive argument, a high-rise building, a waterproof phone
- other nouns used as adjectives to form compound nouns.

a business model, a pilot study, an echo chamber
- past and present participles used as adjectives.

an educated guess, a growing problem
- adverb and adjective combinations.

a frustratingly ambiguous ending, a badly overcrowded train, we are cautiously optimistic that …, highly beneficial effect on the economy

Post-modification:
After a noun or pronoun use:
- prepositional phrases.

The implications for society are … , a course in infant psychology
- relative clauses.

Someone who influenced me greatly was my uncle.
The image you convey will make all the difference.
- infinitives.

Emma needs somewhere to stay.
It'll take a long time to dry.
- participle clauses (replacing relative clauses).

Evidence suggesting a cover-up by the council is emerging.
A tree twisted out of shape by the wind stood on the cliff face.
- adjectives, which are actually relative clauses without *who/which/that + be*. These are often used with pronouns such as *someone, anything, no one*.

The only tickets available are in the stalls. (which are available)
Wear something warm. (that is)
We need someone capable of taking the initiative. (who is)
Did you notice anything interesting? (which was)

5.2 fronting, headers and tails

In English, positive sentences usually begin with a grammatical subject.

I think some TV programmes are too violent.

Fronting
In informal spoken English a phrase can be moved to the beginning of the sentence to make this the topic or to emphasise it, even though it is not the grammatical subject.

Some TV programmes I think are too violent.
Why did she resign? That I really couldn't tell you.

Question-word clauses are often fronted.

When I'm going to do my homework I have no idea.

Headers are a type of fronting where a pronoun or possessive adjective is added later to refer to the initial phrase. Notice the need for a comma.

That man you were talking to, who was he?
One of my sisters, her husband's a lawyer and she …

Tails
In informal spoken English the topic can be put after the main clause. This helps the listener understand what is being talked about. A pronoun is included in the main clause to refer to the final phrase. Notice the position of the comma.

It was the best we'd ever stayed in, that hotel in Crete.
The students like her a lot, our new teacher.

5.3 informal turn-taking

Use the following phrases to keep or to gain the opportunity to speak in an informal conversation or discussion.

Anyway …
Anyway, what was I saying?
Anyway, where was I?
As I was saying, …
To get back to (what I was saying before …)
Going back to …
Like I said, …
That reminds me of …

Actually, that's like …
And speaking/talking of …
Funny you should mention that …
I feel the same way about …
I just want to add …
Oh, I meant to add/say …
Before I forget …

PRACTICE

5.1

A Complete the noun phrases using the appropriate form of the words in brackets and adding words where necessary.

1 A (nurture) environment (characterise / a focus / individuality) makes the course so special.

2 After a (large / dry) start (day) we've got rain (move in / the north) and winds (gust / 100 kilometres / hour).

3 (cut / edge / pilot) studies (conduct / researchers / three countries) support the initial hypothesis.

4 I need more time (relax / let / ideas flow) if I'm going to create something (original / worth / write).

5 We believe there is a (rapid / expand) market (smartphone / app / this / can monitor / blood / sugar / levels).

6 The ideas (we / come up with / yesterday) could help bridge the gap (folk / jazz / audiences).

B Shorten each sentence in the text using noun phrases. The suggested number of words is at the end of each sentence.

[1]People, and I mean the ones who are overwhelmed by pressures from work, they no longer have an excuse for not exercising. (13) [2]Our seven-minute workout, which was inspired by high-intensity interval training (HITT), is the go-to option for people who are busy with packed schedules that leave them with no time for extensive exercise. (25) [3]The workout consists of bursts of exercise that last for thirty seconds separated by rest periods that last for ten seconds. (13) [4]There is scientific support, and it's very persuasive, for the benefits to health of HITT when it is compared to longer activity which is also less intensive. (17) [5]Some people dislike exercise and for those people, there is the attraction which they can't resist, that no matter how bad it feels – it's over before you notice. (22)

People overwhelmed by work pressures …

5.2

A Correct eight of the sentences by adding or crossing out a pronoun (*it, that, someone*, etc.)

1 How he stole we'll never find out – we never got the picture back.

2 I just can't work with, control freaks I mean.

3 They sympathise but say they can do nothing – a lot of good that does me!

4 That pushy colleague of yours, she I just saw her in the café downstairs.

5 Some people I'll never understand them.

6 In general, I don't think it's healthy, putting on a pedestal.

7 The house you've been building, how's coming along?

8 This issue we've gone over again and again, and I think we need to move on.

9 Where it disappeared to I can't actually say it.

10 Most topics I think I'll be able to answer questions on.

B Complete the conversation using the words and phrases in the box. You do not need to use two items.

| challenge enjoyment having an aim having fun |
| other sports that that that's the lessons those |

A: Having a goal, [1]_____ what keeps me motivated long-term.

B: Me too. Well, for gym training anyway, but not for other things.

A: [2]_____, you mean?

B: No, things like learning English.

A: Really? That's what keeps me going, [3]_____.

B: Not me. [4]_____ themselves, I need to enjoy them.

A: So [5]_____, is that what you're talking about?

B: Not necessarily. Really tough grammar tasks, I like [6]_____.

A: Really? [7]_____ I don't get. Grammar's hard.

B: The harder the better! I like the, erm …

A: [8]_____ I think is the word you're after.

B: Yeah, that's exactly the word!

5.3

A Write the letter of a phrase a)–j) in the correct place in the conversation about looking after things/people below.

a) Going back to

b) Oh, I meant

c) As I

d) To get

e) I feel the

f) That reminds

g) Anyway, what

h) I just

i) Funny you should

j) Speaking of

A: [1]__ was saying, it's about companionship, and cats are clearly the best for that.

B: [2]__ mention that, because I read that caring for a *plant* is actually better for people.

C: [3]__ me of my grandparents. They told me that caring for other people kept them active.

A: [4]__ what I was saying about pets, the thing is they're low-maintenance and …

B: [5]__ same way about plants – low-maintenance.

C: [6]__ want to add that being low-maintenance shouldn't be the key factor.

B: [7]__ to say that myself. But the problem with *your* idea is that not everyone has a person to look after.

A: [8]__ was I saying? Yeah, cats are not only low-maintenance but also very rewarding.

B: [9]__ being rewarding, plants can be great in that way.

C: [10]__ back to what I was saying about my grandparents …

GRAMMAR

6.1 concession clauses

Concession clauses contrast two ideas or events. They reduce the force of the main idea/clause.

Concessive linkers

Concessive linkers can be used:

- between two sentences or clauses.

*The offer is persuasive. **However**, the price is wrong.*
*I was given a new dress **when** I wanted a bike.*

- to start a sentence.

***Even though/Although/Though** it's dark, I can see.*
***Even if** he apologises, I still won't talk to him.*

- to end a sentence.

*Economic conditions were bad. The company flourished, **nevertheless/however/though**.*

- before adverbials.

*Sales of electric cars are growing, **though slowly**.*
*Jim has accepted the plan **albeit with some reluctance**.*

- with *while/whilst/whereas* in formal situations.

*Costs are rising **whilst** sales are falling.*

Note: Pay attention to the use of commas in the examples above.

Auxiliary verbs

Add a stressed auxiliary verb or stress an existing auxiliary verb to emphasise a contrast.

*The resort was awful but we **did** like the hotel.*
*I **was** listening to you! Really!*

Fronting

Use fronting in more formal spoken or written situations to show an emphatic contrast. Use:

- adjective/adverb + *as/though* + subject + *be*/verb.

***Difficult as the evacuation will be**, there is no other option.*
***Carefully though we worked**, we had no major breakthrough.*

- noun + *though* + subject + *be*.

***Doctor though she is**, she doesn't know everything.*

- *However* + adjective + subject + *be*/verb. *May* can also be used here.

***However compelling the argument is/may be**, we cannot afford to raise wages.*

- *Though/Although* + adjective.

***Though reluctant** to move, Carla finally agreed.*

- Use *much as* with verbs of liking or hating.

***Much as** I disagree with him, I respect his integrity.*

6.2 indirect speech

When reporting people's speech or thoughts later, change pronouns, tenses, auxiliary verbs, time or place references as logical.

'I think the plan will affect us all.'
*Ali thought the plan **would affect them** all.*
'Why are you laughing?'
*He asked **me** why **I was** laughing.*

Where a situation has not changed, or the present or future situation is still present or future, there is no need to make changes.

*'There will be storms tonight.' The forecast said there **will be** storms **tonight**.*

Past modal verbs don't change.

'You shouldn't have overstated the case.'
*I told them they **shouldn't have** overstated the case.*

Use *whether* (not *if*) in more formal reported questions and also after prepositions.

*The union are talking about **whether** to strike or not.*

Use different patterns after reporting verbs:

- infinitive with *to: refuse, want, demand*, promise*, agree*, threaten*, swear*, vow**

*The rebels **swore to return**. Sarah's **threatening not to come**.*

- object + infinitive with *to: encourage, persuade*, advise*, warn*, remind**; often with requesting verbs: *invite, ask, request, order, command, instruct, urge, beg, want*

*Where do you **want us to sign**?*
*The tour guide **reminded everyone not to take** photos.*

- *-ing* form: *suggest*, deny*, admit*, recommend**

*When do you **recommend visiting** Rome?*

- dependent preposition + *-ing* form: *insist* on, complain* about, apologise for*; or object + preposition + *-ing* form: *accuse sb of, compliment sb on, congratulate sb for.*

*I **apologise for disturbing** you, but I need to speak to you.*
*Allow me **to compliment you on** reaching the finals.*

*can also be followed by a *that* clause. Other verbs include: *add, allege, announce, argue, assure sb, claim, explain, mention, repeat.* Often *that* is omitted.

The doctor assured me (that) the treatment is safe.

6.3 talk about customs

Customary things	Unusual customs
It's a given that … It's expected that … It's customary to … The norm is to … I'm accustomed to/used to (working until …) I've got used to (queuing)	I find some things completely alien, such as … I'm not used/unused to (driving everywhere) I can't get used to (living in …)
	Changing customs
	I'm getting used to (having a …)

PRACTICE

6.1

A Write the words in the box in the correct place in the text. The words are in the same order that they appear in the text.

> ~~as~~ although albeit if however though nevertheless as though do

City dweller

I live in basements. Yes, strange *as* it sounds, I have never lived above ground, I've been offered flats from the ground floor to the penthouse, at prices I couldn't pay. But even the offers were rent-free, I wouldn't have taken them, desperate I might have been at the time. No, I'm not acrophobic, or weird – my friends might tell you otherwise. A basement is cold, damp, and often coated with decades of dirt – I love it. Or should I say I love it all the more? Disgusting you may find it, there's always a firm grip for my hundred legs as I scamper over the surfaces foraging bits of nourishment. Badly you might think of me, I have as much right of abode as you.

B Rewrite each item as one sentence so that it means the same. Begin with the word in brackets.

1 The jury seemed to doubt his testimony. I thought he was credible. (credible)

2 The novel quickly became impossible to follow after the first ten pages, although I enjoyed these. (much)

3 Lia wasn't thought photogenic enough for print work, but she was a catwalk model. (catwalk)

4 On closer inspection it is clear that the new tax laws will have a detrimental effect on less well-off workers, even though at first sight they appear to be progressive. (however)

5 Sam's had remarkably limited success running for office. It's ironic, as when it comes to education, he's a highly influential public figure. (highly)

6 I was glad to have Jenny on my side. Yet she can, at times, be annoying. (annoying)

6.2

A Complete the sentences. Make changes in tenses only where it is absolutely necessary.

1 In 1543 Copernicus / publish / his theory / state / the earth / go / round / sun

_____

2 application form / state / recent photo / must / attach

_____

3 When / we / cross / border / last night / border officials / demand / see / papers

_____

4 When / we / be / young / our father / assure / we / will / never regret / go / college

_____

5 Last night / Sue / explain / me / she / travel / a lot / her / current job

_____

6 When / he / see / broken / window / Mr Harris / ask / whoever / do / it / step / forward

_____

B Find and correct ten mistakes in the article.

Magic bullet shot down

Authorities have cracked down on distributors of the health supplement '*Magic Bullet*', alleging the business making a number of promises it could not substantiate. Company owner Sven Petersen has been formally accused with misleading the public through an advertising campaign that claimed that Magic Bullet will deliver a host of benefits to those who took it regularly. Asked about if he denied the charges, Petersen redupiated the accusations and vowed demonstrating that his company's practices were entirely above-board. Customers voiced support for the legal action, insisting to push for full compensation, though several acknowledged not to have taken the supplement on a regular basis. Authorities are urging users of Magic Bullet come forward to assist in the investigation. Meanwhile they have advised would-be customers to not use the supplement until the case has been fully investigated.

6.3 Underline the correct alternatives. In some cases more than one answer is possible.

Silent year

I took the vow of silence exactly because I'd [1]*become/been/got* so used to the world of sound. I spent the year in a retreat in Nepal, where it's [2]*expected/norm/given* that you not only avoid speaking, but do nothing to provoke others to speak. Of course it wasn't easy to [3]*be/become/get* used to the silence, but I grew to savour it. It was [4]*accustomed/a given/norm* that we greeted each other with only a subtle nod, yet I felt closely connected to those around me.

After that year I [5]*could get/was/wasn't* unused to speaking so I found it completely [6]*alien/alienating/alienated* to use my vocal chords again. For a few days I simply avoided human contact, but lately I'm getting used [7]*to live/living/to living* in a world where the [8]*expected/norm/accustom* is to fill the silences with unnecessary words.

GRAMMAR

7.1 subjunctive

present subjunctive

Use the present subjunctive (the infinitive without *to*, e.g. *they be, he go*) in very formal and impersonal situations. It is only obvious with the verb *be* and in the third person (*he/she/it*) of other verbs.

Use the present subjunctive after:

- reporting verbs: *recommend, suggest, insist, propose, request, demand*

*The Governor is proposing (that) he **extend** his term of office.*
*The authorities insist (that) Harris **be arrested**.*

- adjectives and nouns showing desirability or importance: *vital, crucial, important, imperative, essential, desirable, best, recommended; advice, recommendation*

*It is imperative (that) no one **jeopardise** the plan.*
*Our advice is that she **not speak** to the media.*

- adjectives of annoyance, regret, surprise or inevitability, often using *should: strange, odd, unusual, understandable*

*It is understandable that people **should support** the idea.*
Note: *should* can also be added before any verbs above.

past subjunctive

Use the past subjunctive (*were* or the past simple or continuous form) for hypothetical situations in the present.

Use the past subjunctive after:

- *if, as if/though, suppose/supposing, imagine, if only, wish, would rather*

*We would rather you **paid** in advance.*
*Sylvie treats the kids as though they **were** her own.*

- *it's time. It's time we **went** home.*

fixed phrases

Some **fixed phrases** include a present subjunctive:

*If that's the plan **so be it**. = I don't like it but I'll accept it.*
***Suffice (it) to say**, we were very late. = it is enough to say*
*I'll stay with you, **come what may**. = whatever happens*
***Far be it for me to** criticise, but … = I don't want to criticise you (but in reality that's what the speaker is doing).*
*It is expensive but **be that as it may** we need a new school. = I accept that's true but it doesn't change the situation.*
*We are ready to help, **if need be**. = if it's necessary*

7.2 adverbials

sentence adverbials

Use single adverbs or adverbial phrases at the beginning of a sentence to show the speaker's attitude. These can show:

- surprise or disbelief. *Unbelievably, Difficult as it is to credit, Strange as it sounds, To my astonishment*
- other emotions. *Confusingly, To my horror, Sad to say, With some embarrassment*

intensifying (strengthening) adverbs

Use *very* and *really* with gradable adjectives.
very deceptive, really congested

Use *really* or strong intensifiers with ungradable adjectives.
totally inappropriate, absolutely hectic, completely atypical

Use *quite* with ungradable adjectives. *quite extraordinary, quite perfect, quite fascinating*. The main stress is on the adjective.
*The concert was amazing – **quite** brilliant!*

modifying (weakening) adverbs

Use *fairly, relatively, slightly, somewhat, pretty* with gradable adjectives. *relatively easy, somewhat irritated, fairly shy, pretty stupid*

Use *rather* with negative adjectives or ones expressing difference. *rather difficult/slow/strange*

Use *quite* with gradable adjectives. *quite pushy, quite conventional*. The main stress is on *quite*.
*The lecture was OK – **quite** interesting.*

collocations

Many adverbs collocate strongly with:

- adjectives. *closely associated, inextricably linked, perfectly clear, utterly exhausted, heavily dependent, widely/readily available*
- verbs. *vaguely/distinctly remember, instantly evoke, thoroughly recommend, fully appreciate/ understand*

7.3 telling anecdotes

Use the following features when telling informal anecdotes.

Reported speech	Vague language
Be like instead of *says/said* to report what was said. *She **was like** 'Who are you?'*	Expressions such as: *stuff/things like that, I think it was, sort/kind of* *A year ago, **I think it was**.* *Bring food and drink and **stuff like that**.*
Determiners	**Expressions to involve the listener**
This instead of *a/an* in a neutral way. *There was **this guy** standing there and …* *Some* instead of *a/an* to say it doesn't matter who/what the person/thing is. *Some* can also show annoyance. ***Some guy** tried to chat me up.*	Adjectives such as *strange* or *funny*, to start a sentence. ***Strange**, I didn't ask her name.* Expressions such as *you know what I mean, it was (just) one of those things* to show shared experience. *We clicked straightaway. **It was just one of those things**.*

PRACTICE

7.1

A Find 11 verbs that can be changed to the subjunctive and make changes to give the text a more formal style. If the change to the subjunctive does not change the verb form, use *should*.

FOR INTERNAL USE ONLY
Guidelines for films prepared for re-distribution via streaming

---

To maximise commercial viability, we recommend that an editor keeps the following in mind:

- It is imperative that total length is cut to 90 minutes.
- While it is understandable that some directors prefer a slower pace, it is best that the editor omits or greatly curtails overlong scenes.
- It is vital that product placement is taken into consideration and that relevant scenes aren't removed.
- Our market segment demands that offensive elements are minimised, thus we advise that the editor cuts any scenes containing violence or nudity entirely.
- We ask that commercial breaks are kept under consideration; while currently it might seem odd that an advertisement breaks up a paid-for-view film, we anticipate that this will change.

B Replace the crossed- out phrases in the sentences with a phrase which means the same. The first words are in italics. Add two more words.

1 We'll hold the picnic ~~regardless of the weather~~ *come* _____.
2 The company can provide additional financing ~~in an extreme situation~~ *if* _____.
3 There's snow and public transport is shut down? Well, ~~nevertheless~~ *be that as* _____, we should still hold the open day event.
4 You crashed your car … again? Well, ~~it's not my position~~ *far be it* _____ to say but perhaps you're getting too old to drive.
5 We expected 200 and only 17 showed up. ~~I could say more but all I'll say is~~ *Suffice (it)* _____ we were disappointed.
6 The whole staff is quitting? As of today? Well, if that's the case, ~~there's not much I can do so I accept it~~ *so* _____.

7.2

A Put the words in order and cross out the extra word in each group of underlined words.

1 <u>horror to very his</u>, Charlie realised the brakes had failed.

_____

2 <u>credit as to its difficult is it</u>, Stella was once an A-lister.

_____

3 <u>it sounds just as strange</u>, I actually like winter more than summer.

_____

4 <u>my be to much astonishment</u>, I won.

_____

5 <u>say sad to you</u>, Roger passed away last year.

_____

6 <u>embarrassment with your some</u>, I have to admit that I haven't even started yet.

_____

B Complete the adverbials in the art review.

Art Review

[1]Strange as it mi_____ so_____ for an art critic like myself, it disturbs me that children's drawings are [2]en_____ absent from art criticism, so I was keen to attend a nursery school art show. I arrived [3]to_____ exhausted, and found myself instantly uplifted by this [4]ut_____ delightful event. The young artists were present, some [5]fa_____ shy, some [6]re_____ poised and outgoing.

As any parent with an eye will [7]fu_____ appreciate, children's art can be [8]qu_____ fascinating and sometimes [9]de_____ moving, particularly the odd ones, the ones that are [10]co_____ atypical. One never forgets that a child's approach is [11]in_____ linked to their world view, and I felt [12]hu_____ privileged to peer through the eyes of these budding artists.

7.3

A Complete the story with the words/phrases in the box. Two words/phrases are not used.

| Funny | I think it was | some | sort of | stuff like that | things | this | was like | were like | you know what I mean |

This happened a few years ago when Robbie our son was about three, [1]_____, and I drove with our five kids to the supermarket. It's [2]_____ tricky to shop with five kids, [3]_____? Anyway I did the shopping, got the usual 10 litres of milk, five boxes of cereal, tons of pasta, [4]_____. Packed it all in the car, kids climbed in and we got home. As I parked, I turned around and I [5]_____ 'Uh, where's Robbie?' and the four kids [6]_____ 'How should we know?', and I realised of course that I'd left him in the supermarket. [7]_____, driving back I felt completely calm. Robbie was fine of course – still by himself in the cereal aisle, trying to open [8]_____ box of cereal.

GRAMMAR

8.1 understanding complex sentences

Complex sentences can be challenging to understand. Typical problems arise with:

- relative clauses.

When the relative pronoun is omitted, two nouns/pronouns can occur next to each other.

The wallet a boy found outside was left in my office. (which)

This can be particularly problematic if a relative clause ends with a preposition.

The role model Jane most looked up to was her mother. (who)

- past participle clauses.

The relative pronoun <u>and</u> the auxiliary are missing and the past participle can be mistaken for the main verb.

People caught hunting will be prosecuted. (who are)

Phones hacked into included those of celebrities and ordinary people. (which were)

- *that* clauses.

That can be omitted, making the sentence tricky to disentangle.

Did you know [ ] people are saying [ ] Jill believes [ ] she's going to be sacked?

- long sentences separating subjects and verbs.

Long subjects can include subordinate phrases and clauses with the result that the key noun can be separated from its verb and a closer noun can be mistaken for the subject.

<u>Residents</u> living in blocks two and three of the condominium who have mounted a long campaign to keep pets <u>have succeeded</u> in getting the rules changed. (it is not the pets who have succeeded)

- sets of examples separating the subject from its verb.

<u>A mother</u> who responds actively to her baby by using musical speech, non-verbal gestures, reassuring facial expressions and physical touch, such as hugging the child, <u>is</u> constantly <u>teaching</u> emotional awareness. (it is not the child who is teaching)

- long adverbial clauses before the main clause.

Standing in the middle of the jungle and surrounded by lush vegetation and the sound of parrots squawking, she felt a sense of growing excitement at the adventure ahead.

8.2 prepositional phrases

dependent prepositions with adjectives, nouns and verbs
Use prepositions after:

- adjectives. *accustomed to, angry about/with, annoyed about/with, aware of, amazed at/about, ashamed of, based on, certain of/about, committed to, concerned about, conducive to, confident of/about, conscious of, convinced of/about, eligible for, guilty of, horrified at/by, indicative of, justified in, keen on, mindful of, terrified of/about, proud of, typical of, upset about/at*
  *He is **guilty of** not giving detectives the full story.*

- nouns. *necessity of, talent for, motivation for, hope of, a consequence of, the risk of, hesitation in, implications for*
  *There are long-term **implications for** the farming community.*

- adjectives + *for* + object. *essential*, vital*, crucial*, important*, (im)possible, normal, common*
  *It's **impossible for me** to answer that question.*

*can also take the subjunctive in formal texts.

- nouns. *anger about, a/no/little chance of, a course in, a hint of, an increase in, no justification in, the likelihood of, a possibility of, a reason for, a regret about, the thought of, a focus on*
  *There's **no hint of** the strike being called off.*

- verbs. *believe in, benefit from, compliment on, decide on/against, depend on, dream of/about, insist on, plan on, pride yourself on, result from, struggle with, specialise in, succeed in*
  *I think the soup would **benefit from** more salt.*
  *Mum **prided herself on** how she brought up us kids to have good manners.*

8.3 giving opinions

Asking for an opinion	Expressing disbelief or belief
What's your take on this? How do you see this?	I'd be surprised if that was the case. That doesn't surprise me in the least.
Giving/Justifying an opinion	**Prioritising facts over supposition**
I'm really against any form of … Why should it be any different with … ?	On the face of it, it seems … but actually … Well supposedly so, but look at the facts.
Agreeing	
In that respect I'm with you. No one would/could disagree with that.	

PRACTICE

8.1

A Put the phrases in the correct order to make a complex sentence. Then write the sentences out in full to check, adding commas where necessary.

1 ¹is likely to be a one-off event / ²A statement / ³the gas cloud / ⁴is unlikely to be acceptable / ⁵reassuring local residents / ⁶coming off the sea yesterday

   *2,*_____

2 ¹made in the sixteenth century / ²opens next week / ³to work with hospital patients / ⁴exploring the 500-year-old story / ⁵resembling a monk / ⁶An exhibition / ⁷to robots created in labs / ⁸ranging from a robot / ⁹of humanoid robots

   _____

3 ¹currently making a fortune / ²never came to her / ³to pay for the patent / ⁴the woman / ⁵for manufacturers around the world / ⁶because she couldn't afford / ⁷The money owed to / ⁸who invented the spinner toy

   _____

4 ¹rescued / ²about their ordeal / ³after monsoon flooding / ⁴to collapse / ⁵More than a dozen people / ⁶talked to reporters / ⁷caused a building

   _____

B Make the text below easier to understand: a) underline six hidden relative clauses, then add the full clauses b) add *that* in three places c) add six commas.

Four people charged over their role in toppling a monument first erected in North Carolina several decades after the American Civil War have turned themselves in to the authorities.

Standing outside the courthouse protesting in support of the people arrested a crowd of about 200 sympathisers including people from around the state not even there when the statue was destroyed demanded they should also be arrested. Declining to allow any of the 'volunteers' into the courthouse an officer claimed the reason was the risk of fire with such large numbers. The situation brings into sharp relief the choice facing many societies: is it right we judge history by today's standards?

8.2

A Add eight missing dependent prepositions to the text.

How our heroes have changed
In ancient mythologies, such as Indian or Greek, heroes tended be humans who benefited the support of gods and goddesses and succeeded destroying their enemies on an epic scale. These days we are becoming more accustomed women wielding weapons as well as men. The rise in cinema of the female hero may be indicative women's changed role in society. And our heroes tend to be people who show courage in the face of adversity and are committed acting for society's greater good: a charity worker in the field or a first responder at the scene of a terrorist attack. Our modern-day notion of a hero is based the saving of lives as opposed to a focus how many enemies or monsters a hero can slay. One thing we can be certain is that humans will always have an innate desire for a hero to look up to.

B Rewrite the sentences so they have a similar meaning. Use the word in brackets and a dependent preposition.

1 It's impossible for you to get an interview with her today. (chance)
2 Pictures in magazines are very often manipulated. (common)
3 Anyone caught up in the mis-selling scandal can get compensation. (eligible)
4 The landlord is within his rights to raise rents annually. (justified)
5 What do you hope to focus on in your third year? (specialise)
6 You'll win the contract as long as you don't gloss over the problems. (depends)

8.3

A Correct one word in each sentence (1–10).

Conversation 1
A: ¹What's your mistake on this?
B: ²On the fate of it, it seems a good idea to go vegetarian but actually I couldn't give up meat completely.
A: ³In that prospect I'm with you.
B: ⁴And, I'm really against any forum of coercion, like someone telling us what to eat.
A: ⁵No one might disagree with that.

Conversation 2
A: This thing about banning wifi in public spaces – ⁶How can you see this?
B: Well, they bluffed about banning mobiles. ⁷Why should it be all different with this?
A: Bluffing again? ⁸I'd be surprised if that was the base. They've actually created wifi-free zones in some areas, and it worked, technically I mean.
B: ⁹Well supposedly so, but look at the factors. There's mobile internet …
A: But they can block that. Or they say they can block it.
B: ¹⁰That doesn't surprise me in the last – They'll say anything that's convenient for them.
A: I still think it's a good idea …

VOCABULARY BANK

1 A Match the prepositional phrases in bold with phrases a) or b).

1	The kid was **on the verge of** tears.	**a)**	at the point where something is about to happen
2	We went to Madrid **on impulse**.	**b)**	without planning something

3	Only armed guards kept the mob **at bay**.	**a)**	having nothing to do
4	I was **at a loose end** and a bit bored.	**b)**	(prevent) from attacking or coming closer

5	I'm **in the dark** just as much as you are.	**a)**	in the same difficult situation as others
6	Most newspapers are **in the same boat**.	**b)**	not knowing because you haven't been told

7	What's up? You're a bit **out of sorts today**.	**a)**	feeling ill or upset
8	The forest is **out of bounds** to students.	**b)**	it's forbidden to go there

B Complete the sentences with the prepositional phrases above. You need to change the form of one of the phrases.

1 I think we're _____ of a full-scale riot. We can't hold the crowd _____ for much longer.

2 Sorry, but everyone's feeling slightly _____ today. We're all _____, workers and management alike, worried about losing our jobs.

3 We were _____ on Sunday, nothing planned, so _____ we decided to get in the car and head for the beach.

4 The border area is _____ to journalists, completely off-limits. I have no idea why. I'm as much _____ as you.

C What is each situation in Exercise 1B and who is talking to whom? Complete the person's response for each sentence.

1 Then we should …

2 OK, give me a call when …

3 Oh, you're always so …

4 Maybe there's a …

1 A Cover Exercise 1B and look at the pictures. How could you complete the idioms?

1 I had to _____ _____ £60 for the ticket.

2 The _____ _____ is on the driverless car. It's the best investment you can make.

3 She's _____ _____ _____ _____ from her new café, it's become so popular.

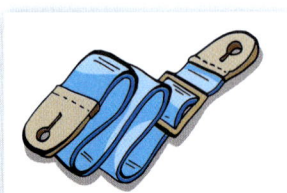

4 I'm _____ _____ cash at the moment so can I owe you?

5 Jen is travelling _____ _____ _____. She hardly has any money at all.

6 I'll _____ _____ the tab.

B Check your ideas. Match idioms a)–f) in bold with sentences 1–6 in Exercise 1A.

a) **on a shoestring:** without spending much money

b) **strapped for cash:** to have little or no money available

c) **the smart money is on/ says:** experts think this is the best choice

d) **pick up the tab:** pay the bill for something, especially when it's clearly not your responsibility

e) **rake in the money:** to make a lot of money without trying too hard

f) **fork out:** to spend money, not because you want to but because you have to

Lesson 2.1 BODY IDIOMS

1 A Match the idioms in bold with pictures A–F.

1 Olivia's parents' return was **hanging over her head**.
2 Sam and Jen started **on the wrong foot**.
3 Tim was **head and shoulders above** the rest of us.
4 Anna likes to **fly in the face of** convention.
5 We'll be pleased **to see the back of** Fluffy!
6 Let's **play it by ear**, depending on the weather tomorrow.

B Rewrite each sentence so it has a similar meaning, using the words in brackets.

1 The figures contradict our current understanding. (face)
_____

2 I'm going to decide what to do during the meeting, not before. (ear)
_____

3 My exam results – I'm so worried about them. (head)
_____

4 We began our relationship really badly. (foot)
_____

5 Lydia's far better than the other candidates. (head, shoulders)
_____

6 I'm very glad that Pat has left. (back)
_____

C Choose four of the idioms and write two true and two false sentences about yourself. Then see if another student can guess which ones are false.

Lesson 2.2 EDUCATION

1 A Match an item from group A with one from group B to make a compound noun.

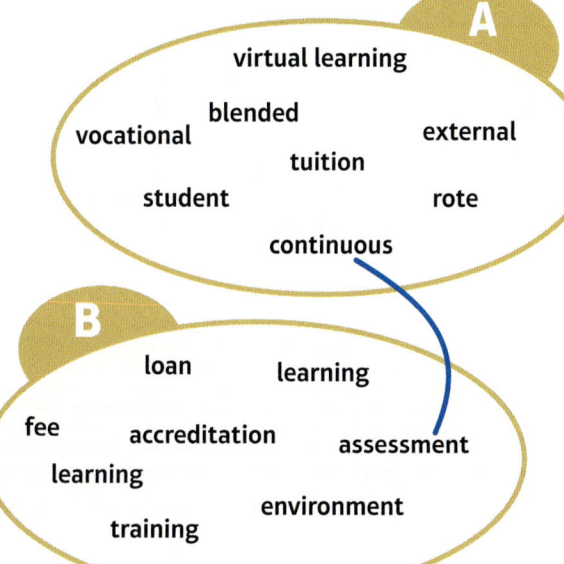

A
virtual learning
blended
vocational   external
tuition
student   rote
continuous

B
loan   learning
fee   accreditation   assessment
learning
environment
training

B Write the compound nouns next to the definitions.

1 Money paid to a university or college for its courses.
2 Money borrowed from the government or a bank to finance studies.
3 Judging ability by a person's coursework rather than by an exam.
4 A web-based study platform for the digital aspects of a course.
5 Learning based on the skills needed to do a particular job.
6 A combination of online and face-to-face studying.
7 The memorisation of information based on repetition.
8 Objective confirmation of someone's standard by an independent person or organisation.

C Which of these do you have experience of?

VOCABULARY BANK

1 A Which game/sport in pictures A–F is connnected with each expression below?

1 follow suit
2 quick/slow/first off the mark
3 skate around/over
4 lay (your) cards on the table
5 plain sailing
6 let/get someone off the hook
7 back on an even keel
8 below the belt

B Replace the phrase(s) in bold with the correct form of an expression above.

1 Look, after a while we just have to **explain our intentions clearly and honestly** and maybe the other side will **do the same as us**.
2 It was a tough meeting but we managed to **avoid** the issue of redundancies.
3 OK. I'll **allow you to get out of this difficult situation** just this once but I expect you to be on time from now on.
4 The next few weeks of the project will be the most difficult, but after that it's all **very easy** and things will be **steady again, with no sudden changes**.
5 Ouch! That remark was **unfair and cruel**.
6 You'll have to be **fast to react** if you want find a new apartment.

1 A Complete the information with words from the box.

ballot constitution hard/far left liberal lobbyists monarch polls progressive regressive right spin state vote

1 A socialist party is one which is **on the** _____ of political beliefs, and a conservative party is _____-**wing** in its beliefs.
2 Even though **exit** _____ aren't official, they're often a good indication of the final result of a vote.
3 A member of the _____ **right** or **left** holds more extreme views.
4 Most nations have a **written** _____ of the basic laws and principles by which it is governed.
5 The **head of** _____ can be a president or a hereditary _____.

6 The union leader is elected **by secret** _____, where every union member can **cast a** _____.
7 _____ **policies** are fair to all members of society while _____ **policies** affect the poor more than the rich.
8 Those with _____ **political views** share a belief in liberty and equality for all.
9 In politics, party leaders usually try **to** _____ any defeat to make it sound positive.
10 Lawmakers can be influenced by **professional** _____ who push to have laws passed that are favourable to whoever is paying them.

B Use a minimum of eight phrases (including the words in bold) in Exercise 1A to describe the current state of politics and the political system in your country.

Lesson 4.1 THREE-PART MULTI-WORD VERBS

bear down on somebody/something   *phrasal verb*

to move quickly towards a person or place in a threatening way
a storm bearing down on the island

come down to somebody/something   *phrasal verb*

if a complicated situation or problem comes down to something, that is the single most important thing
It all comes down to money in the end.

come in for something   *phrasal verb*

come in for criticism/blame/scrutiny – to be criticised, blamed, etc., for something
The government has come in for fierce criticism over its handling of this affair.

fill in for somebody   *phrasal verb*

to do another person's job for a short period of time because they are not there or are unable to do it
The supervisor is forbidden by the union contract to fill in for an employee who is on a break.

lead up to something   *phrasal verb*

if a series of events or a period of time leads up to an event, it comes before it or causes it
the weeks that led up to her death; the events leading up to his dismissal

listen in on   *phrasal verb*

to listen to someone's conversation when they do not want you to
It sounded like someone was listening in on us.

play up to somebody   *phrasal verb*

to behave in a very polite or kind way to someone because you want something from them
Connie always plays up to her parents when she wants money.

tie in with something   *phrasal verb*

to be similar to another idea, statement, etc., so that they seem to be true
Her description tied in with that of the other witness.

Source: Longman Dictionary of Contemporary English

1 A Use the dictionary definitions above to complete questions 1–8 with a multi-word verb in the correct form. Add pronouns where necessary.

1 Were you the kind of kid who _____ your teachers in the hope of getting better grades?
2 How does learning English _____ your hopes for the future?
3 Do you sometimes enjoy _____ people's conversations? When did you last do so?
4 Think of a major change in your country or in your life. What events _____?
5 Would you be willing to _____ your English teacher for a day if he/she was sick?
6 If you had to choose between job satisfaction and a high salary, what would your decision _____?
7 You're on a beach and a hurricane is _____ you. Do you panic or keep a cool head?
8 Have you ever _____ a lot of criticism? When?

B Answer each question using the multi-word verb.

Lesson 4.3 ADJECTIVES: QUALITIES

1 A Choose the correct alternatives to complete the description of a good presenter.

A [1]*mediocre/captivating* speaker keeps everyone's attention and will convey their ideas in a(n) [2]*assured/self-deprecating* manner with [3]*expressive/stiff* body language, using their face and hands to illustrate their point. They will have a [4]*muddled/cogent* argument which is well thought through and easy to follow. They will support points with [5]*pertinent/flimsy* examples and may include a number of anecdotes or [6]*subtle/crude* jokes, ones which are clever, not obvious, and certainly not offensive or rude.

B Complete the conversations with the other adjectives from Exercise 1A.

1 A: How was the lecture?
   B: Hmm. I found it rather confusing and _____. I couldn't really follow her argument.
2 A: How was the comedy club?
   B: Mixed. Mostly fine but the last guy used really _____ language so we walked out.
3 A: How was your meal?
   B: Nothing special, quite _____ in fact.
4 A: How is the court case going?
   B: Well, I think. The evidence against my client is very _____ and unconvincing.
5 A: How was the play?
   B: Not bad. The only problem was the main actor. He was too _____ and formal for the role.
6 A: How is your new boss?
   B: I like him. He has a deceptively _____ manner which masks his obvious expertise.

VOCABULARY BANK

1 A Complete the information about fitness classes with the words in the box. Then match the photos with the fitness classes.

> Aquarobics   Boot Camp   Boxercise   Circuits
> Pilates   Spinning

1 _____

Train indoors on bikes to great soundtracks. Vary the intensity through adjusting the bike. Good for cardio.

2 _____

Work at your own ability and move from station to station to build up strength and endurance.

3 _____

Group fitness class, includes press-ups and squats interspersed with running and competitive games. Builds strength and toning in a convivial atmosphere.

4 _____

Emphasis on breathing, alignment and coordination and balance. Builds strength, develops control and flexibility.

5 _____

A water-based workout to music: cardiovascular and muscle conditioning.

6 _____

High-energy, weight-losing, non-contact training, combining boxing and aerobics. Emphasis on cardio fitness rather than technique.

B Which classes have you tried or would you like to try?

1 A Complete the compound adjectives with *full-*, *far-* or *hard-*.

1 _____
- headed
- hitting
- earned
- wired

2 _____
- fetched
- flung
- reaching
- sighted

3 _____
- blown
- fledged
- page
- scale

B Replace the phrases in bold with a compound adjective from Exercise 1A. Make any other necessary changes to the sentence, e.g. word order or prepositions.

1 As a leader, Gandhi was **wise and knew what would happen in the future**, and realised it would take some time before India became a **completely developed and established** independent power.

2 The government has just produced a **strong and critical** report about pension provision, which will have **very influential and extensive** effects on today's working population.

3 My grandmother travelled to **very distant** corners of the African content.

4 Wanda's theory about a meteor collision next year is **extremely unlikely to be true**.

5 We'd like to take out an advert **which covers the whole of a page** in your newspaper, defending workers' rights, **which have been achieved after a lot of effort and difficulty**.

6 The army has launched a **complete and thorough** attack on the rebels in the hope of avoiding a **complete and advanced** crisis.

7 The ability to learn a language seems to be **something people are born with, which cannot be changed** in our brains.

8 We need to make a **practical, not influenced by emotion** decision about the new high-speed rail link.

C Look at the sentences again and write the nouns that collocate with the compound adjectives. Use your dictionary to find two other nouns that could go with each adjective.

1 *A far-sighted leader, politician, investment*
2 *A full-fledged power, member, economy*

Lesson 6.1 BINOMIALS

1 A Complete the sentences with the words in the box.

> balances choose clear dance
> dried forth large learn shut
> sweet tear true

1 It's not complicated at all, in fact the situation is completely cut and _____.

2 Alright, you can make a speech but we don't have much time, so keep it short and _____.

3 The jury only needed a half-hour to decide. It was an open and _____ case.

4 My company compensates me for petrol but they don't give me anything for the wear and _____ that comes from all the driving.

5 I'll tell you once more, and I'm going to say it loud and _____: Don't touch my stuff!

6 My wife and I went to the same school but only met later, while travelling in Europe. Strange but _____.

7 A couple of students take notes by hand, but people by and _____ use a tablet.

8 A few mosquito bites isn't a big deal. Cut the song and _____.

9 The old woman said nothing, just stared, rocking back and _____ in the creaky chair.

10 Don't think you can pick and _____. We don't have enough time, or money for that matter.

11 There's no single person making a final decision. There's a system of checks and _____ where the decision-making is a shared responsibility.

12 OK, so my interview was a disaster, I was completely unprepared. Next time I'll know what to do. You live and _____.

B What's the relationship between the two words in each binomial above? Is it related to meaning or sound?

Lesson 6.2 MULTI-WORD VERBS FOR REPORTING

1 A Match the captions with the cartoons.

1 Do fill me in on what's happened in the past 1.5 million years.

2 Erm, remind me why you talked me into this …

3 It wasn't you who ate all the ice-cream? Sure, I'll back you up on that.

4 What tipped you off to the fact that I was the escaped prisoner?

5 Jack entertained the guests by reeling off the names of his 298 grandchildren.

6 Protesters are calling for a ban on margarine.

B In each caption underline the multi-word verb and circle its object. How many of the verbs are separable?

C Match the multi-word verbs with the definitions.

a) say or show what someone is saying is true

b) persuade someone to do something

c) ask publicly for something to be done

d) warn someone secretly, especially about illegal activities

e) tell someone about recent events, especially if they have been away

f) say a lot of information quickly and easily, often from memory

VOCABULARY BANK

1 A Complete the headlines with the past participles in the box to make compound adjectives.

| acclaimed   controlled   deserved   disturbed   held   motivated   needed   worded |

1 Internationally _____ scientist joins Bilkent University

2 Police say high-street attack was racially _____

3 STRONGLY _____ EMAIL WARNS STAFF – NO SHORTS!

4 Well _____ award goes to eighty-year-old charity worker

5 Urgently_____ medicine reaches besieged city

6 Mentally _____ patients to be moved from prisons

7 STRICTLY _____ GM CROP TRIALS ON FARMS NEXT YEAR

8 Widely _____ belief in millennials' selfie obsession challenged

B Which headline are they talking about? Write the number.

a) 'After all he's done, it's the least they can do for him.'

b) 'Everybody thinks it's true. I did, and I still do.'

c) 'She could have said it in a nicer way. She offended everyone.'

d) 'That's hopeful, as maybe at least some of them may get proper psychological support.'

e) 'But they can't prevent seeds from blowing onto land outside the test area.'

f) 'There have been a lot of incidents recently. People are so ignorant, judging others just because they're foreign.'

g) 'What a relief. They were really desperate.'

h) 'Wow, even I've heard of her!'

Lesson 7.3 TRAVEL: ADJECTIVE COLLOCATIONS

1 A Look at the photos. Then complete the definitions of the adjectives in the collocations.

a pristine beach

a dense forest

a rambling farmhouse

a well-appointed hotel room

a rugged coastline

a barren desert

1 _____: having an irregular shape and covering a large area

2 _____: land or soil that has few or no plants growing in it

3 _____: in the same condition as the original; extremely clean and new

4 _____: rough and uneven

5 _____: made of or containing a lot of things or people that are very close together

6 _____: having a good standard of furniture and/or equipment and all necessary amenities

B Cross out the noun which does not usually collocate with the adjective.

1 rugged – mountain, hill, building, good looks

2 dense – undergrowth, beach, smoke, population

3 rambling – museum, trail, discussion, furniture

4 well-appointed – spa, exhibition, quarters, conference centre

5 barren – landscape, town, wilderness, hillside

6 pristine – coffee, rainforest, condition, white shirt

C Write a minimum of two adjectives that collocate with the noun you crossed out in Exercise 1B.

Lesson 8.1 CONNOTATION

1 A Cross out the item that is not possible. What is wrong?

1 The house is quite *lone/isolated/secluded*, with no neighbours nearby.
2 Go round the field *anti-clockwise/counter-clockwise/the wrong way round*.
3 The company is *taking up/going ahead with/embarking upon* a period of restructuring.
4 My client *subscribes to/concurs with/sees eye to eye with* the view that climate change is still a question of debate.
5 *Take-home/Take-out/Take-away* deliveries – all city zones!
6 The neighbour's kid, he's such a little *brat/devil/urchin*.
7 Need to sort something with the mayor? Ask Jack to help, he's got a lot of *influence/persuasion/clout*.
8 The shortage of nursing staff is a *worrying/vexing/concerned* problem.

B What differences are there, if any, between the two correct answers? Think about shades of meaning, formality and British or American English.

Lesson 8.3 ANIMAL IDIOMS

1 A Complete the idioms with the singular or plural form of the animals in the photos. You can use two of the animals twice.

1 hold your _____
2 a _____ in _____'s clothing
3 till the _____ come home
4 cry _____
5 the _____ in the room
6 take the _____ by the horns
7 the _____'s share
8 wouldn't hurt a _____
9 get someone's _____
10 a cash _____

B Replace the text in bold with the correct form of one of the idioms above.

1 Don't trust him just because he smiles and seems helpful. He's **dangerous even if he looks nice**.
2 If I were you, I'd confront your boss about this issue. You've got to **take control of the situation**.
3 At first, Jody was worried about her start-up but in fact it was **a brilliant business idea and brought in a huge profit**.
4 You can wait **for days and months and years**, but I'm not going to change my mind.
5 He's always taking credit for my ideas. It really **annoys me**.
6 Don't keep **telling me there's a huge problem when there's not**. I won't believe you when there really is an issue.
7 Now **wait a second**, I haven't agreed to getting married! There's a lot to talk over first.
8 I know, he barks a lot and shows his teeth, but he **would never do anything that would harm someone**.
9 The company gives them all sorts of perks – free lunches, a company car and phone – but they're ignoring **the biggest and most obvious problem that no one seems to want to talk about** – the gender pay gap.
10 The workers' salaries aren't bad but are only a fraction of the owner's income, who still takes **the largest portion**.

COMMUNICATION BANK

Lesson 1.1

4 A Which is the correct answer? Sometimes more than one is possible.

1. a) Malala Yousafzi   b) Indira Gandhi
   c) Margaret Thatcher
2. a) Steve Jobs   b) Tim Berners-Lee
   c) Mark Zuckerberg
3. a) the five hundreds   b) the sixteen hundreds
   c) the seventeen hundreds
4. a) the cart   b) the horse   c) the wheel
5. a) Donald Trump   b) Barack Obama
   c) David Cameron
6. a) The Eiffel Tower   b) The Berlin Wall
   c) London Bridge
7. a) penicillin   b) DNA sequencing   c) vaccination
8. a) hydroelectric generators   b) wind turbines
   c) solar energy

Lesson 1.2

7 A Student A: read the information below and make notes. Prepare to explain the situation to Student B.

Paul, from Wellington, New Zealand, is a widower of thirty-five with a ten-year-old son who is suffering from mental health problems, including severe depression since the death of his mother. Paul works two jobs: by day he's a builder and in the evenings he works as a cleaner. Even so, he is only just able to make ends meet. He's unable to spend sufficient time with his son – they haven't had a holiday for the last two years, and he knows his son would benefit from intensive, but expensive, one-to-one counselling sessions. He is at the end of his tether and doesn't know which way to turn.

B Work with Student B. You can only help one of the two people. Argue the case for your person, and in the end agree who to help.

C Tell the rest of the class what you decided in the end and why.

Lesson 1.2

8 C Features of an informal article

1. A catchy title
2. Informal rhetorical questions
3. A question-answer sequence
4. Addressing the reader directly
5. Quotations
6. Examples
7. Informal sentence starters
8. Contractions
9. Informal lexis and lexical phrases

Lesson 2.1

4 B How many a) answers did you circle?

4–5: Very uptight. Look, no offence, but you're really expecting too much of yourself and others. We all mess up from time to time – take it easy, we're only human!

3: Somewhat uptight. You seem to be able to accept our human foibles some of the time, and that's promising. You have some work to do though!

1–2: Verging on tolerant. It's completely human to find it difficult to accept our humanity from time to time, and that's where you're at. And most of the time you're not so quick to judge.

0: Tolerance personified. You're a poster-child for acceptance and you're going to live a long time!

Lesson 2.1

6 A Student A: work with Student B. Read aloud the first word in each pair in the list below. Student B will guess a related word. After he/she has guessed, tell him/her the word you have on your list.

A: pond   B: pond, water   A: no, pond, frog

1. pond – frog
2. fruit – date
3. bus – diesel
4. problem – dilemma
5. bird – beak
6. sound – footstep
7. language – slang
8. ice – slippery
9. tired – yawn
10. police – speed limit
11. green – lawn
12. theatre – surgeon
13. picture – fake
14. start – kick off

Lesson 2.2

8 B

DON'T teach:

Memorising facts

- not relevant now

- 100 years ago: no access to facts when needed – someone chose key facts we needed to learn

- when things no longer needed we don't notice immediately

- X times tables, spelling, grammar

- He's misunderstood – stop teaching, not Ss stop learning, √ use assistive technology so children learn what they need, e.g. spellchecker

DO teach:

Ability to tell difference: information needed/not needed, right/wrong

Lesson 5.3

6 B Student A

You're a member of management and you want to go for cheap options. You need to show a good face in terms of the company's desire to provide for its employees, but meanwhile the owners need you to keep costs down or you may lose your job. Look at the list and decide which options are acceptable for you, and jot down some arguments to support those and reject the others. Prepare to argue your points, and make sure you get enough time to speak!

Lesson 6.2

3 B Student A: complete each sentence with your own idea. Then work with Student B and take turns to read a sentence. Student B will summarise each sentence. Tell your partner the verb in brackets if necessary.

1 I think English is relatively easy, for example … (illustrate)
2 We need to have a public debate about … (call for)
3 You shouldn't have … (reprimand)
4 I promise from the bottom of my heart that … (vow)
5 All my friends say this too, that … (echo)
6 In my opinion … (voice)

A: I think English is relatively easy, for example nouns aren't all masculine or feminine.
B: You illustrated why you think English is relatively easy.

Lesson 6.2

5 Student A

Situation 1

You are a manager. Speak to B, a staff representative. You are annoyed because some of your employees copy everyone into every single email they send. It's a waste of time and you want everyone to stop it. Say this in your own words. You start the conversation.

Situation 2

You are the husband in the middle of divorce negotiations. Listen to your lawyer's (C's) message from your wife. Repudiate your wife's story, then insist on what you want in return for agreeing to her request. Use your own words.

Situation 3

You are a journalist. Listen to C, a member of the public talking about B, a local politician. Then speak to the politician and tell him/her C's concerns. Use *criticise* and *call for*. Listen to the politician's answers and tell C what was said. Use *thank, echo (your proposal)* and *suggest*.

Lesson 2.3

6 B Roles

A • You are leading the discussion. Welcome the participants and keep them focused throughout, making sure everyone gets a chance to speak. Have someone take notes and, at the end, they recap on the ideas.
  • Start by choosing some expressions you'd like to use from Exercises 3A and 4B on pages 26 and 27. Practise saying them to yourself.

B • You are enthusiastic about the topic and want to put ideas forward. You interrupt, sometimes speaking over other participants.
  • Start by listing your own ideas about the topic.

C • You have ideas but they are sometimes off the topic.
  • Start by listing your own ideas about the topic.

D • You are reticent to speak but you do have ideas. Try to interrupt politely.
  • Start by listing your own ideas about the topic.

Lesson 7.3

5 Student B

1 Read the story. To make it sound more informal, change or omit the underlined words and add phrases where there are gaps.
2 Imagine the story happened to you and practise telling it alone, using informal language.

This story is _____ depressing. A few years ago my friend Dan and I were hitchhiking from Santiago, Chile, to Córdoba in Argentina. We got stuck for a while somewhere, and spent hours standing there with our big cardboard sign that said 'Córdoba'. Finally a car pulled over, a beautiful Mercedes _____, driven by a really nice Argentinian guy. He was an architect and on his way to Buenos Aires for an important meeting, a big job that was going to change his life. He was a fast driver too, and we got to Córdoba by late afternoon. He dropped us off in the city centre, we said goodbye. _____ We didn't exchange numbers or anything, and I wish we had. Anyway, Dan had the sign and found a rubbish bin to throw it into, but then he said, 'Hey, what's this?' and then 'Oh, no …' Then he showed me: It was the architect's cardboard portfolio, full of the drawings that he was taking to his meeting. Somehow we had picked it up instead of our sign. _____ I just wanted to die.

Tell each other your stories, incorporating the informal features from Exercise 4B. Discuss. What do you think happened next in each story?

COMMUNICATION BANK

Lesson 3.1

9 A

Assistant Hotel Manager for small hotel in Ireland

You will need to enjoy a busy, hands-on environment in this 20-bedroom family hotel close to a National Park. You will be responsible for assisting the General Manager to ensure the smooth operation of the business and will have previous experience of management or of working in a hotel.

Duties include:

- running reception and the office in the mornings
- organising part-time staff
- helping out in the reception, restaurant, bar, etc. when busy

Skills: good communication skills, face-to-face and online; management skills, knowledge of at least two languages including English.

Posted 2 days ago

INTERPRETERS NEEDED!

Graduate positions in the interpreting/translation industry. Requires two languages, one of which is advanced-level English.

Human Resource Allocation is a leading provider of language services within the social services sector. We are currently recruiting for interpreters for various assignments. You will be responsible for providing face-to-face interpreting in meetings and appointments. The work is primarily within the outer London area, and having your own transport and being flexible about timings is an advantage.

Skills:
– fluent English plus one other language
– excellent communication skills
– good organisational skills
– ability to work with a range of people
– discretion with regard to confidentiality

Lesson 3.1

10 A Student A

1 You are the interviewer. Look at the job adverts above. Decide with Student B which job you will interview him/her for.

2 Work with other interviewers interviewing for the same job. Prepare questions for Student B. These could include: reasons for applying for the job, qualifications, relevant experience, skills and personal qualities relevant to the job.

3 Think how you can put the candidate at ease at the beginning of the interview.

4 Conduct the interview.

Lesson 3.2

1 B Student B: read the article and write five words for each story to help you remember it.

Buck up, buckaroo!

After six years of living off of disability payments from his private insurer, James Bowman got <u>caught red-handed</u> – on a horse. His Facebook photos of riding a bucking bronco at a rodeo didn't quite match with his claim of chronic whiplash and depression. His insurer took notice and Bowman's benefits were terminated faster than you can say 'Yee-ha!' Bowman calls the decision unfair. 'I've been having work done on my back and the therapist recommended the rodeo.' His insurer says 'People should realise there's a lot to be said for honesty. It really is the best policy in the end.'

LIKE 👍

He only had eyes for FB

Ankit Patel, a junior manager with a city firm, called in sick, claiming that an infection had left him with eyes swollen shut and severe headaches. Well, apparently his eyes weren't THAT shut, as his colleagues noticed him making regular Facebook postings. This was brought to the attention of the head manager, and the deception cost Patel his job. 'Not being given a second chance is just plain wrong,' said Patel. 'OK, maybe I <u>overstated</u> how sick I was, but there's no way I could have gone to work.'

LIKE 👍

A costly nap

Some people just can't take a joke. Office worker Cristina Diaz posted this picture of herself with the comment, 'My job is SOOOO challenging sometimes!' Unfortunately for Diaz, her boss is an active Facebook user

and now Diaz is unemployed and looking for a new job. Perhaps she should try a mattress showroom? Diaz said the experience has made her afraid of using social media at all. 'Can't someone post something without fear of being spotted by Big Brother?' she said. 'I'm a conscientious worker and it seems wrong that I've <u>lost face</u> over a silly joke.'

Lesson 3.3

8 B Student A: you are a politician and you are going to take part in a radio interview. Your task is to avoid answering the question. To prepare, make a list of things you can talk about that are related to the topic, i.e. that you can talk about <u>instead</u> of directly answering the question. Use the article in Exercise 3B to get ideas on how to avoid answering.

Lesson 3.1

10 A Student B

1 You are the interviewee. Work with Student A and choose one of the jobs on page 130.
2 Work with other candidates for the same job. Prepare answers to possible questions.
3 Then, prepare two or three questions specifically related to the job and company you are applying for.
4 Go to the interview.

Lesson 4.1

8 Student A: ask student B the questions below.

 When did you last?

a) catch up on things with your best friend?
b) back out of telling someone your true feelings or opinion?
c) cancel a plan because you didn't feel up to it?

 Do you find it difficult to

a) come up with ideas under pressure?
b) live up to your ideals?
c) face up to your weaknesses?

Lesson 7.3

5 Student A

1 Read the story. To make it sound more informal, change or omit the underlined words and add phrases where there are gaps.
2 Imagine the story happened to you and practise telling it alone, using informal language.

This happened when I was in Algeria with some friends quite a few years back. We had <u>a</u> great idea that we'd buy a donkey and walk along the coast. It seemed like a good idea at the time, _____ romantic and natural. So we bought <u>a</u> donkey from <u>a</u> man we met and started walking along the deserted coast. We saw hardly anyone or any houses. It was fairly typical of the area. So each night we'd camp on a beach and each night the donkey would run back to its village. _____ I can't remember why but we just walked back to the village each time and when we got there we'd find a group of villagers almost weeping with laughter. They <u>said</u>, 'What do you expect from a donkey? That's how they are.' On the fourth night _____ the donkey ate its saddle. _____ We just all looked at each other and decided enough was enough _____.

Tell each other your stories, incorporating the informal features from Exercise 4B. Discuss. What do you think happened next in each story?

Lesson 5.3

6 B Student B

You're a health freak and you love some of these ideas, especially the more expensive ones; you have a taste for luxury and you also think your employer owes it to the employees to provide the best. Look at the list and decide which options you prefer, and jot down some arguments to support those and reject the others. Prepare to argue your points, and make sure you get enough time to speak!

Lesson 6.2

5 Student B

Situation 1

You are a staff representative. Listen to A, your manager. Then tell C, a member of staff, what the manager said. Use *complain* and *ask*. When C tells you his/her reasons, go back to the manager and report what was said. Use *apologise* and *explain*.

Situation 2

You are a wife sorting out a divorce. Tell the lawyer that you want to keep the cat. Emphasise that this is non-negotiable and is very important to you. Reproach your husband through the lawyer for his behaviour and relate a story to show why he shouldn't have the cat. Use your own words. You start the conversation.

Situation 3

You are a local politician. Listen to a journalist (A) giving you a message from a member of the public. Ask A to convey a message: Thank the member of the public, and offer to organise a public meeting. Suggest a time/place. Use your own words.

Lesson 8.1

7 B Student A

acquiesce *formal* to do what someone else wants, or allow something to happen, even though you do not really agree with it
Instead, I acquiesced in her authority and I quietly did as I was told.

buckle to do something that you do not want to do because a difficult situation forces you to do it
A weaker person would have buckled under the weight of criticism.

capitulate *formal* to accept or agree to something that you have been opposing for a long time
Helen finally capitulated and let her son have a car.

give in *phrasal verb* to finally agree to do or accept something that you had at first opposed, especially because someone has forced or persuaded you to
Bob's wife went on at him so much that eventually he gave in.

http://www.ldoceonline.com

COMMUNICATION BANK

Lesson 5.3

6 B Student C

You think the whole thing is a bad idea and like things the way they are. You don't think that people should be telling you how to keep healthy, especially not your employer! Jot down some points about why all the ideas on the list are bad. Prepare to argue your points, and make sure you get enough time to speak!

Lesson 6.2

3 B Student B: complete each sentence with your own idea. Then work with Student A and take turns to read a sentence. Student A will summarise each sentence. Tell your partner the verb in brackets if necessary.

1 I'd be so grateful if you gave me a chance to … (plead)
2 I absolute reject the idea that … (repudiate)
3 As I've said before, I have never ever … (maintain)
4 He'll deny it, but yesterday my neighbour … (allege)
5 It's true, I've made mistakes with … (acknowledge)
6 Here's a story that sums up my childhood in three sentences. You see … (relate)

Student B: *I'd be so grateful if you gave me a chance to work here.*
Student A: *You pleaded for a chance to work here.*

Lesson 2.2

5 c

1. ELEMENTS OF A SOLE

- indoors, in a classroom, computers, kids
- a 'big' question, e.g. hair Q
- students work out answers on their own
- no adult present in classroom
- a granny on Skype (Granny Cloud) helps if needed

2. WHERE GRANNY CLOUD IDEA CAME FROM

- experiment in India: uni-level genetics content given to 12-year-old Tamil kids
- pre-test score: zero   after researching: 30%
- local woman (22) joined, only gave encouragement
- score after 2 months: 50%

3. CHILDREN'S FEELINGS ABOUT SOLE

- no teachers – Ss feel they have more control
- at first thought really strange
- 'cool'
- Ts like tried-and-tested methods, Ss get bored
- at first frightened/curious; now not frightened

Lesson 4.2

11 c

RECOMMENDATIONS

In light of the above, I am offering the following recommendations:

- Stop following 'friends' who use the platform to show off.
- Limit the amount of time you spend on social media.
- When you meet friends in person, switch your phones to mute.

I believe that active users of social media, if they follow these guidelines, are likely to experience a noticeable decrease in some of the negative effects.

Lesson 5.1

3 c

1 American author Jim Fixx's best-selling book *The Complete Book of Running*, published in 1977, helped start the fitness revolution in the USA and promoted the significant health benefits of jogging.
2 In 1967 the 35-year-old, 97-kilogram, chain-smoking Fixx made a decision to start running, losing 27 kilograms and quitting the habit by the time of the publication of his book ten years later.
3 Fixx's unexpected death at the age of 52 from a heart attack while running on a country road in Vermont (USA) stunned the world, but medical results showing a congenital heart disease supported the notion that Fixx may in fact have extended his life because of his dedication to the sport that he made so popular.

Lesson 6.2

5 Student C

Situation 1

You are a member of staff. Listen to B's message from the manager. Then apologise and explain your reasons for emailing that way. Use your own words.

Situation 2

You are a lawyer in a divorce settlement. Listen to B, the wife, and then pass the message on to A, the husband. Use *emphasise*, *reproach* and *relate (the story of …)* when you are summarising what was said. When you have heard what A says, report back to B. Use *repudiate* and *insist*.

Situation 3

You are a member of the public. Tell A, a journalist, how angry you are about plans to close your local hospital. You're also demanding to know when your local politician is going to reduce crime in your area. You're calling for a public meeting about both issues. Use your own words. You start the conversation.

Lesson 4.2

8 B Key points to keep in mind when writing a report.

a) Give an overview of the report at the beginning, including purpose.

b) Use headings to help the reader follow the structure of your report.

c) Use bullet points to concisely summarise and highlight key information.

d) The style should be formal and impersonal, but most importantly should reflect your target audience.

e) Give examples to help the reader understand your data, but do so sparingly – don't overdo it.

f) Do not give your opinion, only convey the results of your research; the recommendations section will reflect your opinion and that too should not be overly subjective.

g) State your recommendations at the end.

Lesson 2.1

6 A Student B: work with Student A. Student A says the words in the list. Repeat the word and say the first related word that comes to mind. Student A will say the answer he/she has. Make sure you understand the word, but don't write anything. Then continue.

A: pond   B: pond, water   A: no, pond, frog

1 pond – _____
2 fruit – _____
3 bus – _____
4 problem – _____
5 bird – _____
6 sound – _____
7 language – _____
8 ice – _____
9 tired – _____
10 police – _____
11 green – _____
12 theatre – _____
13 picture – _____
14 start – _____

Lesson 8.2

1 A

Mostly a)s: You're extremely thorough in preparing for things and perhaps a bit of a perfectionist. You have a strong belief in, even a reverence for, the power of the written word. You probably have a good-sized library at home and never throw out a book.

Mostly b)s: You don't like to push yourself with reading, and often do 'just enough' – in fact that's how you are with a lot of tasks, just doing enough, not more. You may nevertheless be an avid reader of fiction.

Mostly c)s: So reading is not your thing, or at least the written text is not your favourite way of getting and giving information. You're a pragmatist about everything, dealing with issues as they come up and not really worrying about problems unless they're real.

Lesson 8.1

7 B Student B

discerning showing the ability to make good judgments, especially about art, music, style, etc.
... an ideal tour for the discerning traveller ...

finicky too concerned with unimportant details and small things that you like or dislike
She's very finicky about what she eats.

fussy very concerned about small, usually unimportant details, and difficult to please.
A lot of small children are fussy eaters (= they dislike many types of food).

picky *informal* someone who is picky only likes particular things and not others, and so is not easy to please.
He's a very picky eater.

http://www.ldoceonline.com

Lesson 8.2

9

An introduction can follow this suggested pattern, as the model essay does:

1 Connect with the audience by using an example relevant to them <u>and</u> the topic.
2 Comment on the example.
3 State the dilemma, either as an indirect or a rhetorical question.

A conclusion can follow this suggested pattern, as the model essay does:

1 Summarise broadly the two sides of the argument, making your position clear.
2 Make a clear statement of your opinion.

Lesson 8.2

8 C

For:
hard to resist distractions; need to connect with people
multi-tasking a myth; brain can switch but lower mental performance
hyperlinks make reading inefficient, content hard to remember

Against:
people need to get used to handling distractions in 21st century, part of life
people can't concentrate for extended periods, not realistic to expect it – checking emails/FB is a good refresher
internet convenient source of info needed for work/study, can enhance productivity

AUDIO SCRIPTS

Unit 1 Recording 1

1 Her election as prime minister had a profound impact on girls' expectations.
2 This person is a pioneer in the field of social networking websites.
3 In this period, the conventional wisdom was that the world was flat.
4 This stone-age invention was game-changing for travel.
5 His election brought about a paradigm shift regarding political campaigns.
6 Its destruction in 1989 set in motion a series of events that transformed the world.
7 The discovery represented a major breakthrough in eliminating polio.
8 Scientists are conducting pilot studies to see if this could replace fossil fuels.

Unit 1 Recording 4

AM = Aasmah Mir   JT = Jamie Thurston

AM: Now wouldn't it be fantastic, don't you think, if we could help someone or change someone's life for the better every single week; not just occasionally but every single week. Well, Jamie Thurston tries to do that through her website 52 Lives where a story is posted every week, detailing the specific things that somebody needs, for example a gift card, a pram, a vacuum cleaner or some toys, and Jamie I suppose that's the key, it's very simple, isn't it? It's putting the power in people's hands and saying, 'have you got this?'

JT: It is, it's about spreading kindness really, and, as you said, trying to change one life every week and we do that with the help of almost 100,000 people now who follow the website and follow our social media pages and offer help to people that they've never even met and who'll never thank them. You know, it's complete, pure kindness.

AM: How many people have been helped?

JT: This week is week 122.

AM: Wow.

JT: A few weeks ago we helped a little girl in Hull called Josie. She's got a very serious genetic condition. She's in bed a lot of the time and her family spend a lot of time in the bedroom with her. It's kind of become their living room, I guess. And it was in a really poor state and they didn't have the money to fix up her room. So we had painters and decorators, artists, people buying furniture, we've completely redone her room for her. But what people, but what I've learnt over the weeks I guess at 52 Lives is that even though we give people tangible things and things that they need, that hasn't been what's changing their life … it's the kindness that people are showing; that's what's changing their life. Because if you're going through quite a hard time and complete strangers, you know, offer you something or are kind to you, that can really change your life.

AM: Mmm. And I mean, how did this all start?

JT: It started off as a Facebook page for my friends and family. I got the idea when I was shopping online for some second-hand furniture and I saw a 'wanted' ad and it was a lady saying that she needed a rug, she was hoping someone would donate a rug to her. She said her floor was all broken, there were nails coming through, her children were cutting their feet. And I didn't have a rug but I contacted her and said 'if you find someone to donate it, I could pick one up for you,' because I knew she didn't have a car. And we got chatting and I learnt more about her situation, and her and her children had escaped quite a horrible domestic violent situation. They'd lived in a garden shed for a little while. They'd … it was a horrible state, and as I learnt more about her, I just thought between my network of friends and family, I thought if people knew about her, they would help her and so I started a Facebook page. We did help her and I thought between my friends and family we could do this every week. We could do something to help people. And then it grew and grew and we've got almost 100,000 supporters now.

AM: What are the latest things that people have been asking for? And, in fact, what is the most unusual thing that anyone has ever asked for, because people's needs are so … can be very simple but can be so different?

JT: One of the more unusual things we've given somebody was some teeth. There was a man called Victor in America, he's from Alabama, and he'd had heart surgery and he had to have all his teeth removed before his heart transplant and I think it was to minimise the risk of infection or something and he didn't have any money to replace his teeth so he was just going to have no teeth for the rest of his life and so we set up a fundraising page for him and we raised money and we bought him some new teeth.

AM: What do you think this idea, this website, will be doing five years from now? Have you got plans to expand it?

JT: Well, we've just launched a school kindness project …

Unit 1 Recording 5

W = Woman   M = Man

W: … and the next section was particularly interesting. On the whole, people expressed a curiosity about businesses that had less relevance for them. So, they wanted to know more about services that they were in fact unlikely to use, which was surprising for us. To cite one example, people who don't have pets tended to be particularly interested in getting information about the pet-related services. Our impression was simply that these businesses had some novelty for them, and their interest presumably reflected amusement more than a genuine desire to use the service. One person said, 'It just never occurred to me that such a business would exist.'

M: Another illustration of this is the number of people who asked for more information about the parking services, who, as it turned out, don't actually have a car. Generally speaking though, when we asked people about actually using the services, there was limited interest in trying out ones that the survey participants hadn't used in the past. The consensus seems to be that people are partial to what they already use or know about, and are satisfied with the service they're getting for the price they're paying. One might speculate that this reflects human nature – People don't like to go out of their comfort zone – but having said that, some people were drawn by alternatives to services they already use, such as HomeExchange instead of AirBnB.

W: Yes, and in that case there's a real difference in the way the services work, since with AirBnB you pay for what you use, and with HomeExchange you only pay a membership fee, and after that the services are free. Now moving onto the next question …

Unit 1 Recording 7

A: I have a lot of friends who are musicians and it always strikes me how much they struggle to find a space where they can rehearse and develop new material.

B: Yeah, and actually not have music as sort of a secondary thing in their lives. I mean if they can't make enough money from it to live and have to get a job, they might not be able to find a place or time to practise.

A: That's the thing, I think it's the ideal group for a co-living space, they need a kind of a space that addresses their specific needs …

B: … yeah and they can understand and sort of put up with each other. The irregular daily timetables, the noise …

A: Don't call it noise …

B: OK, the sounds … erm, the music, the cacophony of … sound …

A: Anyway, let's talk about facilities. Practice rooms.

B: Definitely, lots of soundproof rehearsal spaces …

A: Small ones, one or two big ones …

B: Maybe no small ones. You know, I think their private spaces, their bedrooms can actually double as their private rehearsal spaces. If they're soundproofed.

A: That sounds good. So, a few big rehearsal spaces and then each resident has their own soundproofed bedroom or private space. That would seem to me to be the key consideration. It's kind of the main need they have in their private space.

B: Along with the usual peace and quiet. And for sleeping, it's good because if others are rehearsing at 3a.m. and you want to like, sleep, you can.

A: So what about communal spaces, besides rehearsal rooms?

B: Well, I wouldn't put kitchens in the individual bedrooms …

A: No …

B: … I'd have one big communal kitchen, really well equipped, a big eating area.

A: Good idea. How about a dining area that doubles as a performance room?

B: So, with a stage at one end …?

A: Yeah, a stage, and some attention should be given to acoustics.

B: An acoustic ceiling.

A: If it's in the budget. How about other recreation?

B: Like a cinema? That would make sense. For watching DVDs and I'm thinking DVDs of performances.

A: So really amazing sound system.

B: Definitely.

A: So let's talk about services.

B: Well it's not exactly a service but I was thinking how important it would be to connect with the local community in a positive way. I mean, people living around this residence might have an issue with the noise and the kind of people living there. So residents could provide free concerts …

A: … a sort of open house …

B: … yeah, every Saturday or something.

A: And music lessons for local kids.

B: Yeah, brilliant idea. That would solve the public relations problem for sure.

A: And it gives the residents their regular audience.

B: Kills two birds with one stone.

A: So what other problems do we need to think about?

B: Knowing my musician friends, the biggest problem would actually be personality clashes that are about the music, you know, it's like 'I really don't agree with your style.'

A: It's an approaches and taste thing.

B: Yeah but we're talking about professionals sort of, or not professionals but people who have extremely strong feelings about their profession, about their art.

A: That can lead to a lot of tension.

B: Not sure what to do about it.

A: On-site mediator?

B: Or something like that. These kinks can be worked out in practice.

A: Yeah, a few hiccups are inevitable. It's hard to know what to do before you're in the situation.

Unit 2 Recording 1

1 **A:** How often do you point out other people's mistakes?

B: Seldom, if ever.

2 **A:** How many spelling mistakes are there in your emails?

B: Few, if any.

3 **A:** You aren't going to complain about the soup, are you?

B: I certainly am, whether you like it or not.

4 **A:** How would you feel if you didn't get the top grade?

B: I'd feel as if I'd let everyone down.

5 **A:** You think you've made a mistake in a dish you're preparing, but you're not sure.

B: If in doubt, I'd throw it away and start again.

6 **A:** There's a small stain on one of your tee-shirts. Would it bother you?

B: No, as long as no-one could see it.

Unit 2 Recording 4

BBC = Sarah Montague   SM = Sugata Mitra
T = Teacher   L = Lucie   G = Granny
Th = Thomas   B = Boy

BBC: Professor Mitra, welcome to *The Educators*.

SM: Thank you.

BBC: Now last year, you won, from the online lecture series TED, a one-million-dollar prize for a project that you wanted to do which was to build what they've called 'Schools in the Cloud' and as a result you are in the process of putting seven schools in the cloud. And the way they work, you call them 'SOLEs', which is 'Self-Organised Learning Environments'. Explain how they work now.

SM: The Self-Organised Learning Environment tries to simulate the chaotic environment of the Hole-in-the-Wall Experiment which was computers outdoors with no supervision and children accessing it. The SOLE attempts to do the same inside the classroom. So, you have a few computers, you have lots of children usually, and you trigger the whole system off with a big question.

BBC: Give us an example.

SM: You could for example ask them, 'Why does hair grow?' A typical nine-year-old will say 'Whaddya mean?' so I you know, the hair on your head, keeps on growing longer and longer and longer and then you have to cut it off. Why on earth does it do that? It doesn't seem to do that on animals. And then the magic starts off.

BBC: So what, you leave them alone in the room with a computer and they have to work out how to answer the question.

SM: We call these the big questions. A big question is something that a child is attracted by and to which preferably no one really has the right answer.

BBC: Now one of the things you've established in these cases that you're talking about there's no adult involvement, you did discover that actually sometimes children do need a bit of help, and this is where what you've called the Granny Cloud comes in which is this idea that there's a little bit of help from the British granny I think was your perfect model.

SM: Well, that came out of an experiment in India which was designed to fail. I said I'll give the children a task that is so hard that they couldn't possibly do it. The task I chose was undergraduate-level genetics, in English, for 12-year-old Tamil-speaking children in an Indian village. You know I had a test at the end of it which they'd gotten a zero in to start with, and they got 30 percent so I didn't want to stop there, I said but how do I get that thirty up further, because thirty's a fail, so what I got was a friendly local girl, she was twenty-two years old and a great friend of the children, they used to play together. And she said 'Biotechnology? I don't know anything about it! I didn't even have science in school.' I said, 'Look, you're the best I have here. You don't understand the subject, doesn't matter. Can you just go on encouraging them?

BBC: So go on, what happened?

SM: Fifty percent in two months.

BBC: Purely from the encouragement.

SM: Just from the encouragement.

BBC: So, somebody just saying to the children, 'Well done, you're doing really well!'

SM: Yes …

BBC: … and they carry on doing it and they get their score up.

SM: Anyhow the *Guardian* was interviewing me and I said 'Will you put in just a couple of lines at the bottom saying that if you are a British grandmother, if you have broadband and a web camera can you give me one hour of your time, for free, because I needed a million of them.

BBC: So you created this Granny Cloud effectively on Skype.

SM: It became the Granny Cloud.

BBC: Look, let's hear how one of your classrooms as they've been called 'School in the Cloud', it's a 'Classroom in the Cloud', how it's gone down at Greenfield Community College in Newton Aycliffe in County Durham.

T: Right, we've got Max? Yep, Max is here …

L: My name's Lucie McCormick and I'm thirteen years old and we're in room thirteen. Room thirteen is a room where the pupils come in to ask a question from a granny who is in different parts of the country and they have to find out the answer independently.

G: You kind of work in groups and use the computers but talk to each other about …

L: In room thirteen there are no teachers because the pupils feel that the teachers give them a specific website to look on and they don't like it. In room thirteen when the teachers aren't here you feel more open to what you can look at and what you can't look at because you're learning yourself and finding out what not to look at and what to look at.

T: My name's Thomas Gally. I'm fifteen. Well, when we first heard about it we thought 'Oh, I don't really want to do it because it sounds really strange compared to normal lessons,' but when we got in it was really cool.

B: I know it's a balance between traditional ways of learning and modern because teachers like to stick with the tried and true methods and stuff but in all honesty they do need to move forwards with the lessons because we get bored really quickly.

L: I never thought my education would include a room without a teacher in. It was frightening at first because I think we were all curious on what it was all about but 'cause we've had quite a few sessions in room thirteen we know what it's all about now and we're not frightened to come in here without the teacher.

Unit 2 Recording 5

BBC = Sarah Montague   SM = Sugata Mitra

BBC: You've even said that memorising facts or solving problems alone are terrible ways of being educated. Why are they so terrible?

SM: Well, perhaps 'terrible' is not quite the right word, but memorising facts and being able to repeat them years and years later is something that we needed to do about a hundred years ago, because we didn't have access to facts at the point of need. So, it was important that for the first fifteen or sixteen years of life somebody should decide the key facts that need to get stored in our brains.

BBC: You've said that we still learn these things because we have a romantic attachment to the past and that's making us hang on to skills we just don't need anymore.

SM: Yes, yes, and I don't know if it's romantic, I think it's just that when things become obsolete or not needed, we often don't notice that for a while.

BBC: Are you suggesting that that's what's happened to times tables, that there's no longer any po – you're nodding. We shouldn't be teaching our children the times tables?

SM: Absolutely not. I can't see a single reason why we should. I …

BBC: What about spelling?

SM: The same, unfortunately.

BBC: Grammar?

SM: Erm … Also the same.

BBC: You'd stop teaching any of those things.

SM: No. I'm misunderstood on this point very frequently. I'm saying we don't need to teach spelling. I'm not saying children don't need to learn spelling. I'm saying that if a child grows up with a spellchecker, his spelling will automatically get better. You misspell a word once, you misspell it twice, you don't misspell it the third time. I've been trying to say this all around the world, that assistive technology teaches. It doesn't make you stupid.

BBC: So what should we be teaching our children?

SM: We should teach them how to discern the information that they need from the information that they don't. And that's a very difficult skill at this point in time. It has to become mainstream.

BBC: So it's just a question of a judgement on what is presented to them. It's the difference between knowing this is a reliable website and this one is not.

SM: We have access to anything we want at the point of need. All we need to know is how to distinguish between the right and the wrong.

Unit 2 Recording 6

A = Amy   C – Chad   P = Pete   S = Sarah

A: Umm, let's get started. First of all shall we just introduce ourselves? I'll start, I'm Amy and I'm a parent here.

C: My name's Chad and I'm a trainee teacher.

P: Yes, hi I'm Pete. I have one teenage son here.

S: Um, hi I'm Sarah I'm twenty-one and I'm a student.

A: Perfect, OK, um, so our task today, is to discuss these two questions: the first being 'Does traditional education leave enough room to develop children's imagination, their creativity, or does it actually stifle it?' In your opinion. And the second question: 'Should any changes be made to our curriculum and if so,

what are they?' So, what I'd like to do I think is start with question one and I'm going to be making some notes as we go along so don't let that distract you. Umm, right Chad.

C: Yeah.

A: What do you think about question one?

C: Err, traditional education, my opinion about traditional education is even though I don't have kids myself …

A: Umm.

C: is that it's, er, it's very rigid. It's very rigid. There is a lot of testing early on.

A: Umm.

C: Umm, even from year one, let alone with Pete's child here is in secondary school, but even from much further back they're testing and assessing children's abilities right from the very beginning and it's not only the, the amount of testing but also what they're testing them in.

P: And, what's, what's wrong with that?

C: Well, I just think that, er, children learn very differently and umm …

A: Could you explore that point further, cause I think that's important is that …

C: … the difference in …

A: … you're suggesting that some children actually may benefit, some not.

C: Umm I think that if you, I think that from a very young age and even, even I have some friends who have children who are also in secondary school and they don't test very well and yet they are perfectly capable – they learn very well but they don't test very well. It's they don't regurgitate the kind of facts that they are told to kind of just memorise and just spit it back out.

P: Can I just check where you're coming from? Are you suggesting that there should be less testing or no testing or that testing should be done in a different way?

C: Yeah, I think in a different way, I think its good to do some kind of assessment but I think the, the rigid way that the assess the assessments are done at the moment …

A: Let's, let's stay focused a minute, Chad.

C: … don't help every child.

A: Chad, sorry. Sorry to interrupt you but we are actually look at crucially whether it develops the children's imagination. Not necessarily how the testing is done but whether you think in essence it's, it's a good thing for their imagination.

P: Well we, we may be going down a sort of testing rabbit hole here that's that isn't entirely helpful because the question is, er, does the curriculum itself encourage creativity or stifle it. Surely …

A: Umm.

P: … that is to do with the emphasis and the energy that the individual school or teacher places on the subject. So umm if, if a school is, is focusing on on stem subjects on science and technology, English and maths …

A: Oh could you run …

P: Yeah …

A: Yeah, sorry carry on.

P: … erm then, then, then you could argue perhaps that, that the creativity is being squashed but many schools, erm, focus very

much on on the arts and and en-encouraging those, those those subjects so if you look at, I've made a note of what I consider to be creative subjects here.

C: Yeah.

P: Drama, dance, music, media studies and photography. Umm, you know there's plenty …

C: Mine are …

P: … opportunities …

C: True, but all …

P: … provided, provided the organisation of the school or the leadership of the school is focusing on those and giving them enough energy.

A: Right, OK let's let's look at that further but I want to bring in Sarah at this point because you looked as though you wanted to add something. Do you want to add something now there?

S: Umm, well I can I can see both sides of the argument but umm I think it's up to the individual. Umm for instance I, I was very much more into the arts, a friend of mine was more into science and maths and um you know the the testing that we did …

P: I'm not sure you …

S: … can't …

P: Wh, what argument we're actually having here but that …

A: Sorry, Peter can …

S: … erm …

A: … we just hear what Sarah's …

P: Sorry, course …

A: … got to say, thank you.

S: Um, I was just saying that it it depends I think some testing can be useful to see where how far a student is progressing.

A: Well that's certainly worth considering as well.

P: But don't you agree that as a young person entering the world of work that being familiar with the idea of evaluation, of being appraised, it's something that's gonna stand you in good stead.

C: Yeah, it will.

S: Umm possibly …

P: No, I was asking her.

C: Yeah.

P: No, sorry.

S: Err, umm, yeah I …

A: I think we might be digressing a little bit here I think we need to … just stay focused on whether the education the traditional education as it stands does leave enough room.

C: Yeah, I don't think it does. I don't think it does and that comes down to …

P: … but if you look at …

C: … that …

P: … if you look at the split here between the stem subjects,

C: … of actual coursework …

P: yeah, then, then I don't think, I don't think your argument stands up because all of the opportunities for creative subjects are there and they should be properly assessed and rigorously tested as the other subjects.

A: So correct me if I'm wrong, but what you are saying is that, Peter that you think, err, things are fine as they the way the way they are.

P: I do.

A: Is that right?

P: I think …

C: Is that in your experience though from the when your boy was in, er, primary school was he getting a umm a wide variety of different creative subjects as well as those the writing …

P: I think he's getting more now at secondary school than he did …

C: Yeah.

P: at primary school.

A: Thank you, thanks everybody we are going to move on cos I know that we are pressed for time so let's stay focused and we're going to move to question two now: ' Should any changes be made to our curriculum and if so, what?' Who would like to kick this one off?

C: I will, I would love to.

A: Thank you …

Unit 3 Recording 1

MF = Marcus Friedman   W1 = Woman 1
M1 = Man 1   W2 = Woman 2   M2 = Man 2

MF: … and that's the key to finding the career path that's best for you. Thank you all for listening, I'm happy to take questions now. Yes, there in the second row.

W1: My question is about actually getting a job. The job market is so competitive … How can you make yourself stand out when you apply? What are the tricks for getting your CV to the top of the pile?

MF: Well, first of all there are no tricks, really, but your question hits the nail on the head – you do have to understand the job market from the point of view of the prospective employer. These days there are bound to be a very large number of applicants for any given position, and so the person handling all those applications has to narrow down the choice to a small handful of people.

W1: So how can I make sure I'm one of the small handful?

MF: Well, of course it's complicated but I can give you some basic guidance. One area to look at is the buzzwords that come up time and time again in job advertisements. For example, these often refer to 'good organisation and communication skills'. Those are two different things but they're key, the ones you see mentioned the most. Does that answer your question?

W1: Yes. Thanks.

MF: Next question. Yes, the man over there … Can you pass the mike over to him?

M1: I have a question about what you just said. Organisation and communication skills sound so general. Can you say more about them?

MF: Well, let's start with organisation. Think about all the information and data we deal with in our everyday lives, and how overwhelming that can be … Well, it's no different in a job, and it's absolutely essential that you have the skills to enable you to manage large amounts of information efficiently. In many jobs you're going to have a lot thrown at you. So you need to have the capacity to select and prioritise in a way so that nothing gets lost and so that you can trace any item of information quickly.

M1: And 'communication skills'?

MF: Having good 'social skills' and being able to handle people have always been important but what employers are looking for these days is different from twenty-five to thirty years ago, because of changes in how we communicate. Face-to-face, interpersonal skills are part of this – Being able to articulate your ideas clearly is key. You need to be good at getting people to want to listen to you, to get them to feel it's worth their while. If you've ever noticed people having trouble listening to you, it could be that you aren't concise or articulate enough.

M1: I see, thank you …

MF: And then there's … Sorry, just let me finish, this is the important bit online communication. Not everyone is a fan of social networking but this is part of the literacy that's expected of employees, nowadays. It's obviously your responsibility to choose the appropriate platform to convey the right impression of who you are. And of course you should always demonstrate common sense and discretion in controlling the image you personally convey. We all have a massive digital footprint that comes from everything we've ever done online, and that is a commodity for a prospective employer. If there's a problem with your digital footprint, inevitably it will come out at some point. Do you see what I mean?

M1: I didn't really understand the last thing you said. Can you explain a bit more?

MF: Well, who you communicate yourself to be, your reputation if you will, is of a potential value for an employer. Companies talk about their reputational value, their RV, and I always tell my clients, 'Your RV is as important as your CV'.

M1: I get it. Thank you.

MF: You're welcome. Next question? Yes, go ahead.

W2: Another buzzword I've often seen is 'flexibility'. Could you say something about what that means to employers?

MF: Ah yes. I think simply put, that means the willingness to put your hand to anything, to muck in. You might be asked to take on a range of tasks and do this with enthusiasm rather than grudgingly. Saying, 'I'm not going to do this because it's outside my job description' will not go down well. And it's good on your CV if you can show you've done this in the past.

W2: So, it's like being a good team player?

MF: Exactly. That's another very common phrase in job adverts. At the same time, of course it's also good to be able to be a self-starter and be able to take the initiative where needed. It's the flexibility to take on a range of different roles as needed. Does that help?

W2: Yes, thanks.

MF: Yes, the man in the red T-shirt.

M2: Every job advert I've looked at says you're supposed to have experience and a 'proven track record'. I'm in my final year of university and apart from summer jobs, I haven't actually worked.

MF: Many people think a novice can't easily point to things like experience and a track record. But there are skills that a novice to the market can focus on in a CV. The three biggies are the ability to work in a team, motivation and creativity. It's not enough to have knowledge or tech skills or other such hard skills. Employers are looking for soft skills. It's vital that anyone entering the job market, at least in the current climate, understands what these are and applies themselves to developing in these areas. But you can't just say you're creative or a good team worker or motivated, you need to demonstrate practically how you've shown these abilities.

M2: How do I do that? I haven't had a real job.

MF: Well, you mentioned that you have had summer jobs. And you've been at university for what – four years? It seems totally unimaginable that you've never had to apply your creativity, that you've never worked in a team or never shown motivation. Indeed, you may well have done all these things. Reflect on what you've done, be honest with yourself about your weaknesses, but be proud of your strengths and your achievements too. If you're a good candidate for a job, there's a potentially strong likelihood that you'll get to the interview stage.

W2: I see, that's been very useful. And encouraging. Thank you.

MF: You're very welcome. There's time for one more question. Yes?

W3: Speaking of university students, to what extent is it important to have a degree?

MF: Mmm. That's a tricky one. In some countries a university degree is no longer as important as it used to be. That's because a degree means very little after you've been working for a while. However, in some countries it's still a real selling point. And of course it all depends on the job. OK everyone, I think that's it for now. Thank you for …

Unit 3 Recording 2

1 A: You look exhausted. How are things at check-in?

B: Flight delays, angry passengers. I can't think straight.

2 A: I'll go and check the problem with the email server.

B: You needn't bother. I've already done it.

3 A: Sorry, miss. My computer crashed and I lost all my homework.

B: That must have been annoying.

4 A: You'll be alone on the fish counter today. Anna's phoned to say she won't be coming in.

B: Anna again! I might have guessed!

5 A: Can I ask you another question, minister?

B: Sorry, I've got to go now.

6 A: Hi Susie. Er, sorry I was held up in the traffic. Is it too late for you to look at Felix?

AUDIO SCRIPTS

B: You might as well come in.
7 A: It's just an oil change. OK if I pick it up at 9?
B: It may not be ready. Give me a call first thing.

Unit 3 Recording 5

A: Figures coming out today show that the gender pay gap, the difference between what men and women earn, has widened in the last two years and now stands at twenty per cent, up two percent from two years ago, when it stood at eighteen percent. The government in its election manifesto promised to reduce the pay gap within two years. Now, two years on since the election, it seems things have got worse. So what's happened?
We're joined in the studio by Ann Simmonds, junior minister for employment. This figure is shocking, isn't it?
B: Good morning and thank you for inviting me on the programme.
A: Good morning. So, as I said, this figure really is shocking, isn't it? Despite pre-election promises by your party, the gender pay gap is actually getting wider.
B: Well, it would be shocking but this figure has been taken out of context. Let me put it in perspective. In fact, female employment has risen significantly in the past few years and what we're seeing is actually a positive, in that more women are in work than ever before.
A: But surely that's not the point. If women's pay is getting worse in comparison to men, then something is very wrong. In your manifesto your party promised to bridge the pay gap. So why have you broken that election pledge? Why haven't you done anything about it?
B: Well, what we have to take into account is that there can be many reasons for the difference in pay. For example, even in the situation of more jobs for women, women tend to go for part-time work or less well paid work.
A: Yes, so what you're saying is that it's right that typically female occupations, such as a carer or a nurse, are paid at a lower level than say an equivalent male-dominated job?
B: No, not at all. What I am saying is that we have to look at the employment figures overall and particularly we need to take into account our priorities of providing more employment for everyone in this difficult economic sit …
A: Excuse me for interrupting, but figures show that even in the same jobs women tend to earn on average fifteen percent less than men. For example, when they're CEOs of companies.
B: Those figures …
A: The opposition is calling for radical changes to be made to regulations affecting pay in both the public and private sphere.
B: The opposition would say that. But one might question just how far the government should go in dictating policy and enforcing regulations in the private sector.
A: Minister, with all due respect, we're talking about a fifteen percent pay differential for the same job. How can that possibly be acceptable?
B: Well, it plainly isn't acceptable and I'm glad you've brought that up because there's another point that needs addressing, which is that research shows that men tend to be more assertive in asking for pay rises and this is something we need to educate employers in so that …
A: Forgive me for interrupting, but I'm sure our listeners want to know the answer to one simple question: What are you are going to do about the problem?
B: Before I answer that, let me just add to what I was saying. I think your listeners would agree that the situation has changed since the election and the main focus at the moment should be on providing employment for everyone. And that's what we're doing as a government.
A: I don't wish to be blunt but you haven't actually answered my question. Are you going to do anything about the gender pay gap? Yes or no?
B: Well, what we plan to do is to set up a review to look into the issue and to investigate possible ways forward. We are currently allocating more resources to studying and addressing the issue.
A: That could take another year or two.
B: All I'm saying is that the government admits there is a problem. The review will be thorough and wide-ranging and we will take its findings very seriously.
A: Thank you, Minister.

Unit 3 Recording 9

A: … and as a career consultant that is definitely the most common question I get from clients, and the most relevant.
B: OK, so how DO we future-proof our career choices? How can we be certain that the career path we choose won't peter out somewhere down the road?
A: Well, in many cases we can use common sense to work out likely scenarios.
B: Could you explain what you mean?
A: Well, we can take a handful of jobs and look at where they might go in the next five to ten years, in terms of automation. Let's pick from different fields, just for the sake of illustration, so let's say musician, erm, financial advisor …
B: Can I throw in a couple? Like tour guide …
A: And one more.
B: Chef.
A: Alright. So musician, financial advisor, tour guide, chef – Who is going to find themselves out of a job in ten years, or at least struggling because of the way automation has taken over their tasks? So, to start with it's old news really that factory jobs have mostly been replaced by robots.
B: But none of these are factory jobs.
A: No, but what I was getting at is that if you look at the jobs that have a repetitive component, for example some sort of manual activity that could in theory be done by a machine, these seem to be the most vulnerable to automation.
B: Oh, you mean like musician …
A: Yes, interestingly that would be one. A big part of a musician's job is actually repetitious. A lot of what a musician does has long ago been automated, like with synthesisers.
B: So, it's the mechanical, repetitive element that's most vulnerable. Manual labour essentially.
A: One might think so but in fact it's not just manual activity at all. Financial analysis has long been done by computers.
B: So, financial advisors are doomed! I've heard of those, robo-advisors. They're supposedly at least as good as humans.
A: Some people aren't comfortable with a robot making decisions about their money, but that career area has been impacted by automation and I think we've only just seen the start of it. Computers will be able to make much better judgements than human beings.
B: Well then, financial advisor – not a good career choice.
A: I wouldn't say that, as someone has to write the programs, and maintain them.
B: A financial wizard with programming skills.
A: That, for example, would be a strong combination of skills.
B: So, your point is that um, well, what do we call it then, as opposed to manual labour?
A: Intellectual work?
B: Yeah, so you mean intellectual work is as vulnerable to automation as manual work. Maybe even more so.
A: There are a lot of variables, so I wouldn't go with a simple comparison like that. Look at the other two jobs on our list, tour guide and chef. I wouldn't call either of them intellectual OR manual.
B: No, well, with chef it depends on the kind of chef, doesn't it? A lot of a chef's job is manual, in any case. All that washing and chopping veggies …
A: Probably most kitchen staff in a restaurant do tasks that can be automated. It's a tough career, unless you're a top chef or a celebrity chef. In reality the genuinely creative jobs are reserved for the lucky few.
B: How about a tour guide?
A: Of course there are free and low-cost computer tour guides, you know, interactive maps, recorded guided tours, all that stuff, and that's taken away a lot of the jobs in the travel industry. But if you put cost aside, a good tour guide can bring something very personal to a visit to a new place.
B: That's true. When I have a tour guide, a good tour guide, I feel so much more in touch with a place, my visit stops being a virtual one.
A: Yes, what a human can bring to guiding a tour that a robot can't is that human touch, and that underlines a key point in future-proofing a career: think in terms of the human element, and bring that to whatever you do. Provided you've chosen a job where that's a premium, you're less likely to be bumped off by an app.
B: That's encouraging. Well, from our list, it seems like if any job is safest from automation, it's … being a tour guide?
A: Being a good tour guide, yes – compared

to the other jobs we discussed. It's not highly lucrative but you can live off of it, and if you have language skills you'll always be in demand.

B: And which of the four is the most vulnerable do you think?

A: Well it's hard to give a cut-and-dried answer to that as there are other factors …

Unit 4 Recording 2

1 Do you feel up to …
2 Can you hold off on …
3 I need to catch up on …
4 Nothing makes up for…
5 When I can't think of a new recipe I often fall back on …

Unit 4 Recording 4

BF = Bobby Friction   JB = Julian Baggini
NL = Natasha Lomas   EP = Eli Pariser

BF: Most of us are now only communicating with those within our own social media bubble. So what impact is this having on us? Philosopher Julian Baggini.

JB: We know from lots and lots of research in psychology, we have a tendency anyway to seek out views which reinforce our own and we have a tendency to discount evidence which contradicts us. So we're up against that bias whatever happens. Now if, in addition to that we are actually being fed more of the stuff that supports our view and we're having the views of the contradictors hidden from us in some way, that just magnifies the effect even more and so the dangers I think are clear. You know, if you end up only exposing yourself to a narrow range of views then first of all, you are not exercising your critical thinking faculties, and secondly, contrary views are going to seem not just wrong, but they're going end up seeming bizarrely wrong in the end because you won't even understand how anyone even begins to think something different to yourself.

BF: I like Julian's idea that things outside your bubble don't just look wrong but might start to look weirdly wrong. It's something we'll come back to later on but it starts closer to home than you might think. It's time to talk about your friends again, you know the ones you talk to on social media. It's really satisfying to do this and it's what I love doing, but …you're not actually talking to all of your friends.

NL: You think that you're, you know, you're keeping up with all of your friends when it's in fact only a sort of small subset and perhaps not even a subset. It can be quite shocking really. The average person, the consumer on the street, has very, very little idea. Perhaps slightly, increasingly, there's an increasing awareness perhaps, but the vast majority of Facebook users have no idea that they're seeing an algorithmically filtered feed.

BF: So the algorithm kicks in and that's what's choosing what I get to see or don't see.

NL: When Facebook first launched, it was effectively a chronological feed of everything

and you could keep up with all your friends' comings and goings and you know, new births and birthdays and so on but it's, things have shifted over the years but the education has not been there to sort of tell people how it's changed so the whole usage of the site has evolved without them really knowing it. Really the onus should be on the social networks to sort of better inform their users about how these sites function.

BF: So just to be clear, not only have I created a bubble around myself by selecting my friends, I'm only interacting with a handful of them, only getting to see their news on my timeline. But … social media isn't the only place where I'm in a bubble. Think about everything else that you use the internet for. The searching, the shopping, the information gathering. Bubbles exist there, too.

EP: For a lot of us, we assume that, you know, if we google Barack Obama, that the result that's going to come up at the top is kind of the most authoritative result on Barack Obama and that's just not always the case anymore.

BF: I had no idea about this bubble that Eli Pariser told me about.

EP: So I asked a bunch of friends to google the same thing at the same time and send me screen shots of what they found and when I saw those screenshots side by side and saw that different people were really getting very different results, that's when it really sunk in for me.

BF: And this is what really freaks me out. Every time I use search engines some of the information is actually hidden from me. The algorithm is deciding what's best for me.

Unit 4 Recording 6

1 There could come a time when …
2 I'd like there to be more …
3 There seem to be a lot of problems with …
4 There isn't any point in complaining about …
5 Is there anyone who doesn't have … ?

Unit 4 Recording 8

A: I'd like to tell you about escape rooms, which have become one of my favourite free-time activities and which I think some of you might really enjoy. They're everywhere now, and big cities have literally dozens of them. So what are they? Well, escape rooms are basically these small rooms or floors, usually in rundown or abandoned buildings, and each escape room complex has different rooms with different themes. What you have to do in each one is the same. You go into the room with four or five other people, so you go in with friends, so it's a good social experience. You're locked in the room for 60 minutes and your task is to find a way out of the room. And to do this you have to engage in lots of puzzle solving, collaborate puzzle solving, so you do it together.

The rooms are elaborate. It's like this huge 3D puzzle, and each room is a different theme. To give you an example, let's say the theme is Ancient Egypt. The room is the office of a professor of Ancient Egypt, and you're surrounded by locked cupboards. All you have is one key hanging down and there are padlocks everywhere, so you have to find the right lock for the key. Eventually you find it, you open the cupboard and there you find another key or a piece of paper with numbers on it, or a paper trail of clues that need some lateral thinking. You've got to communicate a lot with the others, like 'Why do you think we got this piece of paper?' or 'What's this number? Hey, this number's the same as that number over there, do you think there's something in that?'

All the while you can see that the clock's ticking, and it gets a bit frantic. But you can't panic, you can't get out, and you can't stop working as a team.

If you succeed, it's great, you did it as a team, and you feel really good about it. If you fail, well that's a shame, but you did it as a team, and you feel really good about it. In other words either way, it's the feeling of teamwork that you take away. And you go for a drink together and talk about it. For hours.

So that's how an escape room works. And who does it suit? Well, it suits people who like doing hands-on work, people who like looking around and taking it all in, trying to connect the dots, and most of all it suits people who like working in a team. If that's not you, then perhaps escape rooms aren't for you. You have to enjoy the team element, and finding your role in that, whether your role is the foot soldier or the general.

The thing is, it's cooperative, it's collaborative, it's <u>not</u> competitive.

In short, escape rooms are certainly worth trying once. Not only will you have a unique, exciting experience but you will also share an experience with friends that you'll be talking about for years. I guarantee it.

Unit 5 Recording 2

BBC = BBC interviewer   VD = Victoire Dauxerre

BBC: Now it's one of those dreams that goes through the heads of teenage girls: You're walking down the street with your mum. A talent scout stops you and says 'You're so beautiful, you could be a successful model.' That's exactly what happened to Victoire Dauxerre on the streets of Paris. She became a leading model at the age of seventeen. She's now twenty-four and has written *Size Zero: My Life as a Disappearing Model*. Victoire, what happened that day when you were out with your mother?

VD: Well, exactly what you said. Actually I was literally walking in the street. I was preparing my A-level and I wanted to go to a famous uni in France, so I actually never dreamt of becoming a model. That's why maybe it worked for me, you know? And so I was in the streets of Le Marais in Paris, shopping with my mum, and a man came to me and said to me 'You have an incredible nose. It will take the light perfectly, and you are going to become the next Claudia Schiffer.'

BBC: So what was your experience with trying to stay slim enough to satisfy the demands of the industry?

VD: Well, I have to say it was quite awful actually because I couldn't eat anything, because you have to be so skinny, you know, to fit into these clothes.

BBC: So, what was your daily diet?

VD: So, I ate three apples a day, and I couldn't eat anything else, or I was going to gain weight, and that's why I fell into anorexia.

BBC: How did you manage to just function on three apples a day?

VD: Well you don't really, you know I fainted all the time, I fell down in the street, and my agent actually only gave me a piece of chicken, he didn't even give me sugar. What I did with that, I had the little voice, you know, in my head, the voice of anorexia actually, who was, which was the voice of my agent telling me 'You're going to gain weight, you won't fit into the clothes'. And so, when you are anorexic then I tried to like throw up, and it didn't work, and I took laxatives, and then my body was used to it, so I took two pills, and four, and five, then I had to go to the hospital.

BBC: How did you get well again?

VD: So, I spent three month at the hospital, and doctors saved my life, you know because my body was so damaged. I actually had the body of, I mean the skeleton of a seventy-years-old woman when I was nineteen. I had lost my hair and all that, so I had to take like many pills to build all this up again.

BBC: In France there are rules about not having women who are, or girls, who are too thin. How well does that work in France?

VD: It doesn't work. So, the law is not applied, actually. I helped the deputy who wrote the law, that's why I wrote my book. It all came from that, from this law. It's not applied at all. I had a meeting with the minister of health and women's rights and she literally told me that she had a meeting with all of the designers, and they told her, if you do apply this law, we won't do the Fashion Week in Paris anymore. So it's all about money, and nothing about health, because the fashion industry has so much power.

BBC: Victoire Dauxerre, thank you very much indeed for being with us this morning.

Unit 5 Recording 7

M1 = Man 1   M2 = Man 2   W = Woman

M1: What I've found really works for health for me, man of a certain age, erm, putting on a few pounds and stuff is, err, the 5:2 diet. I dunno if you've tried it but basically the idea is you fast for two days, you eat normally perfectly, whatever you wanna eat for the rest of the week the five days and then on those two days you just limit what you're eating to five hundred calories.

M2: I find that, uh, I wasn't very good at dieting and things like that.

M1: Hmm.

M2: And I started doing Bikram yoga. Don't know if you've ever tried that.

M1: Bikram, no I don't know.

M2: So basically, umm, it's yoga but it's much more intense the, it's set in a heated room a carpeted room that's 39 degrees and it's just twenty-six positions, but every time you go to the class it's the same twenty-six positions.

M1: Oh my …

M2: But you burn a thousand calories a class, you sweat so much and they say you can't drink water within the first twenty-five minutes but …

M1: … but …

M2: … you come out of that room feeling amazing.

M1: … but …

W: That reminds me of, erm, so I've joined a choir and I think that is really really good for your health actually. I'm not that into dieting not that much into exercise but it's the same thing, um, when I come out of the room I just feel completely lifted.

M2: Well I feel the same way about …

W: Really happy.

M2: … Bikram yoga cause it's it's just something that you can go, you don't ah, you don't have to think about it, there's an instructor there, you meet people but you don't talk throughout the class so it's something you can just do yourself and it's not …

W: Mmm …

M2: … of course you exert energy while doing it.

M1: Yeah. But to get back to I mean like with the 5:2 the advantage of something like that is you it's not actually something extra in your … I mean like for me, my day is busy and if I had an extra thing like singing to go to or had to go to a class I don't think I got time for that.

W: Going back to the choir thing, I think I like it because it is a part of my day that isn't work or isn't a commute or anything like that. I can just go and be in this room, I meet people; it's a really joyful experience.

M2: It's funny you should mention that actually cos, I feel the same way about Bikram yoga about you don't have to fit it into your day, I actually enjoy that because you know I'll be at work all day it's really stressful environment you know living in the city and things like that actually taking that hour and half to go, a form of meditation, breathing and relaxation just really you know centres myself.

W: Actually that's like with singing, it's really good for, it's really good physically, mm, because you, you're talking about, mm, your whole body so it's not just for happiness, it's physically actually it's really good for your, your complete self. It's a bit like exercise.

M1/M2: Yeah.

M1: Well, going back to, mm, going back to the 5:2, apart from the weight loss, it does have proven and you know they've done tests to … proven benefits in terms of you know your insulin levels your heart conditions so it benefits you, you know, in all sorts of other ways.

W: As I was saying that's exactly the same as singing, they've proven that it's, it's really good for your whole body, your whole self.

M1: Mm.

W: Physically, mentally.

M1: Have they?

W: For mental health it is absolutely because if you can regulate your breathing, you can, you can control panic – you can do all kinds of things.

M2: Anyway, I just wanna add about the Bikram yoga is that it's, it's not just about going to a yoga class.

W: Yeah.

M2: And it's a form of …

W: … to get back to what I was saying before that's the same with the choir you learn songs that you can then take home, you know, you can practise at home but then you've also got this lovely community …

M2: That reminds me …

W: … together.

M2: Well, that reminds me of going to Bikram yoga, it's that community – you tend to be at the same classes. I mean we've all got our strong points to offer but I do think Bikram yoga is the way forward.

M: Well, for you.

Unit 5 Recording 10

Hmm, a food memory… Well, the first thing that comes to mind is this dish my mom used to make on special occasions, a dish called Coquilles Saint-Jacques, which is a French dish, I guess, made from scallops and white wine and a few other ingredients. Mmm, I can just taste it now. I remember when I was very young and I didn't like seafood, this was the one kind of seafood I loved, which is ironic really, since the scallops are cooked in white wine. Anyway, it's pretty simple, just some scallops, my mom used the big white sea scallops, and she'd make this amazing sauce, onions and mushrooms and butter and cream I think, and the wine, and cooked it all together. It's ages since I've made it, actually, so I'm just trying to remember … Oh, it's coming back to me now, how it tasted, but what really made it was the presentation. She served it in these big scallop shells, and there's mashed potatoes around the edge and the scallops in the middle, then cheese and breadcrumbs, I think, on top. Then it's baked in the oven. My mouth waters just thinking about it. Imagine this dish served in these big scallop shells, incredibly succulent, decadently rich, really … When I used to smell this cooking, I knew it was a special occasion, like someone coming for dinner, and whenever my mom asks what I want for my birthday dinner it's Coquilles Saint-Jacques. I'll always associate this dish with home, and special occasions, and family. I've sometimes tried making it but it never comes out the same.

Unit 6 Recording 3

I = Interviewer   A: Alan Danes

I: Simultaneous interpreting is something that's always fascinated me. What is it like to sit in a booth all day at the United Nations or in a conference translating at the same time as people are talking? What sort of problems do the interpreters face? Joining me in the studio is Alan Danes, who is an interpreter for international conferences where he translates between Spanish, German and English. Alan, welcome to the programme.

A: Thanks.

I: So, what would you say are the main challenges you face when you're interpreting?

A: That's a question I get asked a lot. There are quite a few challenges. Some might surprise you. For example, you know how people tap their microphone, you know, 'testing, testing'? Well, in conferences nowadays, the sound levels have been carefully checked and are set for voice level. So if a speaker taps his microphone or shouts into it, it can cause serious injury to the interpreter. At the very least it's extremely painful.

I: I'd never even considered that. Of course, you're sitting there in your booth with your earphones on. Very vulnerable. So, so what can you do?

A: Well, it's crucial to educate the speaker and of course, the organisation. I kind of shock them. Tell them that their behaviour can incapacitate the interpreter and in the worst case scenario there's a risk of actual hearing loss, of the interpreter actually going deaf.

I: Are you serious?

A: Yes.

I: So, what other things can the speaker do wrong?

A: One of the worst is when they insist on speaking a language they're incompetent in, and they're really not good at. I remember one very high-powered professor from … well, I won't say the country … but her English was impossible to follow. I just had to make an educated guess as to what she was trying to say. Normally in that kind of situation I'd ask the speaker to give me the speech in advance so I could translate from the written word.

I: And I suppose sometimes people speak too fast for you to follow?

A: Yes, to a certain extent, but from experience I've found there's no point in asking them to slow down. Everyone has a natural pace of speaking so the best thing to do is not try to translate word for word but to summarise what they're saying.

I: Right. I can understand that.

A: And then of course there are cultural differences. Humour is an interpreter's nightmare. There's a risk of humorous sayings from one language getting completely lost in translation. Humour doesn't travel well and jokes are often just not funny.

I: So what do you do if a speaker is telling a lot of jokes?

A: I'll try and see if I can find an equivalent in the audience's language but if I can't think fast enough, I'll fall back on the old

interpreter's rule of saying, 'the speaker has just made an untranslatable joke. It's about … such and such. Please laugh.' That seems to work.

A: Now one really problematic area is when the speaker uses lots of metaphors or cultural references. For example, if a U.S. speaker starts using metaphors from American baseball. Something like, 'I'll take a rain check on that.' Now most audiences won't have a clue about this so I have to translate it as something like 'He would like to accept your invitation at a later time.' You have to be very quick-thinking and versatile. You also have to have a broad knowledge of culturally specific things.

I: Is there anything else you can do about that?

A: Again I try to educate the speaker. I suggest that they should steer clear of cultural references which seem familiar to them, but may not be understood in a different context; instead they should find references to people or places or events that the audience will understand. But of course, often I only meet the speaker on the day of the conference so I don't always have a chance to help them prepare for the process.

I: That sounds like a lot of problems.

A: Yes, but most problems are fixable as long as there's mutual respect between us, between the speaker and the interpreter. Understanding that we both have an important job to do.

Oh, and there's one more I really must mention. It's a problem I take home with me. You see, I get so used to thinking ahead and predicting what people are going to say that I tend to do the same at home. I anticipate the end of a sentence, so my wife is always complaining: 'You never let me finish!'

I: Well, this has been a real insight. Thank you very much for joining us today.

A: My pleasure.

Unit 6 Recording 5

I = Interviewer   S = Sign interpreter

I: That's interesting. But what made you choose this line of work in the first place?

S: Well, I always had strong feelings about equal opportunity, that everyone should have the same access to information and official processes. My mother is deaf and I saw how she was often left out of things – for example the parent-teacher meetings when I was at school.

I: Is that how you learnt to sign?

S: Yes, I grew up signing. It was natural to me, so I had no problem with fluency or with switching between speech and signing.

I: I see. And what are the ups and downs of the job?

S: Oh, there are plenty of positives – I've helped people understand their doctor's instructions about taking medication, so they could do so confidently and independently. The other day I interpreted at a job interview for quite a high-up position. The candidate, who was deaf of course, prepared a fantastic

presentation, and my translation helped them get the job. I've also done signing for births …

I: That's incredible. It's just never occurred to me how useful it must be to know sign language.

S: Oh yes, like knowing any language.

I: So what's the downside of the job?

S: Well, there are some tough situations I've handled, for example translating for terminally ill kids, or divorce cases. These really drain me.

I: Is it the signing?

S: No, it's the human emotion. And maybe being the mediator, and the way signing is so physical, maybe I internalise some things I shouldn't.

I: Otherwise it sounds like a great job.

S: It is. Oh, except the travel – it sounds glamorous, when I get these jobs abroad, but I prefer to sleep in my own bed.

I: Well thank you for talking with us …

Unit 6 Recording 6

1 S = Suzie   D = Dan

S: So it was when I was in Egypt, and I think it was the first or second session I had with the group …

D: What were you doing out there again?

S: Just some training with staff at a bank there. Same bank I work for here.

D: The bank, uh huh …

S: Anyway there was this one woman, and she was quite quiet, so I just went up to her at the beginning of the lesson, I was trying to make small talk, so I complimented her on her jewellery, I said 'Oh, I really like your bracelet, and your earrings.'

D: Were they really nice?

S: Awful. These big ring earrings and a bulky bracelet.

D: Ugh.

S: Anyway she was happy, and I forgot about it, until the last day of the course when she came up to me with her hands clasped and she said 'I want you to have these' and she opened it and it was these horrible great big earrings and bracelet that I talked about.

Dan: Oh no.

Suzie: I felt really guilty, 'cause they were her favourites, and I'd got them and I didn't want them.

Dan: How awkward.

Suzie: A couple of days later I was telling a friend of mine about this, an Egyptian friend of mine, and she said that basically in Egyptian culture if you tell somebody you like something, the norm is to give it to you.

Dan: Really? I've heard that but it sounds like a stereotype.

Suzie: Well, it was an Egyptian friend who told me.

Dan: Do you really think it's always the case? I mean is it something most people would do?

Suzie: I don't know. Good question. Anyway, I was really careful about giving people compliments on their possessions after that, but you know it's difficult, you go to someone's house and it's natural …

AUDIO SCRIPTS

Dan: It's natural, yeah.

Suzie: I'm accustomed to saying something positive, you know, you say 'What a lovely vase' and just as the words slip out you realise you may be obliging them to give it to you, and it feels awkward.

Dan: Awkward, yeah. I don't think I could get used to that. But I still wonder if it's really that common …

2 S = Scott   A = Ann

A: … so was there anything there that made it hard to get used to?

S: In Japan? Well it's funny, I found so many things completely alien but I never felt out of place. I felt really at home.

A: That's good.

S: But still I can remember a lot of times when I got it wrong, I just didn't pick up on the signals or I didn't know what I was supposed to do.

A: Like when?

S: For example I was teaching a company class at a car manufacturer, a group of eight or nine engineers, nice guys. We sat at desks in a rectangular shape, me on one side sort of alone.

A: Right.

S: And at the end of the first lesson, I said thank you to everyone, see you next time, and then I started jotting down notes about the lesson as I always did. Then I noticed they were all still sitting there, so I said thank you again, the lesson is finished. They didn't budge.

A: Oh.

S: So I quickly finished my notes, I felt really awkward and mystified, and finally I stood up to put my things in my bag, and the second I stood up all eight guys jumped up, grabbed their stuff and zipped out the door.

A: What was that about?

S: Just shows my ignorance of course. I'm used to students leaving before me. It's commonplace in Australia/Canada/New Zealand, but one of the guys explained to me later that it would have been rude for them to stand up first, no matter what. It's a given that they defer to the teacher, they wait for the teacher to lead.

A: … defer to the teacher, right. Is that a general Japanese thing, I mean is it really generally part of the culture?

S: You mean is it a stereotype? Well, I think …

A: Somehow I doubt it's generally true.

S: I don't know, it was my general impression, there was this dynamic between students and teacher …

A: Don't you think it depends on the situation?

S: I suppose so, I'm really not sure …

A: I always wonder about these things …

S: Yeah. Well, anyway, I felt bad. I mean poor them, I think they all missed their bus home. I felt really foolish.

Unit 6 **Recording** 7

1 The norm is to stand up when the teacher arrives.
2 I'm accustomed to taking my shoes off for class.
3 I got used to cleaning the classroom after the lesson.
4 Singing a college song is completely alien to me.
5 I'm used to wearing a uniform.
6 It's a given that everyone arrives early or on time.

Unit 7 **Recording** 2

On the positive side, this review gives a clear sense of what this film is like, and why you'd recommend it, so the message comes across clearly. I like the bit of background information about Jarmusch, since readers might not know him – That's a good bit of content. Your language is rich, some beautiful expressions, so most of it's actually a pleasure to read.

In terms of things you need to change, the main thing is that it's just too long in places, and you've packed too much into each paragraph, all except the last. I found that as good as the writing is, there's too much detail in places, and you need to cut that back. Now to do this, I don't suggest fiddling and cutting words here and there – you risk losing coherence. You can achieve more, and with less work, by cutting a whole sentence from each paragraph. The way I suggest doing this is … Let's see, here in the first paragraph you start out with this scene-setting about indie films, and that's all that sentence does, it sets the scene. You could just cut this first long sentence and start from here … Well, cut 'meanwhile' and start with 'relatively few …' Now in each of the second and third paragraphs there's a sentence you can cut …

Unit 7 **Recording** 4

A: I love this poem. Unsurprisingly, it's a classic and often features in people's top ten poems. It's written by Yeats, one of greatest poets of the English language, although he himself was Irish.

It's such a rich poem, rich in imagery, that's one thing I love about it. The writer is trying to express the depth of his love for a woman. So he compares his love to the sky, the universe and the stars. And he pictures it as a beautifully made and embroidered cloth. I suppose that makes me think of someone helping another person by spreading a cloth under their feet. But his cloth is the whole night sky with the stars. It's a dark, deep, deep, vast thing. There's no compromise. It's absolute.

But then the poet contrasts this with what he can *really* offer her. '*Had I …*' he means '*If I had such a precious thing*', but of course, he doesn't. He has no wealth to share with her. So all he can share with her are his hopes and dreams and he places them under her feet. It's an act of immense … well, I suppose 'trust' is the word. Yes, incredible trust. I think

we can all relate to that, it's a universal theme. We're all painfully aware of how easy it is for a loved one to hurt us. She could walk all over his dreams, she could hurt him terribly, so he begs her to 'tread lightly', to treat his dreams with care. Those last lines really resonate with me. Sad to say, Yeats himself was deeply in love with a woman who did not return his love.

And I love the way the poem is written, the elegance of the language, especially the opening lines … 'Had I the heavens' embroidered cloths, enwrought with golden and silver light …'. For me it's the richness of language which is deeply evocative. It's amazing how words can paint such a beautiful picture. And if you examine it closely, you see it's impossible to read it fast. Because of all those slow words with their slow stress and no rhymes but the repetition: '*cloths, light, feet, dreams, tread.*' It moves me deeply every time I hear it.

B: This is one of my favourite poems and I first read it when I was fairly young, about fifteen. I suppose it's not exactly a 'classic' poem, well, but I think it's a *modern* classic. It's written by Roger McGough. He was one of the Liverpool poets and started about the same time as the Beatles in Liverpool.

Anyway, when I first read the poem, I just instantly loved it. It just so clearly – and sweetly – describes how there can be a breakdown in communication between people in a loving relationship, that for example a quiet explanation is perceived as shouting. There's no sense that they can ever meet halfway. Probably because it is a loving relationship and because such important emotional investment has been made, we react so differently than when we're in a relationship with, say, just a friend. So much is at stake, I guess, and we have such high hopes that the smallest hint of a criticism can put a terrible strain on the relationship and seem utterly devastating.

I love the way it's described as if from the outside. He's not blaming her, he's acting as an observer of their behaviour. We never really have such clear insights into the situation when we're *in* it. If only we *could* have that clarity about ourselves and what's actually happening.

I love the directness. I love the contrasts between what one person thinks they're doing and a very different way this is perceived by the other. But I like the way it's described directly – just the actions are described as seen by each person, with no interpretation. It's quite simple language really – lots of conversational phrases – and I think the simple title is quite perfect too, and also the way each line ends with either 'You' or 'I'.

I like the lightness of touch and almost humour. No, that's not the right word. Showing the contrast, well more like a paradox, really: being aware of our foolishness but unable to act differently.

I guess I like the way there's no attempt to suggest a solution and that's entirely right. This is just how things are. Although I do think that reading this poem is a little bit of enlightenment in itself. As much as we can hope for? I did feel and still do feel a kind of gratitude for this poem.

Unit 7 Recording 5

1 A: I think poetry and song have very little in common.
B: I agree. They're fundamentally different.
2 A: I won't be going to the Dylan concert. It costs too much.
B: Yes, it's prohibitively expensive.
3 A: Your brother must be upset about missing the festival.
B: Yes, he's bitterly disappointed.
4 A: You look wet. So, your tent isn't all that good?
B: No, it's hopelessly inadequate.
5 A: The speakers at the Slam Poetry session were mostly women, then?
B: Yes, they were predominantly female.
6 A: Pablo Neruda is a highly respected poet around the world.
B: Yes, he's greatly admired.
7 A: It's essential that all kids have the opportunity to play a musical instrument.
B: I agree. It's vitally important.
8 A: Students should choose if they want to learn a poem by heart and not be forced to do so.
B: I agree. That's infinitely preferable.

Unit 7 Recording 6

The Trans-Siberian railway is definitely one of those classic journeys that every traveller dreams of taking. I finally got the chance to do so a few years back. Some friends who had done it were like, 'yeah, it's amazing but it's actually quite tedious. A whole week of looking out of the window staring at birch trees going by.' So I wasn't sure about it before I started, but in fact it turned out to be really fun.

I went on the most basic version of the train. No luxuries. So before I left Beijing I stocked up on supplies, just instant noodles and jasmine tea. I knew I'd be able to get hot water on the train but I'd heard that the dining car wasn't always reliable, especially when we crossed Siberia.

Anyway I was in a four-bed sleeping compartment, and I remember that when we left Beijing, the other three fellow travellers, let's see, there were two young Chinese guys and this Russian guy, a really nice guy, more on him in a minute. No one spoke any English. Fairly typical situation for a traveller in an exotic context, you know what I mean? You'd think it was awkward, the lack of a lingua franca I mean, but to the contrary, it was really nice, sort of relaxed, like 'we're all in this together and let's just enjoy it'. In fact, we did make many attempts at communicating, especially me and the Russian guy, by drawing pictures of things, maps showing where we were from, writing dates for major events in life, family tree and all that. Funny, I don't remember much about him now but I remember understanding quite a lot

about his family, his kids, his house, job, stuff like that. I also remember that he was a really warm-hearted guy and loved to share everything, for example on the second day I think it was, he pulled out a whole roast chicken, still warm, not sure where he got it, and simply split it into four pieces, and gave each of us a piece, me and the two Chinese guys.

Every day on the train was the same really. Got up when I felt like it, went to the loo, made some tea and noodles, and stood at the window staring outside, waiting for the noodles to cool down. Once in a while we'd stop in a station for a bit, and I usually got off to stretch my legs. I had brought stuff with me like chocolate and chewing gum, some guy I met in Beijing told me it's a good idea to have stuff to give to kids or even sell. The first time we got off and there was a bunch of kids around, yelling for gum and whatever, and I really felt awkward, I didn't want to just sprinkle the gum around and watch them wrestle for it. Then I spotted this kid on his own. He was standing by himself outside of the group, and I managed to make my way over to him, and then when no one was looking I gave him all the gum and chocolate I had. Stupid thing to do, maybe, but it was one of those moments when you realise you're so out of your element that you have to just let go of whatever scenario you've written in your head and go with an instinct. I wonder what he did with all that gum.

Unit 7 Recording 10

A: I was on this flight to Argentina – a long-haul flight and I'd just settled into my seat. I'd been working quite hard the few days before then so I was quite tired. Anyway, there was this baby in the seat ahead of me and it was crying. I went 'Uh-oh' and braced myself for a bad flight. Then the baby threw up all over its mum and so I went forward to help. The airline staff gave the woman some clothes to change into and I spent the remainder of the eighteen-hour journey helping out with the baby and getting to know the woman. You'd think I'd have been annoyed but to the contrary … This was one of those times where you feel an event connects you with someone. It was as if I was in an altered state of mind, suddenly totally focused on this baby and her mother, totally alert, not thinking about things like a good night's sleep or whatever. The whole thing had an aura of destiny about it.

Anyway where was I? Oh yeah, her name was Martina Martinez and she was Argentinian but married to a French guy. She went back to Argentina once a year to visit her folks. So that was fine and she was able to help me out when we arrived at Buenos Aires airport and I needed some directions. We exchanged business cards and I thought nothing more of it.

Anyway, it's a year later and this time I'm flying to India for a holiday. And I hear two people talking and I think 'that voice sounds familiar' and this guy calls the woman 'Martina'. And there she was. This time two

rows in front of me and with her husband and toddler. Different airline, different time of year, different destination. Talk about coincidences!

B: I was staying in this hotel in Scotland, at some sort of conference. I can't remember exactly where it was. And I was at dinner and I realised I didn't have my wallet. I'd had it before dinner so I knew I hadn't had it outside of the hotel and I reckoned it must be in my room. I went back there but I just couldn't find it. I can tell you, I turned that room upside down. I looked through all the drawers, the wardrobe, everywhere. I was staying there with some colleagues and I met one of them on my way down to reception to see if the wallet had been handed in. I was in a real panic as the wallet had all my cards in it plus quite a bit of money.

Anyway, his name was Rob, and he was like, 'give me two minutes in your room and I guarantee I'll find it for you.' I reckoned I had nothing to lose so I said, 'OK. Go ahead.' I went down to the TV room and began to watch the sport. It seemed like a minute later when he came into the room brandishing my wallet. I was gobsmacked. I was like 'No! Where did you find it?' and he said 'On top of the wardrobe.' And then of course I remembered I'd put it there for safe-keeping, right at the back of the wardrobe. When I'd checked I only checked the front. Rob said it was easy, he does this sort of thing all the time, like he's got some sort of radar for objects or something, or perhaps more like a radar for human behaviour, you know, where would someone hide a wallet … ?

Unit 8 Recording 2

MR = Michael Rosen   NB = Professor Naomi Baron   LW = Dr Laura Wright

MR: So, having studied all the research, Naomi, what do you think are the differences that you've been able to pinpoint between the actual experience of reading a print book and an e-book in terms of, well, let's say concentration?

NB: I did a lot of work surveying university students in five different countries around the world, more than four hundred of them. And they all said very similar things about their experiences. I asked them, 'What is the one thing you like most about reading in print?, What is the one thing you like most about reading electronically?' and then, 'What do you like least about those media?' And you had an incredible number of eighteen- to twenty-four-year-olds, the digital millennials, telling you they liked the 'smell' of a book. I knew about fifty- and sixty-year-olds saying that. I did not know about young adults saying it. They talked about the tactile experience. They said it's 'real reading,' which I found interesting, 'to read in print'. For e-books what they liked most was 'It's very convenient. I can carry lots around without it weighing a lot.'

But when I asked 'What is the medium on which you can best concentrate when you read?' and they had the choice of print or an e-book or a tablet or mobile phone or laptop, 92 percent of all the subjects that I surveyed said 'I concentrate best in print.' Now in a way that's not surprising because the medium of print gives us the opportunity to concentrate, should we choose to. On the other hand, digital media are created more for skimming and scanning and scrolling. They're not designed for concentrated reading and not surprisingly, that's what eighteen- to twenty-four-year-olds are telling us is their experience.

LW: How about comprehension between the two forms? Do readers take in what they read on an e-reader just as well as they take in printed matter?

NB: It's a wonderful question on which we have conflicting research. Most of the research that's been done that gives a passage to read and then questions to ask afterwards shows that there is pretty much the same score that you will get whether you read that text on an e-reader of whatever sort, on a computer screen or you read it in print.

However, a really interesting study done in Israel after doing that version of the study said, 'take as much or as little time as you want for reading the passages and then we'll give you the comprehension test.' Students who could take however much time as they wanted spent less time with the digital version than they did with the print and did worse on the comprehension.

MR: Is there a difference in emotional response?

NB: That's a tricky question because it has been said that no one ever cried reading an e-book. Whether that's true or not remains to be seen because I'd also have to ask, 'How many people today will ever cry over a book?' I've asked a number of my colleagues and they say 'I get emotional reading an e-book,' and I say 'OK let's talk about it.' 'Or reading on my phone.'

And they say, 'I get involved.' I say, 'What's the difference between getting involved in a plot, you know, not wanting to be distracted and really being emotionally drawn in, having the rest of the world go away, getting lost in the book?' And they often step back and say, Yeah, there's a little bit of a difference. If I hold that print book in my hand I'm more emotionally connected because I'm physically connected.' But again we do not have good studies here and I look forward to getting them because my hunch, I'm putting my money on, not getting as involved in reading emotionally when we're reading on screen.

Unit 8   Recording 3

1 I'm not aware of any problems.
2 There's some likelihood of rain.
3 There are many reasons for learning English.
4 I haven't got any regrets about the past.
5 It's indicative of a new fashion.

Unit 8   Recording 4

A: So what's your take on this article about the numbers of wolves in Europe increasing? I mean it seems very worrying to me that, that there's no control around this, that that …
B: Mmm …
A: Wolves just seem to be naturally increasing their numbers within, you know, within tens or hundreds of kilometres of, of large urban populations.
B: Well, I feel like wolves just have a bad name to be honest, you know, you look at any, any film or story depicting a wolf, it's never positive.
A: Er, no, but there's a good reason for that which is they're dangerous wild animals and …
B: Mmm …
A: they've got no place, erm, next to populations of humans that's just, that's just asking for trouble, isn't it?
B: Well, maybe it's just me but it feels like the danger is always exaggerated to me, you know, certainly, erm, in the media they'll blow up any story even if one person has a really minor injury, suddenly all wolves are bad. You know, I think it's time to get the balance back and give nature a chance to fight back. I don't think it's fair.
A: Well, I'm no expert but, but I think it's important that the risk is properly accessed and I think if you, if you look at where, er, if you look at the statistics of, of human wolf interaction, erm, obviously wolves often come off worse because they end up being shot by, by hunters and the like but where you …
B: Well, I'm really against any form of hunting, in fact any form of culling them at all. I just don't think that's an answer, is that what you are saying?
A: And would you feel the same if, if those populations of wolves were not in remote wildernesses but were on the doorstep of large cities and potentially taking people's livestock, pets, children?
B: It's not a cut and dried question. I just don't think it's that simple. I don't think all of a sudden they're in the city, you know, when they were always, … I just don't think it's that simple.
A: I don't think there's evidence that they're in the city, the evidence is they are close to the cities and therefore if you look at what's happened with foxes for example which were previously traditionally rural animals, they, we now talk about urban foxes, they are they're a part of our lives but they, they can be dangerous, they do take, erm, people's pets. There are stories about them attacking children, and that's a fox! If you've got a wolf in the same sort of situation, um, I'm guessing that could cause you a real problem.
B: Erm, I'm, there are some things that I agree with, but I just think that tourists, for example, erm, bring money to places and it's actually a plus to have wolves because people are actually going to the country to see them, did you ever think of it that way?

A: Yeah. Actually in that respect I'm with you. I, I think this probably eco tourist benefits that could come from having a population of wolves nearby but they'd need to be controlled in some way or …
B: Erm …
A: … penned in to a particular reserve …
B: No one would disagree with that. Obviously you've got to have some sort of controls but I just think we've taken it out of all proportion, recently.
A: Er well, no I would be surprised if that was the case I, I don't think we we've, we've got it out of proportion. I think that we need to ensure that if we want to live, erm, alongside animals like that we need to take necessary precautions and potentially, erm, think about culling to keep the numbers, erm, within reason.
B: Do you not agree with me?
A: On the face of it, it seems like the only way to stop this problem is to kill animals, but actually I think there are lots of other things you can do. I just think that's really, really inhumane and too simple. It's not the right answer.